ABEL
FERRARA

THE KING OF NEW YORK

NICK JOHNSTONE

OMNIBUS PRESS
LONDON · NEW YORK · PARIS · SYDNEY

Copyright © 1999 Omnibus Press
(A Division of Book Sales Limited)

Edited by Rob Dimery
Cover designed by Michael Bell Design Ltd
Picture Research by Nikki Russell

ISBN: 0.7119.7652.X
Order No: OP 48135

All rights reserved. No part of this book may be reproduced in any form
or by any electronic or mechanical means, including information storage
or retrieval systems, without permission in writing from the publisher,
except by a reviewer who may quote brief passages.

Exclusive Distributors
Book Sales Limited,
8/9 Frith Street,
London W1V 5TZ, UK.

Music Sales Corporation,
257 Park Avenue South,
New York, NY 10010, USA.

The Five Mile Press,
22 Summit Road,
Noble Park,
Victoria 3174, Australia.

To the Music Trade only:
Music Sales Limited,
8/9 Frith Street,
London W1V 5TZ, UK.

Front cover photo: Ronald Grant Archive

Every effort has been made to trace the copyright holders of the photographs in this book but one or two were unreachable. We would be
grateful if the photographers concerned would contact us.

Typeset by Galleon Typesetting, Ipswich
Printed in the United Kingdom by Redwood Books, Trowbridge, Wiltshire

A catalogue record for this book is available from the British Library.

Visit Omnibus Press at www.omnibuspress.com

ACKNOWLEDGEMENTS

Thanks to: Chris Charlesworth, Rob Dimery & Omnibus Press; my agent Tanja Howarth; Reel-Com (the coolest video search on the planet); the Cinema Bookstore; staff at BFI Library; Moviefinder; *Time Out* Library; Alina in Los Angeles for all the contacts; the helpful East and West Coasters who tried to move mountains; Crazy Larry for early encouragement; all the helpful folks at various film festivals; the Cinema Store; Angela Smith for pulling this together; John Cale for the Zoë Lund story; Mark Eldridge for Crockett assistance; Kim's Video & Music on Bleecker; Dan Taylor and the folks at Exploitation Retrospect; Louis Yansen for the info; Simone Monetti for fixing me up with the Mylène Farmer material; James in Minneapolis for the Nine Lives info; my parents and most of all, my wife Anna, for constantly doing her Reno "Hey Man" impersonation to keep me smiling and for successfully executing Operation Pasolini.

CONTENTS

THE CAST OF CHARACTERS

Victor Argo, Actor
Argo, a veteran of films like *Taxi Driver* and *Mean Streets*, acts in *King Of New York, Bad Lieutenant, Snake Eyes* and *The Funeral*.

Michael Barofsky, Sound Mixer
Barofsky was Production Sound Mixer on *Bad Lieutenant, Snake Eyes* and *Body Snatchers*.

Bojan Bazelli, Cinematographer
Bazelli brought his flashy, polished camera skills to *China Girl, King Of New York* and *Body Snatchers*.

Paul Calderon, Actor
Calderon acts in *The Home Invaders, King Of New York, Bad Lieutenant* and *The Addiction*.

David Caruso, Actor
Caruso acts in *Crime Story, China Girl* and *King Of New York*.

Nicholas De Cegli, Actor
De Cegli acts in *Bad Lieutenant, The Addiction, The Funeral* and *The Blackout*.

Joe Delia, Soundtrack Musician
Delia is to Ferrara what Peer Raben was to Fassbinder, serving as a one-man soundtrack scoring machine. Delia scored the soundtracks to *Nine Lives Of A Wet Pussycat, The Driller Killer, Ms. 45, Fear City,*

China Girl, King Of New York, Bad Lieutenant, Body Snatchers, Snake Eyes, The Addiction, The Funeral and *The Blackout*. His soundtracks for the earlier Ferrara films positioned him as a kind of rough edged, post-punk Bernard Herrmann.

Nancy Ferrara, Wife of Abel/Actress
Nancy Ferrara acts in *Snake Eyes* and *The Blackout*. According to Ferrara, he met Nancy when, "she was acting in a theatre production." They were married in the late Eighties and adopted two American-Indian children in the early Nineties.

Marla Hanson, Screenwriter
Hanson wrote *Love On The A Train* and co-wrote *The Blackout*. She was also Ferrara's girlfriend during his separation from Nancy circa 1996-97.

Paul Hipp, Actor
Hipp acts in *China Girl, Bad Lieutenant* and *The Funeral*.

Nicholas St. John, Screenwriter
Ferrara's high school buddy and long-term collaborator St. John has written many of the screenplays for Ferrara's best-known films: *The Driller Killer, Ms. 45, Fear City, China Girl, King Of New York, Body Snatchers, Snake Eyes, The Addiction* and *The Funeral*. Interestingly, he has never written for any other director. He lives in New York State and teaches Catholic catechism for a living, writing the screenplays around this full-time commitment. Ferrara told *Cahiers du Cinéma* that: "He (St. John) is very Christian, faith is an integral part of his life. The Bible for him is the truth. He knows exactly why he believes. We've known each other since we were 15. It's a very long friendship. We have two completely different lives but we stay close regardless." St. John can be seen acting for a split second in *Ms. 45* where he plays the younger of two detectives, hanging around in the background of the scene. *Film Comment*'s David Chute described him as: "small, stringy and intense, but he's better dressed and groomed (than Ferrara), less of a punk and more of a smoothie." Ferrara also described St. John to *Film Comment*'s Gavin Smith: "Nicky is an artist, a guitar player, a writer, to me that's an incredible person . . . There are periods of our lives where we see each other a lot or we don't see

each other; we work in a lot of ways to try and come up with the goods. We've tried every way, we work together, we work on the phone, we work by fax, he writes things, I work on them again, I come up with ideas and he looks at them."

Mary Kane, Producer
Kane has worked in varying producer roles on *Ms. 45*, *China Girl*, *King Of New York*, *Bad Lieutenant*, *Snake Eyes* and *The Funeral*. According to Ferrara: "She's someone I've worked with for a long time. She keeps a low profile on a shoot, she never meddles in artistic things. Mary Kane is my friend, a very old friend."

Harvey Keitel, Actor
Keitel acts and digs "down into fucking hell" in *Bad Lieutenant* and *Snake Eyes*.

Ken Kelsch, Cinematographer
Ex-Marine Kelsch brought what Ferrara has called his "rock'n'roll" camera style and his "guerrilla" working methods to *The Driller Killer*, *Bad Lieutenant*, *Snake Eyes*, *The Addiction*, *The Funeral*, *The Blackout* and *New Rose Hotel*.

Charles M. Lagola, Production Designer
Lagola worked as a production designer on *Bad Lieutenant*, *The Addiction* and *The Funeral*.

Jimmy Laine, Director/Actor
Jimmy Laine is Abel Ferrara's pseudonym. Under this moniker, he acted the part of Reno Miller in *The Driller Killer* and a rapist in *Ms. 45*. It is also the credit that appears on the film *The Nine Lives Of A Wet Pussycat*, only abbreviated to 'Jimmy Boy L'. The pseudonym also regularly surfaces on the soundtrack credits, whereby Ferrara either plays guitar or co-writes material. The reason for this pseudonym was probably inspired by Fassbinder who used the pseudonym 'Franz Walsch' (a double who has 9 credits in Fassbinder's filmography) as a means by which he could edit, write, act, direct and do just about anything else he wanted to do.

Zoë Lund, Writer/Actress
Zoë Lund a.k.a Zoë Tamerlis a.k.a Tamara Tamerlaine acts in *Ms. 45*
and has a brief cameo role in *Bad Lieutenant*. She also co-wrote the
screenplay for *Bad Lieutenant*. Previous to starring in *Ms. 45* (aged
19), Lund had shown an early talent as a musician before being
seduced by film, as she told *Exploitation Retrospect*: "I could write a
concerto with 17 violins that could be more powerful but film works
on a more visceral level where I can go into the collective audience
and make sure my point gets across." She made an early decision after *Ms. 45* that she didn't want to become part of what
she calls "Abel's stable" and has since acted in the *Miami Vice*
pilot 'The Prodigal Son' as well as in many independent European
and American films such as Temistocles Lopez's *Exquisite Corpses*
and Larry Cohen's *Special Effects*. She has written several novels, a
pilot for ABC called *Crackdown*, a rough screenplay for Ferrara's
proposed film about the last few days of Pasolini's life and also a
screenplay called 'Curfew USA' which she unsuccessfully tried to
sell during the early Eighties. Zoë Lund has said of Ferrara: "He has
always been a close friend despite the fact that there are times when
I have wanted to decapitate him. He can at times be quite sadistic,
not in any sort of exciting way, just in a mundane and hideous
fashion, even to his own detriment. He'd be the first to cut off his
own nose to spite his face if it gave him a sadistic thrill, but at the
same time he can be fired up by the essential questions like those
asked by Christ and the (Bad) Lieutenant."

Long after I had finished writing this book, various American
sources got in touch to inform me that Zoë Lund died in a Paris
hospital in early May 1999. She and her husband Robert had
apparently moved from New York to Paris three years earlier. After
almost a week in hospital, she died of heart failure. She was only 36.

John Paul McIntyre, Grip/Sound Technician/Creative Consultant
Ferrara and St. John's high school buddy John Paul McIntyre brought
his technical talents to *Ms. 45*, *China Girl* and *Bad Lieutenant*.

Edward R. Pressman, Producer
Pressman, who has past credits on his resumé such as Terrence
Malick's *Badlands*, Brian De Palma's *Sisters*, Fassbinder's *Despair*,

Oliver Stone's *Wall Street* and Sam Raimi's *Crimewave* as well as blockbusters like *City Hall*, *Hoffa* and *The Crow*, funded a work of genius when he sent Ferrara a cheque for $40,000 to start work on *Bad Lieutenant*. A relationship bloomed and the pair have since worked together in producing *The Blackout* and *New Rose Hotel*.

Anthony Redman, Film Editor
Redman has worked as editor on *Fear City*, *China Girl*, *Cat Chaser*, *King Of New York*, *Bad Lieutenant*, *Body Snatchers*, *Snake Eyes*, *The Blackout* and *New Rose Hotel*.

James Russo, Actor
Russo acts in *China Girl* and *Snake Eyes*.

Randy Sabusawa, Producer
Sabusawa acts in *China Girl* and *Snake Eyes* (as the producer double-dating with Sarah Jennings and Eddie Israel). He was co-producer on *Bad Lieutenant* and *The Funeral* and casting director for *Snake Eyes*.

Schoolly D, Soundtrack Musician/Rapper
Hip hop legend Schoolly D's gritty raps have appeared on the soundtracks to *King Of New York*, *Bad Lieutenant*, *The Blackout* and *New Rose Hotel*. He told *Uncut* why he works with Ferrara: "Abel's like me. He came to his chosen art form with a vision, his own particular slant of doing things and he's never compromised that for anybody. That, if you're an artist who cares about your work, is the only way to go about it."

Annabella Sciorra, Actress
Sciorra acts in *The Addiction* and *The Funeral*.

Christopher Walken, Actor
Walken acts in *King Of New York*, *The Addiction*, *The Funeral* and *New Rose Hotel*. He has written a screenplay about the life of porn star John Holmes which Ferrara intends to film.

Christ Zois, Screenwriter
Zois co-wrote *The Blackout* and *New Rose Hotel*.

1

NOTES ON FERRARA

"I love life fiercely, desperately. And I believe that this fierceness, this desperation, will carry me to the end. Love of life for me has become a more tenacious vice than cocaine. I devour my existence with an insatiable appetite. How will it all end? I don't know. I am scandalous. I am so to an extent to which I stretch a cord, an umbilical cord, between the sacred and the profane" – Pier Paolo Pasolini.

Abel Ferrara. Director-Auteur. The King Of New York. Manhattan's Pasolini. A Godard disciple. A Times Square Polanski. A man with Fassbinder's zest for life in the fast lane. A student of Bresson's style. A documentor of low-life. A man whose films struggle with the thin line between good and evil, beauty and ugliness, love and hate. A lapsed Catholic trying to find redemption through the lens of a camera, grace in the quiet hum of a film projector. A film-maker who, like Pasolini, stretches a 'cord between the sacred and the profane'. A director whose films wallow in the mire of urban realism. A man who makes films about characters who can't communicate, who have been abandoned, who are afraid, who are vulnerable, who are in pain; characters lost in the crude glare of city lights. A director who makes his characters suffer, who makes them journey into the darkest corners of human existence, who shrouds them in misery and alienation – and then, only when they've been to hell and back, offers them redemption, usually followed by death.

Abel Ferrara's films are all about absenteeism; the absence of love, family, faith, justice, loyalty, respect, God, purity, feeling, law and order, security and safety, balance. When Susan Sontag described Robert Bresson's films as being all about "the meaning of confinement and liberty", her words might just as easily apply to St. John/Ferrara's recurring themes. Ferrara's work splits into two halves: everything before *King Of New York* and everything since. The first half of his career places him somewhere between Martin Scorsese pre-*Raging Bull* and Roman Polanksi. The second, more mature half of his career has seen him re-position himself somewhere between Jean-Luc Godard and Pier Paolo Pasolini. This mature period has seen Ferrara's control of *mise en scène* intelligently flower, the almost bullying demands he makes of his cast reach a militant plateau and his command of cinematography necessitate longer, more ambitious takes and more elaborate editing finesse. Technique has replaced impatience; consideration has replaced immaturity; impression has replaced the constraints of conventional narrative.

Ferrara's style is equal parts polished and punky, sacred and profane, profound and frivolous. A typical Ferrara film will feature: a shot involving a mirror (usually portraying a character's reflection and hence serving as a symbolic soul); a shot or scene of two women in a sexually intimate clinch; visual representations of Catholic iconography, usually the sign of the cross or an image of the Madonna; a close-up shot of a woman's breast and/or nipple; a shot of a hand or hands framed to quote Robert Bresson; a climactic moment of redemption or salvation; at least one shot of a neon-drenched nocturnal city; a scene featuring prostitutes (a cruder, sleazier reading of Godard's use of prostitution as a motif and metaphor); one scene reflecting the paranoia of urban existence; the flawless use of eclectic soundtrack music; one shot (usually on a bed) of a female character that will recall one of Godard's painterly shots of a woman's beauty; the use of the colours blue and red in lighting composition (reflecting heaven and hell but also paying homage to Godard's fixation with these two colours); a scene featuring either a church or a priest or a nun; a scene of extreme violence and a romantic scene with a sinister, destructive undercurrent. All of these stylistic hallmarks that justify his status as an auteur are played out on Ferrara's palette: a setting of urban realism.

Many admirers of Ferrara's work see his success as inseparable from the screenplays written for him by Nicholas St. John. Like

Fassbinder, Ferrara depends on and uses a small team of regular collaborators in order to shoot quickly and effectively. The consistency of his work, one could argue, is based on this fact. The Ferrara style is a group style, a collective style that bears his signature. Although St. John's writing has provided Ferrara with some of his most concrete and acclaimed work, his masterpiece, *Bad Lieutenant*, did not involve St. John. It is for this reason that we can see that Ferrara's authorship is far greater than those who cite St. John as the brains behind the pair would have us believe. Even when directing a five-minute rock promo video for singer Mylène Farmer, the results are still intensely Ferrara-esque. Ferrara has yet to write and direct a film and always seems to rely on St. John or those in his circle to get the writing done. Ferrara has said of screenplay writing, "I don't really write, it will put you round the bend faster than anything." One of his influences, Robert Bresson, once offered a theory as to why directors didn't write their own screenplays: "I don't understand why it is that those (film-makers) who can write – and many of them can – don't write their own screenplays. I have a hunch the reason they use screenwriters is that if film-making is an art, if the film-maker is responsible for everything he does, then constantly he undermines himself, it is a desperate business, whereas having a mate write the screenplay removes every last scrap of uncertainty, leaving you free to work more lazily."

Maybe it is a question of insecurity that drives Ferrara to depend so heavily on such a tight circle of regulars. He has spoken of his dependence on St. John, Lund, Kelsch, Redman, Delia and Kane as a way to ensure fast and high quality work. This inner circle (see Cast Of Characters) is much like a gang. They are all fiercely private and loyal, their connection based on mutual respect and admiration. As Ferrara says, "Film-making is a communal trip." Ferrara's decision to surround himself with a coterie of intimates also recalls the way his influences worked. Fassbinder used the same names over and over again, ranging from like-minded collaborators to lovers: Franz Walsch, Peer Raben, Ingrid Caven, Gunther Kaufmann, Irm Hermann, Juliane Lorenz, Xaver Schwarzenberger, Hanna Schygulla, Liesgret Schmitt-Klink, Thea Eymesz, Michael Ballhaus and Dietrich Lohmann. Pasolini also depended on a gang of regular faces such as Tonino delli Colli, Nino Baragli, Ninetto Davoli, Franco Citti, Ennio Morricone and Danilo Donati.

Ferrara has remarked that for him, all film is documentary. Films like *The Driller Killer, Bad Lieutenant, Snake Eyes, The Addiction* and *The Blackout* have tended to veer towards a confessional, documentary style. Ferrara's tag as 'auteur' (bestowed on him by *Cahiers du Cinéma* circa *King Of New York*) has blossomed to a greater degree with intense, confessional works like *Snake Eyes* and *The Blackout*. His career readily splits into distinct sections: The Urban Victim Trilogy (*The Driller Killer, Ms. 45, Fear City*), The TV Years (*Miami Vice, Crime Story, The Gladiator*), The Territorial Trilogy (*China Girl, Cat Chaser, King Of New York*), The Redemption Trilogy (*Bad Lieutenant, Snake Eyes, The Addiction*), High Budget Re-Make Disaster (*Body Snatchers*) and what could be called The Damnation Duo (*The Funeral, The Blackout*).

Ferrara the man has been described in many different ways: "almost always dressed entirely in black, Ferrara speaks in a mix of thick New York rap and gangster patter" . . . "he's a big, shambling stumblebum of a guy with a mop of greying Roman curls" . . . "Ferrara and his screenwriter/partner Nick St. John (are like) real life characters from *Mean Streets*: volatile, high strung heavy guys. Like if they weren't making movies they'd be robbing liquor stores" . . . "in his green T-shirt, jeans and sneakers, with a dark smudge of beard on his bony jaw, Ferrara resembles a cross between punk singer Richard Hell and the comic actor Gary Raoul." All observers speak of his restlessness, his workaholic passion for film-making, his fondness for a fast living lifestyle à la Fassbinder. His fondness for drinking and partying has led many to wonder where the line between Ferrara and some of the characters in his films ends.

Abel Ferrara was born in the Bronx on July 19, 1951. He was raised by an Italian-American father (whose profession Ferrara has described as "wheeler-dealer") and Irish-American mother. He has told other interviewers that his father was a bookmaker. The Ferrara family roots go back to Salerno, near Naples. His father, like many Italian immigrants at the time, arrived from Italy and settled in the Bronx. Once married to Ferrara's mother, the couple had five children. Abel was the only son. Unsurprisingly for a film-maker

4

who dwells so heavily on spirituality and Catholicism, he was raised in a strictly Catholic household. He went to the Sacred Heart Catholic school in the Bronx, an education that has marked him for life, as he told *Film Nation*: "I went to Catholic School up until fourth grade, then I escaped. When you were in kindergarten you were in, like, the front row and there was this giant crucifix, about eight feet tall, dripping blood." The earliest film he remembers seeing was Douglas Sirk's *Imitation Of Life* (1959) which starred Lana Turner. Sirk was an enormous influence on Fassbinder, who in turn fascinates Ferrara. As he was growing up, Ferrara was equally fascinated by rock'n'roll and film.

In 1966, when Ferrara was fifteen, his parents uprooted the family and relocated to a small town called Peekskill (population circa 20,000) in the Westchester County region of New York State. Ferrara was taken out of Catholic School and enrolled at Lakeland High School where he formed a small but intense clan of friends. One of them would go on to write screenplays for many of Ferrara's most acclaimed films, under the name Nicholas St. John. It is unclear if this is his real surname, though it happens that St. John is the patron saint of writers so it could easily be a *nom de plume*. Another friend, John Paul McIntyre, would wind up working as a sound technician and creative consultant on many of Ferrara's films. The last of the pack was Richard Shaw, who didn't pursue a career in film. The four friends were inseparable. Ferrara and St. John, who both played guitar, formed a rock'n'roll band that made a Bob Dylan/Rolling Stones-inspired racket for just over a year.

In 1967, when Ferrara was seventeen, he bought a Super 8mm camera. The Super 8mm camera became Ferrara, St. John and McIntyre's primary interest and the rock band fell by the wayside. St. John was writing tiny vignettes which served as screenplays and McIntyre concerned himself with helping Ferrara get the right kind of lighting. Already, each of the three was staking a claim on a particular aspect of film-making. Ferrara talked about this period of his life to *Film Ireland* saying, "We were basically in a rock'n'roll band that wasn't making a living, and we realised that. I think making films is the natural expression for people my age. It just brought everything together. I wasn't into doing something on my own – maybe I was scared to. Maybe I still am. We did the same shit

5

then as we're doing now. We had a film called *The Hold-Up*, that was a good title, about robbing a gas station. The same ideals were there, we were grappling with the same things."

Although the films kept the cine-buff trio occupied, high school was coming to an end and the Vietnam War was looming in the background. Ferrara and his three friends, all from lower-middle class families, were in his words "grade A cannon fodder". They were also fiercely against the war. Ferrara, like many of his generation, had made the trek to the Woodstock festival, had absorbed Dylan's protest messages and was scared to death of getting drafted. He and the gang used the Super 8mm camera and a newly acquired beaten up 16mm camera as media with which to channel their fears about the draft and anger about the war as he explained to *Film Ireland*: "We were totally, vehemently against the war. The films we made at that time were totally focused on anti-Vietnam war stuff – Super 8, 16mm, one-minute, two-minute films."

After high school, Ferrara, also like many of his generation feigned an interest in further education in order to escape the draft. He spent one or possibly two years as a student at Rockland Community College, either bolstering weak high school grades or majoring in Art. Ferrara never went to film school. Instead, like Pasolini, Fassbinder and Godard, he preferred to learn the ropes as he went along. For this reason he has said that Pasolini is a primary influence because, "he filmed his visions and did it without qualifications". Indeed, Ferrara joked in one interview, that in his opinion, film school was simply a place to "acquire" equipment. He did however take a series of short film-making classes that fleshed out what he'd picked up working in 8mm and 16mm, probably during the spell he spent at Rockland Community College. Ferrara, as Fassbinder would often quip, learned to make films by "making films".

Ferrara left Rockland at the turn of the Seventies. He moved back to New York City, most likely with Nicholas St. John and John McIntyre. It was at this point, when the boys were each twenty years old, that Richard Shaw went his own way. The period from then until the 1979 release of Ferrara's first feature film, *The Driller Killer*, is sketchy. Ferrara won't discuss this chapter of his life. There are no facts – one journalist described it as a "black hole" in Ferrara's life – and the few interviews that the director does give never touch on this period. Kent Jones wrote in a piece on Ferrara for *The Hard Press*: "There are rumours that he made porno films before *The Driller Killer* but he won't talk about that (if it's true, it's not much of a surprise)." This rumour surfaced many times while I was researching this book. There is a film which was released in 1976 which is credited to Ferrara by several sources. The *International Dictionary Of Films And Film-makers* contains the following biographical entry on Ferrara's career: "Ferrara began making eight millimetre shorts at high school with his friend Nicholas St John. Their first feature together was *Nine Lives*, a love story with fantasy elements, which they made after forming Navaron Films." A similar biographical entry appears on the Hollywood Online, Moviepeople Database and reads, "Ferrara was born in the Bronx, but he spent most of his childhood in Peekskill, where he met the two young men who would eventually become his screenwriter and sound engineer, Nicholas St John and John McIntyre. As boys, they would play around with 8mm cameras. Later, in (the) mid-Seventies, the three reunited and founded Navaron Films, where they produced *Nine Lives* (1975)." The Internet Movie Database cites the film under the title *The Nine Lives Of A Wet Pussycat* on its Ferrara filmography. They cite its release date as 1975. They state that the film has an 'X' rating, that Ferrara directed under the pseudonym 'Jimmy Boy L', that Nicholas St. John wrote it, that Joe Delia scored the soundtrack and that the actors included Dominique Santos and an uncredited performance by Abel Ferrara. Other websites cite the leads as Dominique Santos and Pauline LeMonde. The Internet Movie Database also offers two buzz phrases for the film: 'pornography' and 'hardcore sex'.

One source summarised the film to me as being about two ex female lovers who correspond by a series of letters which lead to fantasy episodes of a predominantly lesbian theme. According to foreign sources who've seen it, Ferrara acts in the film using the pseudonym Jimmy Laine. The Canadian online video store, Blackest Heart Media, who sell the film, advertise it as follows: "*9 Lives Of A Wet Pussy*. Abel Ferrara, director of such classics as *Driller Killer* and *Ms. 45*, actually starred in a XXX hard-core film, no shit! See

7

Abel fucking! Must be 21 and include age statement." The film, although freely available in the U.S and Canada, is legally unavailable in the UK so I was unable to verify if it is indeed an Abel Ferrara film. The film's importation is also prohibited due to its content clashing with the red tape of the Obscene Publications Act. If this porn film is indeed his work, then it's deliberately separate from Abel Ferrara's work. *Nine Lives* is a Jimmy Laine film, not an Abel Ferrara film, and that is why he won't discuss it. If it is indeed Ferrara's work, then it is a bit of fluff that he shot to pay the rent and no doubt to finance some of the making of *The Driller Killer*. The purpose of this book is to appraise Abel Ferrara's outstanding body of films. This film, which he has never discussed in any interview, is therefore not a film he considers to be part of his work (if it is indeed his work).

The Driller Killer started life as a five-minute short and spiralled out of control. Work was started on the feature-length film circa 1977 – it was shot guerrilla-style on a minuscule budget, partly funded by Rochelle Weisberg, the producer who produced a 1976 horror B-movie called *The Drive-In Massacre* about a killer stalking drive-in movie-goers. Rochelle Weisberg co-produced *The Driller Killer* with Ferrara and St. John's own production company, Navaron Films; they took the name from a lens inscription on a Bauer C-3 Super 8mm camera which reads Neovaron, dropping the 'e' and 'o' and replacing it with an 'a' for 'Abel'. Rather like the equally inexperienced young Fassbinder setting up the no-budget production company, Antitheater-X Film, Ferrara was creating opportunities for himself where there were none.

The shoot took forever, which did nothing for casting possibilities, because no actors or actresses were willing to work as and when the co-producers could next raise enough cash to shoot another sequence. The film was shot using grainy 16mm in either Ferrara's Union Square apartment or on the streets. It's a gritty, punky effort about a painter whose desperate situation drives him to kill what he fears with an electric drill. St. John wrote it and McIntyre handled the more technical aspects of the shoot. Ferrara directed and also took the lead role of Reno Miller – a double homage to his hero at the time, Roman Polanski. Ferrara has since described his team on the shoot as: "a crew of characters from Philly who would keep going off doing mercenary work in Panama and shit."

Louis Yansen, writer and director of *Girl Gone Bad* and co-writer and co-director of *Misplaced*, worked for a few nights on *The Driller Killer* shoot. He told me, "While I was attending the Graduate Film School at NYU, a fellow student needed to replace himself for a few days on a horror film he was working on. In those days, to work on such a film was the last thing a self-respecting graduate film student considered appropriate. Godard, yes. Roger Corman, no. However, I soon changed my mind when I was told that it paid $100 a day, an astronomical figure in those days. So for a couple of nights I was the gaffer (lighting) on *The Driller Killer*. What I remember is that we travelled all over Manhattan filming people (getting) drilled to death, like at bus stops and stuff like that. Ken Kelsch was the Director Of Photography. I think the reason for this was that he owned his own Arri and I think he shot a prior porno film by Abel. He was an ex-marine and had a rather military approach to things. I remember going and shooting some stuff at Abel's loft in Union Square. I remember that Abel had a girlfriend there and I think . . . that she was somehow linked to the porno film he made. The whole thing had a very seedy atmosphere to it. Abel struck me as a competent director, less interested in acting than in getting things done and over with, not impressive . . . Needless to say I was somewhat shocked by his success later with *King Of New York* et al."

When *The Driller Killer* opened in select theatres across the US, Ferrara and the crew were amazed to find that the film generated genuine interest. *The Driller Killer* swiftly established itself as a cult classic, as Ferrara later recalled to *Film Comment*: "The movie opened in about 20 theatres in, like, Portland and Seattle or someplace. They're calling us up for TV spots. We were laughing – you got to be kidding, you're gonna put this film in the theatre, much less put spots on television?" Some reviews were harsh, such as the *Variety* critique: "The most stupid thing about the film is why, when he turns into a murderer with an electric drill, he doesn't go downstairs and eliminate the band, which could have improved the tone of the film by at least a thousand per cent."

Fired up by its success, St. John whipped up a sketchy screenplay for a second feature, about a mute garment worker in New York City who is raped twice in the same day and sets out for revenge on the male gender. Rochelle Weisberg again co-produced with Navaron. The lead role went to 19-year-old unknown actress Zoë Tamerlis who, as she explained to *Exploitation Retrospect*, was involved on *Ms. 45* from the start. "In the beginning stages of the film, the only material that existed was vague descriptions of several scenes. Being that my face is on the camera, without dialogue, for something like 98% of the time, I was involved very much. As to the film being pro-woman, I go beyond that by saying that the film is as much pro-woman as it is pro-garment worker, whatever." The decision to have Tamerlis play a mute part was a risky move for a second-time director, but was undoubtedly inspired by Wim Wenders' 1978 film *The Wrong Move*, in which Nastassja Kinski plays a deaf-mute acrobat. (Several reviewers compared Tamerlis's looks to those of Kinksi at the time.) The film became an instant cult hit when it opened in 1981 because Warner Bros had picked up the distribution option; the film therefore received a wide theatre release. Janet Maslin wrote in her *New York Times* review: "Thana's silence allows Mr Ferrara the chance to demonstrate how skilfully he can communicate a character's thoughts by purely visual means. He has also paced the film crisply." *Variety* garnished even more praise: "*Ms. 45* is an exciting urban thriller that despite many a nod to past suspense classics, manages to leave an indelible original impression." When the film played in Los Angeles, Zoë Tamerlis, by then 20 years old, drummed up some great publicity for the film by pulling up at any theatre which showed the movie in full *Ms. 45* costume and driving a Chevy van that had the *Ms. 45* logo painted on the side. Anyone who tried to interview her had to follow two rules: the interview could only take place after 11pm and only in one particular res-taurant on Sunset Strip. The film wouldn't get shown at British or European theatres until 1985. When it did, London weekly *City Limits* raved, "*Ms. 45* is one of the fiercest films ever to emerge from the twilight zone of the American cinema where exploitation meets Art."

This double success attracted interested parties to the dynamic duo. St. John had already written the screenplay for a slasher on the loose in New York City feature that would become *Fear City* (sometimes known as *Border* or *Ripper*). He got the idea for the screenplay from a real-life incident, as he told *Film Comment* in 1983: "It happened around 1975. There was some strange guy in New York who was infatuated with go-go dancers. He'd go out and try to put the moves on them. The cat would call up these girls, say he was this big Hollywood producer and he'd give them $2,500 to go out to dinner with him. But then he'd, like, take them to Delaware or someplace, tell them to undress, take their clothes and make-up and then go out to his car and split." St John then took this seed, planted it and developed it into a psycho-on-the-loose slasher flick: "We thought it would be more cinematic to make the guy a slasher. We try to give him more of a motive. Like he's sexually maladjusted but he has this mentality that 'I can abuse the law because I'm strong and I'm perfect'. He's more philosophically based. There are three books in his room: *Thus Spoke Zarathustra* by Nietzsche, *Origin Of Species* by Darwin and *Crime And Punishment* by Dostoevsky. So he's a killer but he's also the flower of philosophy."

They signed with Bruce Cohn Curtis, head of Zupnik/Curtis Productions (and grand-nephew of Columbia Pictures granddaddy Harry Cohn) and found themselves shooting the film in both Los Angeles and New York City with a budget of $4,000,000, several more zeros than they were used to. They also had a reasonable cast: Melanie Griffith, Tom Berenger and Rae Dawn Chong. A major report of on-set drama between Ferrara and Cohn Curtis appeared in *Film Comment* in 1983. Ferrara told the author of the piece, David Chute, that *Fear City* wasn't his first choice of film. He had wanted to shoot a "futuristic war movie" (*Birds Of Prey*) but it hadn't found a backer because it was too "anti-corporations". During the interview, St. John revealed one of Ferrara's huge influences when he joked, "Abel really has pretensions of being (Robert) Bresson."

Chute witnessed Ferrara's rebellious attitude when Cohn Curtis arrived on set with an entourage. When he asked how the morning shoot had gone, Ferrara laughed. Then, when Curtis took issue with a shot which was scheduled for the morning but had been postponed, an argument started. According to Chute, Ferrara kept grinning like a naughty schoolboy and Curtis went berserk, shouting that it was his money that was getting wasted by Ferrara's failure to stick to production schedules. Curtis called Ferrara, in

11

front of everyone, a "stupid asshole". Ferrara responded by hurling a handful of the macaroni that he was eating into the producer's face. Chute saw the fireworks that resulted: "Then Ferrara's on his feet lunging for Curtis, slapping at him, catching him across the face and knocking his glasses off. 'You don't call me asshole!' " Initially, it was muttered that Ferrara was going to be thrown off the shoot and replaced by another director, but it didn't happen. Things cooled down. Some of the tension had arisen because Cohn Curtis had demanded revisions in St. John's original 70-page screenplay. Cohn Curtis even forgave Ferrara enough to talk him up to Chute saying, "Abel's a very talented guy, which is why I've given him this big shot, his first big picture." *Fear City* brought the pair to national attention in spite of its early tasters of Ferrara's trademark stylistic traits: sleazy scenes where girls dance in strip clubs, a breast/nipple close-up, scenes of heroin use, a romantic/sexual relationship between two women, stomach-churning attacks by the stalker on the dancers and neon-drenched nocturnal shots of Manhattan. The *Variety* review of the film at the time of its release at the end of 1983 read: "*Fear City* lives up to its title as a tough, nasty, big league meller by throwing every element from the exploitation cookbook – gory violence, straight and gay sex, multiple murders, martial arts, raw dialogue, mobsters, drugs and gobs of female nudity – into the pot and letting them stew."

The modest success of *Fear City* landed Ferrara a major agent and a deluge of offers to work in the world of TV. He accepted three high profile, lucrative TV projects and one pay-the-bills telemovie job, while St. John worked on the screenplay for their next feature, *China Girl*. Michael Mann, Executive Producer of overnight hit TV series *Miami Vice*, approached Ferrara's agent and invited Ferrara to direct an episode of the show, tentatively called 'The Home Invaders'. Ferrara jumped at the chance and started a love affair with Miami which would climax in his 1997 feature, *The Blackout*. His flashy work on the episode led to a repeat offer to direct another episode called 'The Dutch Oven', which screened as part of the show's second season. The worldwide success of the show delivered Ferrara's directorial style into the homes of millions.

Meanwhile, *The Driller Killer* had been thrust to the forefront of the British newspaper *The Daily Mail*'s campaign against the so-called 'video nasties', films which had been released during the early 1980s home video revolution and which were suddenly considered to be a dangerous influence on those who saw them. The rental sleeve to *The Driller Killer* depicted a scene in which Reno drills a bum through the forehead and blood pours into his eye. This image alone catapulted the film to legendary status in the 'video nasties' debate. When I met Mike Bor, the Principal Examiner at the British Board Of Film Classification during the research for this book, he told me that, "*The Driller Killer* was almost single-handedly responsible for the introduction of the 1984 Video Recordings Act."

The Video Recordings Act was the Government's response to the media and public pressure that grew around the snowballing moral outrage that surrounded the 'video nasties'. Amazingly, very few of these self-appointed moral guardians had even seen *The Driller Killer* and were simply basing their campaign on the video sleeve and the fairly unsubtle title of the film, which was a feint homage to Tobe Hooper's *The Texas Chainsaw Massacre*. This legislation appointed the BBFC as censors and examiners of video as well as cinema release titles. The small print reads: "As the authority designated by Parliament with the responsibility for classifying videos under the Video Recordings Act 1984, the Board must first of all determine whether or not a video is suitable for a classification certificate to be issued to it, having special regard to the likelihood of video works being viewed in the home. In making this decision, the Board must have special regard, amongst other relevant factors, to any harm that may be caused to the potential viewers or through their behaviour, to society because of the manner in which the work deals with criminal behaviour, illegal drugs, violence, horror or sex."

As soon as the act was up and running, *The Driller Killer* was officially banned in Britain and withdrawn indefinitely. Prior to the Video Recordings Act, the censorship of film and video was handled by the courts and by the Obscene Publications Act. This meant that the courts decided if a video was likely to "deprave and corrupt"; the Director Of Public Prosecutions kept a list of videos that were found to be obscene by the court and were therefore banned. *The Driller Killer* was instantly added to the list (along with Sam Raimi's *The Evil Dead* and Pasolini's astonishing critique of

Fascism, *Salò*), bringing Ferrara notoriety. Once banned, the film floated in censorship purgatory. According to an oft-quoted comment by BBFC examiner Ken Penry, the film was submitted to the BBFC for reconsideration by a distributor in the late 1980s and was in the BBFC's opinion, "cuttable. We could have taken out that particular (eyeball) shot but the distributor lost interest. From their point of view if they don't keep the goodies, it's just not worth progressing." When Ferrara's first *Miami Vice* episode, 'The Home Invaders', aired on the British BBC network, *The Driller Killer* furore was still simmering away and the BBC made several censorious cuts to the episode which featured actual and implied scenes of torture. It seemed Ferrara had become the censors' public enemy, just like his hero Pasolini.

The 'video nasties' debate that overshadowed The Home Invaders episode of Miami Vice didn't bother Michael Mann who handed Ferrara the much-coveted director's chair for the feature-length pilot of his new TV series, *Crime Story*, set in 1963 Chicago. The dazzling results illustrate just how fast Ferrara's talent and style had evolved. For a film-maker who'd sidestepped a film school education, these TV jobs offered invaluable experience and gave him a grounding that would enable him to "arrive" in grand style with his coming-of-age gangster epic, *King Of New York*, in 1990. Jim Shelley recounted a hilarious story in his piece 'The Abel Guy' for *Neon* magazine: "In 1984 Abel was in the public gallery of a New York court, attending the trial of a gangster as part of his research for the Michael Mann TV series, *Crime Story*. Suddenly, the trial was interrupted when the prosecuting attorney complained to the judge that a member of the public was trying to intimidate the jury. 'They were talking about this guy in sunglasses,' Abel says. 'I turned around to see who it was and there was no one there. It was me.'"

After completing the *Crime Story* pilot, he spent three weeks in Los Angeles making a telemovie called *The Gladiator*, which was based on a television story and screenplay by William Bleich, about an alienated mechanic who turns vigilante when his kid brother is killed by a drink driver. It aired on TV in 1986. Ferrara only did it to buy time for later work: "We did that job because it got us an advance for Nicky to write the first draft of *King Of New York*, so we go to LA and crash cars for about three weeks and everyone has a good time and the film showed it."

The TV run came to an end because Ferrara was ready to film what I have termed his 'Territorial Trilogy': *China Girl*, *Cat Chaser* and *King Of New York*, all films which feature battles over geographical, ethnic, interpersonal, gang, romantic and moral territories. The first part of this trilogy is the St. John-penned *China Girl*, a not entirely successful study of a love affair between two 15-year-olds, one a Chinese-American girl, the other an Italian-American boy. *China Girl* takes the racism which greets the couple from each of their respective ethnic communities and pits it against the mob business that goes on between the Chinese and Italian community elders. Although the film's polished style carries the mark of Ferrara's Michael Mann work, his handling of the young lovers is underconfident. The film was stolen by David Caruso who, after excelling in *Crime Story*, played an Italian-American hood. The film's tale of romance in a racist society would surface again in a similar vein in Spike Lee's awesome *Jungle Fever*, a tale of a love affair between a black architect and his Italian secretary (played by Annabella Sciorra, an important figure in Ferrara's later work).

After *China Girl*, Ferrara was again bombarded with offers of TV work. He considered working on another major network pilot but plans for the proposed show were shelved. Instead, he took the director's job on an adaptation of Elmore Leonard's *Cat Chaser* novel, backed by Vestron Pictures, who were spending money like water after the success of *Dirty Dancing*. The screenplay, which was written by Elmore Leonard himself with help from James Borrelli, is often too elliptical and expects too much of the viewer's imagination. However, Ferrara was a Leonard fan and jumped at the chance to spend more time in Miami. The film starred Peter Weller and Kelly McGillis as lovers kept apart by her former Dominican Republic General husband. Unfortunately, *Cat Chaser* never received a US release because Vestron Pictures folded. Ferrara abandoned the editing stage and left it to the producers to finish up. Their cut was an abomination of Ferrara's work, as he later told *Film Comment*'s Gavin Smith: "*Cat Chaser*'s a tough one to talk about because to me it was a film we never finished. I left the editing because the opportunity to do *King Of New York* came up. And that's a cardinal sin for a director." The film only received a theatre release in Britain, but it was the cut print that showed (complete with a voice-over that the producers insisted on adding). Ferrara admitted that the way the producers cut the film makes it barely comprehensible, acknowledging, "Even I couldn't follow it."

The Italian-backed *King Of New York* kick-started Ferrara's mature work. It was the picture in which his style finally became fully formed. All the promise of the earlier films blossomed in this stunning, operatic tale of a gangster who gets out of jail and declares himself judge, jury, government and God. St. John most likely took the basic idea from Fassbinder's *Gods Of The Plague* which told the tale of a German gangster who gets out of jail and sets about re-establishing his position in Munich's underworld. Christopher Walken took the lead role and under Ferrara's direction, turned in the finest acting performance of his career. The cinematography, use of classical music, exquisite lighting and powerful dialogue and screenplay earned Ferrara immediate praise from respected film journals such as *Film Comment, Sight and Sound* and *Cahiers du Cinéma*. *Film Comment*'s Gavin Smith wasted no time in defining the Ferrara/St. John style: "Imagine what kind of films Martin Scorsese and Paul Schrader might have made together if they had remained in orbit around *Taxi Driver*'s lurid nighttime New York and carried on exploring the pulp violence of *Hardcore* and *Rolling Thunder* and the ethnic obsessions of *Mean Streets*. They'd probably be very like the films made by director Abel Ferrara and his screenwriter and collaborator Nicholas St. John." Not everybody loved the film though. According to Kent Jones' piece in *The Hard Press*, Ferrara's penchant for "tits and ass" caused his wife, Nancy, to "walk out of a New York Film Festival screening of *King Of New York*."

After the critical success of the film, Ferrara was expected to follow it up with a big-budget re-run of similar themes, or to take on a fat pay cheque directing job. Instead, he shot his *tour de force*, independent film masterpiece, *Bad Lieutenant* in a mere 20 days on a minuscule budget that Kent Jones claims in *The Hard Press* to have been approximately $1,000,000. An initial cheque for $40,000 from Hollywood producer Edward R. Pressman got the film off the ground, as Ferrara explained to *Sight and Sound*: "I don't know what possessed him to give me that money . . . Nicky St. John didn't want to write it for reasons of his own. So Zoë Lund, star of *Ms. 45* came in, we worked together. She wrote it very quickly, at least the first draft and we needed a draft in two weeks." Ferrara told *Empire* in typically dry fashion how the writing collaboration worked out: "I'd tell her a bunch of shit and she'd make sense of it."

Ferrara had already conceived the idea for the film from two sources. The first was a Bob Dylan-inspired folk-blues song which he had written called 'The Bad Lieutenant'. The second, which gave the song its subject matter, was a news story that dated back to 1982 about a nun who was raped in Spanish Harlem. Although Ferrara had been as shocked as any other New Yorker by the story, he also wondered why the rape of a nun was elevated to priority police and media status when hundreds of other rapes passed by every week with barely a mention. He combined the story and his reaction to it with another idea about a police lieutenant with every vice known to mankind. Ferrara turned this recipe of ideas into the song 'Bad Lieutenant' (which plays out the alternate cut of the film after Schoolly D's track 'Signifying Rapper' had to be replaced due to legal problems) which, in Ferrara's words, was about a lieutenant with "a wife and five kids and a house by the park" who has a mistress, a drug habit, is completely corrupt and is investigating the rape of a nun. He would later give *Film Ireland* a different theory on where the Lieutenant's character sprang from: "The *Bad Lieutenant* emerged from my imagination and I'm stuck with him. You know people who have all these different vices and you think, 'Man, what if you had one guy who had every one of 'em, and then if he was a cop on top of that, so he has a gun and a badge to go with his womanising and alcoholism and everything else?' I thought that'd make a pretty funny movie. Then we hired Harvey (Keitel) and out went the humour."

Ferrara had Harvey Keitel on his wish-list for actors to play the role of the Lieutenant but didn't expect him to take the part: "When we were writing the script, we thought it was a real long shot he'd do the film because we knew he was booked for a long time." Keitel was in a state of despair over his mother's death when a rough draft of the script was passed on to him by his agent. According to Marshall Fine's biography *Harvey Keitel: The Art Of Darkness*, Keitel was also suffering because his wife, actress Lorraine Bracco, had unexpectedly left him for actor Edward James Olmos (whom

Ferrara had twice directed in *Miami Vice*), taking their five-year-old daughter Stella. He read the script, having just finished work on Quentin Tarantino's *Reservoir Dogs*, a film which, along with *Bad Lieutenant*, would entirely rejuvenate his reputation as an actor prepared to go all the way. The screenplay didn't appeal to him: "I read a certain amount of pages and I put it down. I'm going to get a lead role and do this? There's no way I'm going to make this movie." Slowly, the theme of redemption began to filter through the screenplay. Keitel, struggling to forgive Bracco for leaving him, related passionately to the Lieutenant's struggle to accept that the nun could forgive the boys who had raped her: "The issue of forgiveness fascinated me because I was having a very difficult time in my own existence with forgiving and asking for forgiveness. I found it to be a wrenching struggle." Ferrara found Keitel ready to "dig down into fucking hell" (as Keitel, playing a film director in *Snake Eyes*, would say to his lead actor): "He's an ex-Marine for Chrissake. He said to me when we started filming, 'My sword is sharp, my boots are shined. Just point me to the hill and I'll take it.'" Peter Lehman wrote of Keitel's performance in *The Velvet Light Trap*: "Keitel's over the top performance succeeds as it does precisely because its excesses, replete with gut wrenching moans and groans and muted, twisted, distorted posturings, fit in so well with the overall style of the film."

Ferrara, deciding not to write the screenplay himself, asked St. John to write the screenplay but he turned it down because he said it asked too many questions; St. John prefers to write screenplays that seek out answers rather than those which dig up more uncertainties. His more than capable substitute, Zoë Lund, continued to work on the screenplay while Ferrara added a *cinema-vérité* feel to the film by persuading Detective Bo Dietl, who had headed up the original investigation team working on the nun rape case, to take a part in the film as . . . one of the detectives working on the case. Keitel's own daughter Stella appears in the film as the Lieutenant's daughter. One of the two Jersey girls who get pulled over by the Lieutenant had earlier in the day been baby-sitting Stella for Keitel. It is a case of 'all hands to the pump', the same kind of creative independent film-making approach that Pasolini and Fassbinder had pioneered.

18

Zoë Lund was at the time acting in a low budget independent film. Also working on that film was musician and composer, John Cale, who told me how Lund handled the duel tasks: "Zoë showed up. She was acting in this little film that I did which was done by a friend of mine, France Holland, who had been involved in that Madonna movie, *Desperately Seeking Susan*, that Susan Seidelman did. Zoë was hovering around because she was in the movie. It was all shot out on Long Island. We were in this ramshackle old house from around 1920. It was totally empty and they had brought out these lights. And Zoë's dressing room was on the top floor. Somebody would make a run to the local bakers first thing in the morning to get some chocolate croissants for Zoë. So I would go up to the dressing room too, sitting there and waiting to get called. Zoë would often be there doing her nails for a long time and she would get very, very upset about her nails. And she was saying, 'I've got this script that I've got to finish.' And then invariably, she would come and appear and be in tears . . . She would lose her composure fairly regularly and I could never understand why until somebody mentioned that there was a certain habit that was contributing to all this. So whenever we'd have conversations about the script or whatever, it never got anywhere because she'd be distracted or go somewhere else and I'd never get any sense of reality about it. Then, I went to see *Bad Lieutenant* and I mentioned it to France and said, 'Holy shit, Zoë's in the movies'. And France said, 'Yeah, that was her script.' "

Zoë Lund finished the screenplay and handed her searing portrait to Keitel. She later fleshed out her personal vision of the character to *Interview* magazine: "This is a character who is so flawed that a lot of viewers can't understand how far he goes to seek redemption. People talk about how morally terrible the character is, not understanding what the Lieutenant finally did. One of the things the Lieutenant is raging against is that Christ had already taken this ultimate act of responsibility. Some people wait for the opportunity to do that, but you can't wait. You have to seize the moment. And that is what the Lieutenant finally does." Ferrara also talked to *Interview*, focusing on the Lieutenant's hunger for gambling that eventually kills him: "The gambler has a kind of inner confidence in the beginning because he has a fix on that ball game. He knows

19

who's going to win. (Darryl) Strawberry is not going to let him down. Then again, if anybody is gambling that way, it's almost a desire to lose."

For an independent film, *Bad Lieutenant* gained a lot of attention when it opened at the end of 1992. Martin Scorsese bestowed the highest imaginable compliment on the film by saying, "It's the kind of film I wanted *The Last Temptation Of Christ* to be . . . It's among the greatest pictures made about a man's descent in search of redemption." Janet Maslin wrote in *The New York Times*, "Imagine a series of long, improvised-sounding behavioural meltdowns and you get some notion of what happens when *Bad Lieutenant* goes off the tracks." When the film opened in Britain in early 1993, Mark Kermode wrote in *Sight and Sound*, "Ferrara deliberately distances his latest film from the cosy conventions of the mainstream. Extensive use of a hand-held camera and numerous sparsely edited sequences create a documentary-like quality reminiscent of the director's long-banned debut (*The Driller Killer*)." The film, which had been shown out of competition at the Cannes Film Festival on the same day as *Reservoir Dogs*, led critics to instantly cite Tarantino and Ferrara as kindred spirits, breathing sharp, ultra-violent new life into the exhausted gangster genre; predictably, the heinous tag 'Sons Of Scorsese' was bandied about. Ultimately however, although Tarantino has spoken of *King Of New York* as the best non-Italian gangster film ever made, there is no way that the two directors can be compared.

Bad Lieutenant provoked outrage in Ireland, where it was immediately banned from ever getting a cinema or video release. In Britain, after being passed by the BBFC uncut for theatre release, *Bad Lieutenant* spent six months trapped in the BBFC's system. It was finally passed after substantial cuts had been made to the scene of the nun's rape and also to the prominent depiction of drug use. To date, the BBFC have passed the following Ferrara films to video, all with savage cuts: *Ms. 45*, *Fear City*, *China Girl*, *Cat Chaser* and *Bad Lieutenant*. In short, when you see a Ferrara film on video in Britain, you are unlikely to be watching the film that he made. This enrages Ferrara, as he told *City Limits* in 1985: "It's an abomination, man, when they start cutting, but just fuck 'em. All this makes me say, 'We're gonna make 'em worse.' " The issue of censorship also came up in Tom Charity's 1997 *Time Out* piece, in which Ferrara's attitude veered from angry to dismissive: "I can't even imagine where the censorship of adults comes from. Eventually the films outlive censors, so I don't worry about it. I think the censors are more dangerous than the films." Similar extensive cuts were made to *Ms. 45*: a scene in which Thana saws her attacker's arm off is removed and cuts were also made to both rape scenes. When Warner Home Video released the film under the alternative title *Angel Of Vengeance* in 1998, as part of their 'Maverick Directors' series, a percentage of the initial copies that went on sale were, due to an error, the uncut version that had outraged the BBFC. They were immediately recalled, but a week's sales had already taken place and therefore plenty of Ferrara fans ended up with the uncut edition; it can be identified by the spine notation: '082897'. This version – the one Ferrara made – is the version that I will discuss later on in the chapter on *Ms. 45*. Unfortunately, this hopeless situation isn't much better in the US where all of Ferrara's films, except the re-make of *Invasion Of The Body Snatchers*, have been stuck with the 'NC-17' rating.

Ferrara's battles with the censors echo those fought by one of his acknowledged influences, Pasolini. The latter's contribution to *RoPopag*, *La Ricotta*, was seized in March 1963 by the Italian authorities, who charged Pasolini with making a film that insulted the religion of the state. He was found guilty by the courts and sentenced to four months in jail. Fortunately, the sentence was overturned by the appeals court. *Theorem (Teorema)* was confiscated by the public prosecutor's office in Rome in September 1968 and charged with obscenity. The trial ended and the film, after being judged a work of art, was released from charges. *Salò* remains banned to this day in many countries including Britain even though it carries a '16' rating in France and an '18' rating in Italy. The trilogy that included the *Decameron*, the *Canterbury Tales* and the *Arabian Nights* led Pasolini to be branded a "pornographer" in Italy. Pasolini's many battles with state censorship mirror Ferrara's struggle to get one film released that doesn't get altered by the censors.

Ferrara followed *Bad Lieutenant* with two very different projects that would both surface in 1993. The first was the third remake of

Don Siegel's classic film *Invasion Of The Body Snatchers*. A storyline co-conceived by fellow cult director Larry Cohen and his writing partner recast Siegel's small-town setting to a heat drenched military base. Ferrara, working with Terry Kinney, Meg Tilly and the young Gabrielle Anwar (who had wowed critics in *Scent Of A Woman*) had his biggest budget to date: $20,000,000, provided by Warner Bros. He even managed to get St. John a small writing role on the screenplay team. Unfortunately, *Body Snatchers* illustrated that Ferrara, capable of making a work of raw genius on a budget of $40,000, had no idea how to make a great film with $20,000,000. Even a plethora of special effects and explosions fail to save the film from drifting so far away from Siegel's bristling masterpiece of poetic paranoia that it becomes plain dull. It's not hard to wonder if Ferrara had taken the project for the money, mimicking John Cassavetes who would act in endless awful films in order to finance his independent feature films.

The second project, *Snake Eyes* (later re-titled for TV and video as *Dangerous Game*), crackled with chaotic brilliance. St. John's screenplay is about a New York film director called Eddie Israel (played by Harvey Keitel) who travels out to Los Angeles to direct a film called 'Mother Of Mirrors' about a suburban couple whose marriage is disintegrating. Madonna played an actress called Sarah Jennings who played the part of the wife and James Russo (the *China Girl* veteran) played the actor playing the husband. The wife has experienced a religious conversion and rejected her former decadent, promiscuous lifestyle; the husband still sees drink, drugs and wild sex as "the truth". Ferrara described the film-within-a-film structure as "a cross between *Bad Lieutenant* and *Day For Night*, with Harvey playing Truffaut and Madonna as the actress." The sprawling film, which addressed the blurred line between film and reality, is Ferrara's longest film to date and is heavily reminiscent (in structure and execution though not content) of John Cassavetes' films. The film inevitably recalls other classic films using a film-within-a-film structure, such as *Contempt* and *Passion* by Jean-Luc Godard, Truffaut's *Day For Night* and Cassavetes' play within a film, *Opening Night*. Keitel saw it as being a "story about the complete failure to cope with life's problems. The problems are dealt with in a destructive way." Madonna, who as good as disowned the finished product, was furious with Ferrara's final cut: "It was an entirely different movie when I made it, it was such a great feminist statement and she was so victorious at the end. I loved this character. But the way Ferrara edited it completely changed the ending. When I saw the cut film, I was weeping. It was like someone punched me in the stomach. If I'd known that was the movie I was making, I would never have done it, and I was very honest with him about that." Ferrara responded to her allegations in an interview with Kent Jones in *The Hard Press*, saying, "She's a fuckin' jerk. Like we sit around taking out the best scenes in the movie to spite her. You know how paranoid you gotta be to fuckin' say something like that?" Regardless of the Ferrara-Madonna fall-out, even Keitel admitted that something was missing from the finished film: "I can't say I'm shocked that it disappeared. There were brilliant things in that film, but the central story was lacking. It needed some work, which we failed to do."

Few critics could review the film without seeing it as Ferrara's personal confession. Ferrara has spoken of the way in which the film is filmed as a documentary about the making of 'Mother Of Mirrors': "(Keitel) was basically directing that film, so we were shooting a documentary about the making of that movie, 'Mother Of Mirrors'. And that was Harvey's film. Or Eddie's film." More interesting is the fact that Ferrara let Keitel/Israel do his job for him, as Kent Jones reported in *The Hard Press*: "I heard stories about the shoot, fast single takes, Abel sitting in the corner having a glass of wine and letting the film direct itself. The finished product bears out those stories. This wild, mean, smart movie about confessional film-making and the business around it is the work of a director interested in letting different elements, film within a film, scenes of family life, video rehearsals that may or may not be staged, collide at full throttle." *Cahiers du Cinéma* also saw *Snake Eyes* as a confessional Ferrara work which collapsed all boundaries between the film and the director: "With *Snake Eyes*, Abel Ferrara signs his name to a film, in which he is ultimately not just foreman as well as architect, but also active spectator and implicit and central character."

The casting of Ferrara's wife Nancy in the role of Madlyn, the director's wife, did little to detract from the mood of self-portrait even though she wasn't originally meant to be in the film, as Ferrara told *Cahiers du Cinéma*: "It was Harvey (Keitel) who had the idea. At the beginning, he had thought that Jane Campion would be perfect for the role but she wasn't free. And anyway, Nancy is really good." He did agree that having his own wife play the wife of a director based on himself lent the film an extra layer: "It's evident by the end of the film. Nancy brought something to the role that only she could have brought. It's a voyage of the soul, to go to the heart of a subject like this, with people who you love and who you have confidence in." It also paid homage once again to Ferrara's key influences. Fassbinder often cast his lovers in his films. Polanksi cast his lover Sharon Tate in *The Fearless Vampire Killers* before going on to cast his wife Emmanuelle Seigner in *Frantic* and *Bitter Moon*. Cassavetes cast his actress wife Gena Rowlands in seven of the eleven films that he directed and Jean-Luc Godard cast his wife Anna Karina in many of his ground-breaking early masterpieces. After divorcing Karina, Godard continued this reality/film blurring by frequently casting his second wife, Anne Wiazemsky, in features. His partner after his split from Wiazemsky, Jean-Pierre Gorin, worked side by side with Godard, as did his replacement, Anne-Marie Mieville.

During scenes where Eddie demands more from his cast or baits Sarah into a more intense delivery of her lines, we seem to be edging towards Ferrara's notorious penchant for tearing strong performances from actors' and actresses' souls. The sub-plot, which concerned the breakdown of Israel's own marriage to Madlyn, flirted to sinister effect with ambiguous revelation. When asked by *Time Out*'s Tom Charity if Keitel's director was a thinly veiled Ferrara portrait, Ferrara confessed, "Watching that film reveals a lot about us. But Harvey's directing it, not me. Those are his methods." Again, Ferrara is not accepting authorship for his work here, but attributing it to a 'we', placing himself within his gang of confidantes. Asked by *Cahiers du Cinéma* if *Snake Eyes* was an example of *cinema vérité*, Ferrara replied, "No, it's very styled. Everything is reconstructed."

After this double whammy of critical and commercial flops (neither film gained much of a theatre release), Ferrara kept a low profile until he returned in 1995 with *The Addiction*. During the vacation, he and Nancy adopted two native American-Indian children. By a terrible irony, during the same period Nicholas St. John was devastated by the death of his eldest son. He poured his grief into two screenplays which Ferrara shot back to back, with overlapping casts and crews. The first, *The Addiction*, draws parallels between vampirism and addiction. The second, a stylish period gangster film entitled *The Funeral*, concerns the reactions of two heavyweight gangsters when their 22-year-old kid brother is suddenly gunned down by a rival mobster. Both screenplays were thinly veiled attempts by St. John to come to terms with his loss.

The Addiction was shot in black and white on a $500,000 budget; Def Jam Records mogul Russell Simmons used his affiliations with Polygram to fix Ferrara up with the cash. Lili Taylor was cast as the postgraduate NYU philosophy student Kathleen Conklin. Christopher Walken and Annabella Sciorra, both also in *The Funeral*, took cameos as vampires while Paul Calderon, who had played a cop in *Bad Lieutenant*, was cast as Kathleen's tutor/lover. The decision to shoot in black and white (Ferrara says simply that he 'saw' the film in black and white) clamped restrictions on potential backing, as Jim Shelley mentioned in his interview with Ferrara for *Neon* magazine: " 'No one wants to see black and white anymore,' one potential backer told him. 'What about *Schindler's List*?' Abel asked. 'That was about the Holocaust.' 'Well, this is about the Holocaust,' he insisted. 'My own personal Holocaust.' " Faced with this kind of blanket disinterest, Ferrara had to find independent backing; he got the $500,000 from Simmons and started shooting. His determination paid off, as he told *Film Ireland*'s Paul Duane: "I just went to the crew and said, 'Y'know, let's shoot it.' You wait to see who shows up and who doesn't, and that's when you know who's on your side. Anyway, I told 'em I don't wanna go begging with this script, 'cause nobody's gonna get it."

The finished film was both intelligent and offbeat. The cinematography paid homage to Carl Dreyer's *Vampyr*, Ferrara's Manhattan shot through with a similarly stifling use of shadowplay. In a timely act of fate, it was released in the US at the same time as Michael Almereyda's black-and-white, arty and exceptionally tedious vampire film, *Nadja*, starring Peter Fonda and Elina Lowensohn. Critics latched on to this double whammy of black-and-white vampire revivalism and tried to lump the two films together.

The Funeral was a return to the stylish techniques of *King Of New York*, Ferrara playing it relatively straight after the complex redemption trilogy of *Bad Lieutenant, Snake Eyes* and *The Addiction*. The plot concerns the tension between a gangster's hunger for revenge (Ray, played by Christopher Walken) after his kid brother is killed, and the contrary pleas for peace from his wife Jean (played by Annabella Sciorra). It's a story of the beautiful (Jean) and the damned (Ray). In spite of Jean's pleas, *The Funeral* ends not with Ray's redemption but with his damnation after his brother shoots him and then commits suicide. The performances, most notably Christopher Walken's casket-side monologue (heavily reminiscent of Marlon Brando's monologue by his dead wife's corpse in *Last Tango In Paris*) and Annabella Sciorra's walking conscience of a mobster wife, were again further proof that Ferrara has established himself as a director capable of extracting searing performances from established acting names. This is particularly true of Ferrara's work with Walken, an actor who has seemed cold in films where he hasn't connected with the director. Ferrara and Walken hit it off from the first day they met, as Ferrara has revealed: "Me and Walken, we're like Fassbinder. Just get the cash, get the chicks, call him up and shoot it over the weekend. Just jam." Laurence Fishburne, after working with the pair on *King Of New York*, commented, "Cats like Abel and Walken, they're on the edge, man. They are the edge, man. There ain't shit those motherfuckers ain't seen."

The role of Ray was originally going to be played by Nicholas Cage, as Ferrara bitterly recalled to *Film Nation*: "Cage was in, we were about to shoot the movie and he walked. Not very nice. When Cage pulls a stunt like that it's a nightmare, total nightmare." Faced with a potential disaster, Ferrara and the production team were rescued by Walken: "Walken saved our lives," Ferrara enthused. "We offered that part to him before. The thing is he felt he wasn't right, he was too old, you know? So then we went to Cage. Cage seemed perfect. Neopolitan, the right age, the whole deal. Then all of a sudden, for whatever reason, Cage walks. Walken knows we got our back to the wall, comes back and does the part and kicks ass."

By the time these films surfaced (during the same week in Britain in April 1997), rumours had started to surface about Ferrara's increasingly erratic behaviour. After Martin Scorsese had been unable to attend a film preservation fund-raiser in New York, Ferrara had been drafted in at the last moment as guest speaker. When it was time for him to speak, he got up, thumped the microphone and said, "Can everybody be quiet please. There's something I'd like to say about film preservation." He was ignored by the sea of chattering table-holders. He asked them once again to quieten down but everyone kept on chattering away. Finally he snapped, "Can everybody just shut the fuck up for a minute!" Although this did capture the audience's attentions, it also got him ejected from the building by security.

On a press trip to Italy to promote *The Funeral* and *The Addiction*, Ferrara took his bizarre behaviour to new heights. After making a small legion of Italian journalists wait for over an hour for an interview, he had them all sent to his hotel room, where he promptly climbed into a wardrobe. He insisted that he would only answer questions through the wardrobe door (mocking the 'confessional' aspect of the interview process). The two brave journalists who played along with the madness and conducted their interviews through the wooden dresser were rewarded with one of Ferrara's more lucid interviews. Ferrara hates interviews with a passion. He's too restless to sit still, too excited about his next film to discuss whichever film just got released. He's been making films for twenty years now and there are less than twenty English language interviews with him in existence.

In late 1996 Ferrara was booked to give a talk on directing at the London Film Festival which was showing the British premiere of *The Funeral*. On the appointed Sunday morning, he handpicked a selection of clips from his work. When the scene where the nun gets raped in *Bad Lieutenant* showed, he stood at the back of the theatre and cheered. Halfway through the class and during another clip, he walked out of the theatre and vanished for over an hour. His PR team found him eating pizza and drinking a beer in Leicester Square. Apparently he'd wanted a beer but had been forced into buying some pizza in order to get it. Tom Charity wrote about this incident for *Time Out*: "his vanishing acts became so frequent on this trip that the PRs had to install an icebox full of beer in his car, just to ensure that he'd return to it at regular intervals. Worst of all, during one interview Mr Ferrara dropped off."

When he appeared on the American TV talkshow *Late Night With Conan O'Brien* in late 1997, he was wasted. One observer of the show commented, "Abel was so messed up, but somehow Conan let him on. Abel kept talking about how he was going to do a live show from a strip club so anyone could be on TV, as long as they paid cover and tipped the girls. My friend Sidney was in the green room. She said Abel was blotto. He introduced himself and then zoned out."

Ferrara then took on two shorts. The first was a rock promo video for French-Canadian singer Mylène Farmer's 1996 single 'California' – the video again played with motifs of prostitution and violence, trademark subjects in Ferrara's work. The second was a short film for an HBO presentation called *Subway Stories*, a project for which a series of directors produced a short film about a variety of experiences on New York's subway. The producers had placed a series of advertisements asking members of the public to send in their stories of anything unusual that had happened to them on the subway. Of the 1,000-plus replies that the producers received, a mere ten were filmed. Ferrara picked a story and gave it to Marla Hanson who turned it into a five-minute screenplay. By this time, it appears that Ferrara and Nancy's marriage was in serious trouble and Ferrara had started seeing Hanson. Her screenplay became a snappy, colourful vignette called *Love On The A Train* about a silent, complex affair between a married commuter (more a Hal Hartley character than a Ferrara character) and a stranger (played with typical zest by Rosie Perez). This short marked a new direction for Ferrara, with a lightness of composition that must have been a reaction against the sombre hues of *The Funeral*.

His next feature was a return to the sprawling chaos of *Snake Eyes*. It was called *The Blackout* and owed a debt to Larry Cohen's *Special Effects*, Jean-Luc Godard's *Contempt* and Hitchcock's *Vertigo*. Ferrara billed it as a film about "obsessive love". *The Blackout* returns to the film-within-a-film structure that Ferrara had utilised for *Snake Eyes* and also continued the theme of Hanson's screenplay for *Love On The A Train*, polarising love between 'the wife' and 'the girl'. Ferrara had originally started the screenplay in 1994. At this early stage, the narrative concerned a man who "murders a woman who leaves him, coupled with *The Blackout* story." Having written the first 30 pages, Ferrara handed it over to Hanson. When she and Ferrara broke up, the screenplay took on a new relevance as Ferrara also told Gavin Smith: "The idea was let's do Hitchcock, a take on *Vertigo*, where a guy investigates a murder and he finds he committed it. But then it came back around with the break-up of my relationships with Nancy ... and Marla ...." In light of this, it's hard not to wonder if the polarisation of romantic interest in the film's 'plot' is based loosely on a polarisation of Ferrara's estranged wife and ex-lover.

It was an ingenious bit of casting to have Matty, a Hollywood movie star, played by Matthew Modine, a real-life Hollywood movie star. Modine, who has a reputation as one of Hollywood's clean-cut boys-next-door actors, takes to the role perfectly. His boyish good looks sit uneasily on such a slimy, depraved character, and an endless succession of untrustworthy, mischievous grins gives Matty a perversely boyish air. Modine told *Neon* magazine that his agents were "somewhat nervous" about him doing the film; indeed, it was a risky choice for Modine to play the part of Matty, an alcoholic, junkie actor. However, he told *Empire* magazine that the experience of working with Ferrara ended up shaking both him and his career up: "I couldn't have done *The Blackout* at the beginning of my career. I do feel like this is a rebirth. If the significance of a baptism is to wash something away, this role has changed me. I have a different understanding of myself. I have a different kind of maturity and I'm really glad I met Abel Ferrara."

Modine also told *Empire* that he had many reservations about taking the role, mostly because of the way he felt the script treated women: "I was encouraged to do it by several women I love and respect, which is strange because it's so violent to women, so abusive." In spite of this, Modine was finally persuaded by Ferrara himself, as he told *Uncut* magazine: "He wouldn't stop calling. He's somebody who has the freedom to make the film he wants. And the odd thing, y'know how violent the film is towards women? Well, the first person to say, 'You should read this, it's really good,' was my wife. I said, 'What, are you out of your mind?' I picked page 10, I'm saying to the girl I'm supposed to love and want to marry, 'Why don't you take a knife and cut that baby out of your stomach? Give it to me and I'll cut it out for you!' This is the most pornographic thing, completely obscene. But then several other women said, this is good, read it. While the guys that read it were all sharing my reaction, like, 'Wait, this is dangerous and weird.' "

Modine told *Uncut* how supermodel Claudia Schiffer (another unlikely choice, like Madonna in *Snake Eyes*) wound up with the Susan role: "Abel saw her in a restaurant and she was like, 'Oh I love your movies.' And he was, 'Huh, really?' He couldn't believe Claudia Schiffer watched his movies. He sent her the script and she wanted to play Susan, not the lead, and Abel thought, 'Great I've found this beautiful milkmaid, I want to put my head against her breasts and just go to sleep for the rest of my life.' This wholesome woman was to represent that to Matty; would take care of him and nurture him and wanna save him. Then in rehearsals she said she'd been in a relationship like this, with somebody who didn't love her back, which was painful."

Schiffer played the romantic counterpart to Annie 1, played by the eternally beautiful French actress Béatrice Dalle, who told *Cahiers du Cinéma* how she landed the Annie 1 part: "Abel tracked my number down and called me from New York one Friday night. I couldn't believe it. He said to me, 'Can you come and see me?' I said, 'Sure. Of course I can.' " Dalle's only prior work with an American director was when she played a blind woman in the Paris segment of Jim Jarmusch's *Night On Earth*. She took the first flight out of Paris: "I left on the Saturday morning. I met up with him and he didn't speak a word of French and I only knew three words of English but it went OK. That wasn't the problem really, it was more how I would play a role in English." Ferrara explained to Dalle that he wanted her to play a French actress: "He wanted the character to be believable but also one that I could play." The final key character, that of porn film-maker Mickey Wayne, was played by Dennis Hopper who had problems with what all of the cast have referred to as the total chaos of the shoot. Dalle told *Cahiers du Cinéma* that Ferrara and Hopper argued constantly on the set, each having a conflicting set of ideas about how things should be done. In spite of this, Ferrara sang his praises once the film was finished: "Hopper's dynamite. He's been driving me nuts, busting my chops, but you know, talent rules."

Yet more peculiar stories about Ferrara filtered from the set, such as this one which Modine shared with *Empire*: "I really pissed off Abel when I asked if Jesus had died for his sins. He didn't speak to me for three days. This was after he had got beaten up badly in South Beach. When he came back he was thinking of giving up drink. He wanted a really big cross to keep them [the demons] away, like a vampire. He scared the hell out of me. I'm not Catholic, I'm not into any organised religion but I like that hip dude Christ. And Abel rejuvenated my interest in religion. Or spirituality at least." Modine went on to describe Ferrara in fairly frank terms: "You could look at Abel and say he's a drunk, a junkie or weirdo. You realise he is a brilliant man who is so sharp in a rock'n'roll kind of way. It's not a mistake that Keith Richards or Bono gravitate towards him."

After the midnight screening of *The Blackout* at the Cannes Film Festival in 1997, Ferrara grabbed a guitar, director-painter Julian Schnabel strapped on a bass and the duo started jamming. Claudia Schiffer, Béatrice Dalle and Matthew Modine all sang along with Ferrara's gruff voice, in a display which pretty much baffled the audience. Ferrara's life-long love of rock'n'roll has resulted in him often co-writing soundtrack material with Joe Delia (Ferrara's name often appears in the credits as a musician and songwriter). At the press conference earlier in the day, an out of control Ferrara had babbled so incessantly that Béatrice Dalle had been forced to put her hand over his mouth to get a word in. When *The Blackout* was shown at the Los Angeles International Film Festival in early 1998, it was still without a US distributor, despite the strong cast. A 'Question & Answer' session took place before the film was screened. Somebody in the audience apparently asked Ferrara about the problems with distribution. He explained that corporate giant Tristar had expressed interest and that there had been negotiations which had broken down. The audience member asked why negotiations had broken down. Ferrara said that Tristar, "spend a tremendous amount of money to bury a film" and went on to explain why negotiations came to a grinding halt: "I said, 'Why don't you guys just go fuck yourselves?' "

In September 1998, Visual Entertainment acquired the British rights to *The Driller Killer* and submitted a CBVS (Cut Before

Video Submission) cut to the British Board Of Film Classification's Director, James Ferman, who had long before explained that he would pass the film if cuts were made to the more violent drill killing scenes. Ferman and the BBFC examiners concluded that *The Driller Killer*, complete with the 54 seconds of cuts, was a film that could now be passed for video release. Robert Walak, Acquisitions Manager at Visual Entertainment, told me why he had submitted the film: "These films are getting re-appraised critically so I thought it was high time that *The Driller Killer* was re-submitted. Films like that do have a cultural significance. I can't imagine 15-year-olds going out and renting *The Driller Killer*, it will mostly be for people who are interested in Ferrara and want to check out his early work. In general though, there is a change in attitude towards what were viewed as 'video nasties' and are now being seen in a new light." The master that Walak acquired from Ferrara featured the restoration of approximately eight minutes of lost footage that had been missing from the 1980s print. Consequently the film altered from 85 minutes to 94 minutes in length. It turned out that a dozy projectionist had overlooked an entire reel at the mastering stage and once the mistake was identified it was too expensive to go back and amend the error. Once the certificate was approved, the BBFC issued a press release which stated, "The BBFC has classified the video of *The Driller Killer* as '18' with cuts. This is the first time that this 1979 Abel Ferrara film has been submitted to the BBFC. The film was never issued theatrically in the UK but became notorious as one of the first 'video nasties' when released in an uncut version on tape in the early 1980s. This uncut version was at that time the subject of a number of successful prosecutions under the Obscene Publications Act. The version which the BBFC has now classified has been pre-cut by the distributor to remove the more extreme and unacceptable images."

The press release went on to then explain more specifically why it had approved a certificate: "The Board has concluded that in this present cut version the film is unexceptional compared with many popular modern horror films and has lost much of its power to shock over the years ... The main problem with the original video version was the bloody killings perpetrated with the drill, which formed a large part of the video's original marketing campaign.

These have been significantly reduced. There is little terrorisation or suspense in the film. The violence is for the most part now dimly lit, in long shot and obscured by camera positioning. The Board has concluded that this cut version of *The Driller Killer* is unlikely to produce any harmful effects, either upon its audience or on society more generally." Regardless of the cuts, it was still a major moment in the cooling down of the 'video nasties' cultural hangover.

It's now 1999. Ferrara's loyal following of fans and critics are waiting for *New Rose Hotel* starring Christopher Walken, Willem Dafoe and Asia Argento, to be released. Even though the film won the Elvira Notari Prize and also the Filmcritica Prize at the Venice Film Festival as well as being nominated for the Golden Lion category, it has so far only been released in Italy (in March) and France (in April). The film is based on the William Gibson short story of the same name which appears in his collection of short stories, *Burning Chrome*. Edward R. Pressman has once again served as producer, and bills the film as a "fast paced techno thriller". The mini-web trailer certainly suggests that it's both slick and intense. Walken looks like a well-heeled businessman, Dafoe is icy as usual and Argento smoulders as a "beautiful treacherous woman". The film aired in various forms at The Hawaii International Film Festival, the Hamptons Film Festival and The New York Independent Film And Video Festival in September 1998, before getting its Canadian premiere at the Vancouver Film Festival. It also showed at the Venice Film Festival without end titles and was described by one correspondent on the Corona web-site as the "anti-*Johnny Mnemonic*".

Stuart Alson was responsible for getting the premiere of *New Rose Hotel* to the New York Independent Film And Video Festival. He sums up his relationship with Ferrara thus: "I first met Abel through a mutual friend and decided to screen his film *The Blackout* with Dennis Hopper, Claudia Schiffer and Matthew Modine in the April 1998 New York International Independent Film And Video Festival. It turns out that he is also my next door neighbour. After that we became friends and kept in touch. When it came to our festival in September 1998 we decided to handle the premiere of *New Rose Hotel*. Quentin Tarantino, Sean Penn, Harvey Keitel and many others showed up to the standing room only screening. I gave a small speech to introduce the film, Edward Pressman and Abel. It was the last night of the World Series where the Yankees won but all of Abel's loyal fans and press showed up. His films are great for the New York International Independent Film Festival because we represent cutting edge films that are made independently."

Bruce Fletcher, Programmer and Film Selection Co-ordinator for the Hawaii International Film Festival also told me how his festival came to screen *New Rose Hotel*: "We were able to screen *New Rose Hotel* because Abel Ferrara and Kevin Cherashore (Mr Ferrara's assistant) had just returned to New York from the Venice Film Festival . . . Kevin received the latest issue of *Filmmaker* magazine in the mail . . . (and) noticed the full page ad for the Hawaii International Film Festival at the front of the magazine. Apparently, this convinced them that it would be a good idea to visit Hawaii, so Kevin phoned our office and left [a message on my] voicemail asking whether or not we would be interested in hosting the US premiere of Mr Ferrara's new film, *New Rose Hotel*. I have been a tremendous admirer of Ferrara's work since I first saw *Ms. 45* in the early Eighties, so I immediately returned the call to say that it would be an honour to present the film as a Gala presentation in our primary venue, even though we were within days of our press deadline. Shortly after we went to press, Mr Ferrara offered the work to the Hamptons Film Festival (where it had the main US premiere). Abel and Kevin were both invited to Hawaii for the screening, however, due to circumstances beyond our control only Kevin made it to Honolulu where he acted as the official presenter of the work." The Hamptons Film Festival got to show the film because, "Serendipitously, Abel called us just at the moment we had another film cancel. We filled the slot with *New Rose Hotel*. Abel came from NYC to East Hampton with a crowd for the screening and the press chased him around town for interviews."

According to various rumours, *Strange Days* director Kathryn Bigelow was initially mooted for the film before Ferrara became involved. Likewise, the model Bridget Hall was originally rumoured to be taking the lead role, as was Claudia Schiffer, who'd already earned Ferrara's respect in *The Blackout*. In an interview with *Sight and Sound* in April 1997, Ferrara referred to the film as, "*Alphaville* and *Notorious*" and again, "it's *Notorious* meets *Death Of A Salesman*."

He also spoke of the film's key as being the Sandii role played by Argento: "she's a prostitute, a sleazy, tattooed, acne-faced freak . . . she's gonna have Louise Brooks hair, shades, chewing bubblegum." Another equally interesting yet Ferrara-esquely obtuse summary of the film ran as follows: "When Edward Pressman told us that he was definitely committed to making this William Gibson story, I felt obliged at least to give my opinion. The read turned into a revelation . . . *New Rose Hotel*. Gibson puts you into image overdrive. A tattoo on the inner thigh of a 14-year-old motorcycle magazine centrefold, scrawling Sandii, the girl named in that great Springsteen song and the name of my grandmother, the only Jewish woman to marry into my father's family of six brothers."

Where next? Ferrara has many pet projects that he has been trying to get off the ground for years. There's a St. John screenplay called *Birds Of Prey* which Ferrara has been pitching since 1979 and which he described to Gavin Smith in an interview with *Sight and Sound* as, "a film about revolution in New York, present day, the shit hitting the fan. The United States is run by a corporation and you're either working for the corporation or you're an enemy of the state. It's about those on the outside, who have jumped ship because they feel the morality of corporate America is not in the best interests of everybody. It could be a big budget movie and we could also do it for very little. It's the idea that matters." In another interview he revealed that Christopher Walken was interested in playing the lead role. Ferrara has also expressed interest in doing a sequel to Fellini's *La Dolce Vita* set in Miami, with Marcello Mastroianni as the father and Benicio Del Toro playing his son. Regrettably, the idea died when Mastroianni died. Thirdly, Ferrara has spoken of plans to make a series for a network like HBO which would feature a string of thirty-minute shows filmed in his local strip club. Ferrara imagines it as "a cross between the clubs in *King Of New York*, Dorothy Parker's Round Table and the club at the beginning of *Star Wars*." His fourth pet project is based on the life of porn star John Holmes who died of AIDS. This idea comes from a screenplay that Walken wrote and showed to Ferrara: "It's Chris's take on that person and being an actor and being famous and having a special gift and seeing where that can take you." The fifth project, and the one closest to Ferrara's heart, is a proposed film about the last few days of Pasolini's life, based on a screenplay written by Zoë Lund. Both of them discussed the project with Julian Schnabel in *Interview* magazine. Ferrara: "I have a project for a film about Pasolini. Sometimes I think, 'Why am I doing this? Here's this guy who's dead, didn't know me, never met me, where do I come off robbing this guy's grave?" Zoë Lund then went on to explain why they *did* want to make the film: "All you have to do is go up to a gas station attendant in Italy and say 'Pasolini' and there's immediately an eruption of emotion and sanctity and reverence and titillation and awe and mystery and desire that comes from mentioning that name."

Ferrara could do anything next (and having one of the most powerful people in the American film industry as your agent must surely help). He can pursue his Godard/Pasolini fixations, change tack and direct a big-budget studio number, return to some TV work, shoot some more music promo videos (he followed the Mylène Farmer video by directing a second promo video in 1998, this time for the single 'Iowa' by a band called The Phoids) or tackle any of the projects mentioned above. As Ferrara himself has said: "We're ready, we're rocking, we just want to keep the show on the road. Whatever it takes, we're not hung up on our, quote-unquote, 'cult reputation'."

2

THE URBAN VICTIM TRILOGY

The Driller Killer 1979

"To me it's a comedy. That was our sense of fun! The idea was a documentary about a dear friend of mine. I played the role of my friend. He lived in that attic with those two girls, they were his real girlfriends. We're not violent people ... We're just trying to put over the sense of frustration of not having any money" – Abel Ferrara, *Monthly Film Bulletin*.

"[*The Driller Killer*] is like *Taxi Driver* with a paintbrush; shot like a no-budget porno-abstract, disjointed, minimalist, rough hewn. You wonder if the actors are brain damaged" – *Film Comment*.

"The original video nasty" – *Sight and Sound*.

"In addition to thirteen murders, *The Driller Killer* has a collage of revolting sights and sounds, unmatched since *Peeping Tom* and *Performance* – the buzzing drill, grating punk rock, documentary footage of NYC derelicts, close-ups of disgusting fast food, streets full of garbage, the self-involved chatter of various minor characters and the seediest screen milieu since *Trash*" – *Monthly Film Bulletin*.

"Money is an abominable idol. It is everywhere. The only things that matter are invisible" – Robert Bresson.

François Truffaut once remarked that everything a critic needs to know about a film-maker's style and ambitions can be found in the first few minutes of any film-maker's debut feature. In the case of

The Driller Killer, Truffaut is onto something. A white opening title appears out of a black background: THIS FILM SHOULD BE PLAYED LOUD. This steals the generic rock'n'roll album sleeve-note and pastes it onto the big screen. Already, Ferrara was bringing his rock'n'roll interests to film-making. Church bells chime on the soundtrack, parodying the clichés of the horror genre that so many people wrongly classify *The Driller Killer* under. The screen turns red, then cuts to a blue tinted animal eye. Using a back shot, Ferrara has cinematographer Ken Kelsch film the character he's playing (a painter called Reno Miller, played under the pseudonym Jimmy Laine) as he enters a Church. The crucifix above the altar is drenched in red light. A lone man with a white beard, obviously destitute, sits alone, mumbling prayers like a mantra. Reno walks up the aisle and sits down on the same pew as the old man. Ferrara has Kelsch switch to a reverse shot of Reno staring at the old man whose prayers are now elevated to a disproportionately loud sound level on the soundtrack. A quick shot shows a young woman (Reno's girlfriend, Carol, played by Carolyn Marz) talking with a nun. Reno's hand itches along the pew's rail to take the old man's hand. The old man suddenly grabs Reno's hand. This abrupt act throws Reno into a panic and he runs off down the aisle. To the nun's surprise, he drags Carol out of the Church. The nun, who seems to know Reno by name, and hence suggests that Reno is a regular Church goer and devout Catholic, exclaims, "Mr Miller! Mr Miller! What's wrong?" While she says this, she stands beneath an inscription on the church wall that reads: THERE IS ALWAYS CAUSE TO PRAY. This is the first of a series of visual puns that Ferrara uses in the film and also a technique that he would use again in later films. When Reno is starting to crack, a single, random shot shows a Zeppelin air ship passing overhead with the slogan GOOD YEAR emblazoned on it. In another scene, while Reno drills a wino at a bus stop, an advertisement billboard that reads NEW YORK WINS is never out of the frame. Ferrara is taking a leaf out of Godard's style book and letting advertising do the talking.

Reno and Carol jump into a cab. Reno is freaking out; she doesn't understand why. He says that "some fuckin' degenerate bum wino" touched his hand and that was why he freaked out. In the last shot of the nun's solo monologue, she had made an odd and poorly explained comment about how the old man had had Reno's name and address on a piece of paper in his jacket pocket. What was this to suggest? That the old man was a kind of prophetic omen? A symbol of evil? More likely, the meeting had happened because the nun had found Reno's name and address in the old man's pocket and contacted Reno. This would explain how she knew his name. It would also explain why Carol waited in the Church's entrance, keeping a respectful distance from a possibly emotional encounter with an old face from the past. If this encounter was organised by the nun, then does this suggest that Reno thought that the old man was his father? We later learn in a nightmare sequence that Reno's mother never knew his father. Is the quest for his father a recurring theme? Where is his mother in the film? Dead? Estranged? If the man was Reno's father then it would explain why Reno reacts so savagely after the 'encounter'. He is shocked at the possibility that the down-and-out could be the father he never knew. This explains the random footage of Reno talking with down-and-outs and, in one scene, making a charcoal sketch of a wino. His fascination with these down-and-outs is a search for a father figure that he never had. We also later learn that Reno and his girlfriend (presumably Carol) had recently gone through an abortion which adds intensity to the situation. Why did they decide to abort the baby? Financial reasons? Immaturity of their relationship? Either way, Reno nearly becomes a father. Was that possibility coupled with the chance rendezvous with this old man/father figure the point at which his breakdown begins?

Or is the old man simply someone that Reno once knew? An old face from the past, a symbol of what happens when a person loses their balance on the tightrope walk between surviving and not surviving? Or someone he didn't know who by a strange coincidence simply happened to have Reno's name and address? The old man could have come to have those details from any number of sources. He could have known someone who knew Reno; he could have even copied the name at random out of a telephone book. The possibilities are relentless. The only consistency throughout these possible scenarios is that Reno was terrified of the old man, of what he had become. That an old down-and-out should know Reno, should once have known him or have any connection to him, touches a raw nerve for Reno. He comes face to face with what he fears most. His worst anxiety/fear confronts him in the Church. He gets a taste of what he thinks he might become. It is a common anxiety for most people, especially artists who live from project to project in an insecure world. Rather than spell it out, St. John doesn't follow this up and leaves it as an ominous one-liner, pregnant with possibility.

In the cab, Reno's silver cross necklace is caught in a passing car's headlights and lights up for a split second like a beacon of truth. Ferrara would return to this exact illuminated motif in the masturbation scene in *Bad Lieutenant* where one of the Jersey girls is wearing a silver cross ring on her finger which gets lit up by a street light. Reno and Carol start kissing and then the cab pulls over and she gets out. If this was a possible encounter with a man who may have been Reno's father, then why does Carol abandon him at a time when he would surely be upset? The fact that she abandons him to go and meet her female lover, Pamela, at a club sets up a pattern for the rest of the film whereby Reno always plays second fiddle to Carol's relationship with Pamela. These opening scenes last no more than three minutes but as Truffaut rightly suggests, we can tell a lot about what is to come. We see Ferrara walk into a Church and confront his fears. In some respects, this is what Ferrara has continued to do via film ever since.

Reno Miller lives in a Union Square apartment with his girlfriend Carol and her doped out groupie girlfriend Pamela (played by Baybi Day) who spends most of the film hanging around with the grating punk band Tony Coca-Cola and The Roosters who torment Reno. Carol is separated from her husband Steven and is reminiscent of Ali McGraw; Pamela is a no-brain floozie who comes across as being like a degenerate Goldie Hawn or a smacked out Melanie Griffith. Ferrara's performance as Reno is part Bob Dylan, part period specific satire of an artist circa 1977 on Manhattan's Lower East Side art circuit. Although wooden and nondescript, he makes the best of a difficult obstacle to the film's success (the fact that no actor would take on the role) by injecting Reno with a mock-serious persona.

The film anchors itself around various obvious influences. The coldness between Reno and Carol evokes comparisons to some of the relationships portrayed in Fassbinder's grey, icy films. The

Scorsese *Taxi Driver* influence which would surface as a series of more explicit allusions in *Ms. 45*, appears in *The Driller Killer* in a chain of neon soaked nocturnal street scenes and in the early aforementioned cab scene, where the shot/reverse shot structure recalls the Travis Bickle/passenger scenes in *Taxi Driver*. Two scenes of Carol lying in bed, wrapped in red sheets, allude to the opening scene in Godard's *Contempt*, in which Brigitte Bardot lies naked across red sheets. Some snappy editing lets quick-fire shots of Reno's artwork surface twice in the film as disjointed homages to Godard's experimental use of slogans and single shot images as powerful departures from the conventions of cinematic narrative.

The relentlessly dark lighting in both interior and exterior scenes has been described by Ferrara as an explicit homage to Polanski's adaptation of Shakespeare's *Macbeth*, which uses lighting to a similar (and perhaps more deliberate) effect. Early on, Carol writes out a cheque for unpaid rent and gives it to the superintendent. While she does this, he feeds a rabbit in a cage. Later, he gives the skinned, dead rabbit to Reno as a peace-offering because Reno is complaining about the rehearsing band who have been let the apartment above him. A skinned rabbit also played an important symbolic role in Polanski's *Repulsion*. In a scene which is more disturbing than any of the twelve drill killings, Reno lays the skinned rabbit out on newspaper. He has a series of candles lit around the table. Although this is because the electricity has been shut off due to the bills not being paid, it gives the scene a mood of witchcraft or ritual. After cutting the flesh, he starts to caress the carcass with the knife in a menacing manner. He then starts to repeatedly stab the rabbit, each blow delivered with increasing frenzy. The number of scenes in *Repulsion* that featured the rotting rabbit carcass (which had been left lying out on a dinner platter) served as a raw explanation of how fast beauty salon assistant Carol (played by Catherine Deneuve) was mentally disintegrating. Of course, calling Reno's girlfriend Carol provided another direct homage to *Repulsion*. Lastly, a scene in which Reno applies lipstick and eye make-up, in anticipation of his art dealer, Dalton Briggs (played by Harry Schultz), coming around, quotes liberally from Polanski's actor-director performance in *The Tenant*. In that film, Polanski's character often appeared in drag and Ferrara is playing with similar themes of dissolving masculinity here. The last film-maker's influence to be seen here is that of Pasolini. Ferrara set *The Driller Killer* against a backdrop of Lower East Side squalor, just as Pasolini set his debut, *Accattone*, against a backdrop of the slums of Rome. Ferrara, like Pasolini, also used a cast of unknowns and captured a seediness that you can almost taste.

The Driller Killer is a film about one man's fear of getting chewed up by a society that tosses its victims below the poverty line and forgets about them. Above all else, it is an explicit attack on the American government. Reno, the artist, the painter, is trying to make art in a society that values money above everything else. Reno's art is bastardised by economic restraints. For the entirety of the film, he is primarily working on a painting of a buffalo, whose menacing eye parallels with the camera lens, as an all-seeing observer throughout the narrative. In one telling scene, while the women are next door getting ready to go out, Reno stares at the buffalo. When he feels as though its eye's gaze is fixed on him, he starts to explode. In a warped re-working of the Travis Bickle 'You talkin' to me?' monologue in *Taxi Driver*, Reno asks the buffalo what it is looking at. He then pulls a knife and waves it threateningly at the painted animal. It is as if his art has become his enemy. The muse is driving him closer and closer to the down-and-outs that infatuate him. An early montage throws up the newspaper headline: STATE ABANDONS MENTALLY ILL TO CITY STREETS. Reno's feelings towards down-and-outs see-saw between terror and compassion. An early touching scene has Reno trying to resuscitate a sleeping, probably drunk down-and-out. While he is asking him how he reached such a state, how he can have no one who loves him, how he became so helpless, a gang of club wielding youths come tearing past. Reno and the down-and-out hide in the shadows. Even in 1979, St. John/Ferrara were portraying New York City as a place of constant threat.

The buffalo painting becomes a ticket out of terror. When electricity and telephone bills arrive, Reno complains to Carol and Pamela about the amount they're spending on calls and then, overwhelmed with frustration, throws the telephone through the window. First we see the phone shattering the glass, then we see a reverse shot from street level, of the phone and glass falling through the air. In another scene Reno lashes out at Carol, when she encourages him to finish the painting so his art dealer can buy it and save their dire financial crisis, by ripping up some dollar bills and telling her how much he hates money. Central to their argument is the implication that money becomes a power chip in the balance of a relationship: who earns more, who pays the way the most, who isn't earning. Money is threatening Reno from all angles. It takes away his electricity, it makes him throw his telephone away, it makes his girlfriend return to her husband, it makes a talentless punk singer richer than a painter, it leaves human beings rotting in the gutter, it measures art against commercial value. St. John/Ferrara are as much attacking their own plight as they are making a film. They too had to self-finance the making of the film. They too suffered from a hand-to-mouth existence.

In one eerie montage that is contained within the framework of a nightmare that Reno has (a narratorial technique resurrected by Ferrara for Matty's nightmare in *The Blackout*), we hear a female voice, presumably that of his mother, saying, "I never knew your father." To accompany this random line of dialogue, a baby cries on the soundtrack. There are many suggestions that Reno is still a child inside. When Carol leaves him near the end of the film, he chases after her and begs her to stay. His connection to her seems more like a mother and son connection than a sexual one. Only once do we see them kissing and that's in the early cab scene. When she vanishes into the subway, having left her suitcase behind, he packs up her things which have fallen out of the suitcase like a small boy, wracked with pain at seeing his mother leave him. Back at the apartment, in total darkness, he waves a Star Wars light sabre toy (all the rage for children circa 1977-78) back and forth like a luminous metronome dial. This scene, although fairly ridiculous and absurd, does underscore the infantile aspects of Reno's per-sonality. A few scenes before, he had sat down to eat a take-out pizza with Pamela and Carol. This, like the rabbit stabbing scene, is far more unwatchable than any of the almost camp, bizarre drill killings. Reno wolfs down slice after slice of pizza, at such a pace that the women are left speechless. He has become an animal, he is the buffalo. Carol, disgusted by the display, hurls her slice in his face and goes out. To apologise he paints her a small picture in which the three of them are portrayed standing in front of a white picket pence, regular fairytale home. Across the top of the painting, run the words 'I'm Sorry'. Reno is trying to become something he isn't: a regular American man, like Carol's husband.

Although there is little sexual intimacy between Reno and Carol, there is a far stronger connection between Carol and Pamela. The film's only sex scene is between Carol and Pamela and takes place in the shower. Ferrara unleashes the first of his trademark, signature breast/nipple shots, the camera lingering on their breasts as they make out in the shower. When Reno finishes the painting, he creeps into the bedroom where the two women are sleeping. He looks sad and hurt when he sees that Pamela's arm is protectively wrapped around Carol. He whispers to Carol (just Carol, not Carol and Pamela) that he has finished the painting. He is shut out of his relationship with Carol. She is far closer to Pamela.

Early on in the film, Reno is woken up by the sound of a drill. He goes into the lounge and finds Pamela trying to drill a hole in a door. He takes the drill and asks her where she wants the hole drilled. Every time he drills a hole, she changes her mind and the scene takes on a demented air of comedy, mostly because the viewer knows what significance the drill will later have in the film. As Reno feels himself being drawn towards the poverty line by circumstance, he starts killing what he fears: down-and-outs. He drills the down-and-outs that we earlier see him talking to, sketching and trying to help. He abandons his compassionate mission and takes to killing what he can't bear to see. Of course, St. John/ Ferrara were also crudely satirising the American government's treatment of those who fall below the poverty line. They, like Reno, kill down-and-outs.

When Reno cracks and buys his porta-pak electric belt with which to power his drill, St. John can't resist having the idea sold to him by a television advertisement. Reno and his two girlfriends are watching TV. They look bored. The apartment is seedy, their faces blank, their attention centred on the TV set. It's like a scene in an Andy Warhol film. A commercial break comes up. The porta-pak ($19.95) is advertised as an ideal accessory to an electrical appliance like a drill. The advert is hypnotic, numbing, driving Reno to somnambulistic consumerism. Ironically, not only is St John poking fun at

TV culture, he's also pre-empting the relentless censorship wars that *The Driller Killer* would face when it became the central pawn in the British 'video nasties' furore of the mid-Eighties. What is the stock line that censors give when they refuse to give a film a certificate? They say that certain films are capable of making its viewers recreate the scenes they see. What is St. John satirising when he has Reno buy an electric drill after seeing a TV advertisement? He's satirising the moral overkill of censorship. Reno becomes a psychotic 'driller killer' after a TV advertisement gives him the idea to buy a drill. What use would a drill be to a painter? The concept thus serves as a sly, prophetic poke at the expense of the self-righteous censors.

Why a drill? On one level, it's not dissimilar to an artist's paintbrush. St. John is replacing the fine point of a paintbrush with the fine point of an electric drill. The drill also serves as a motif of male impotence. Reno loses more and more control as each scene unfolds: unpaid bills arrive constantly; the superintendent is always hassling him for unpaid rent; he can't get his 'buffalo' painting finished; the women are getting bored with the poverty; Carol is closer to Pamela than him. He's broke and desperate – Reno has been made impotent by the demands of society, so it's an ironic touch to have him buy a phallic drill: an overly masculine, tough-guy power drill, a plaid-shirt, 'dad-working-in-the-garden' kind of tool. Reno couldn't be further from that world. By having Reno buy this drill, St. John aligns Reno with the bedrock of a society which has given the government the power to drive a wedge between poor and rich. It's a symbol of extermination, of muscular economics, of government power over 'outcasts'. Reno the painter becomes Reno the driller. It's also a satirical inversion of his 'gift'. Instead of meticulously concentrating on each brushstroke, he sloppily drives a drill bit into his victims. Reno spends his time painting an animal (the buffalo) and then goes out and acts like an animal (slaying innocent victims) who society (and the government) sees as animals (the down-and-outs). It's like a food chain gone mad. Reno is treated like an animal by his superintendent and by his art dealer, who both see him as a source of money.

Everybody wants something from somebody. Reno even ends up having to paint a portrait of the Roosters' singer to raise a month's rent. As he sketches and paints the portrait, he first has to put up with the singer's obnoxious ravings, then he has to put up with him playing guitar while he poses. Finally, Reno works on the portrait while the singer and Pamela make out on the floor. Early on in the film, the band move into the upstairs apartment on Pamela's suggestion. They proceed to rehearse at extreme volume morning, noon and night. When Reno complains to the superintendent, he says they don't bother him. What he really means is that they pay their rent and therefore they don't bother him. Reno, who is several months late on his rent, does bother the superintendent. The band, a mix of New York Dolls (whose singer David Johansen was rumoured to be a candidate for the Reno role at one time) and Television, both New York bands of the time, are portrayed as mind-numbingly egotistical and dull. The banality of their rehearsals is deliberate. These scenes where the band stop and start a song or play the same chorus repeatedly, are designed to put us inside Reno's mind. Interestingly, Ferrara wrote some of the music that they play. He is trying to finish his painting; they are disturbing him. He cannot escape them. Due to the money crisis, the trio rarely go out at night. When the band give Pamela three free tickets for one of their shows, Reno can't believe that his only night out in ages has to be a night where he hears the music he hears 24 hours a day. When he is forced into the portraiture commission, he is having to prostitute his talents. Earlier, his smarmy, camp art dealer, whose office is decked out with art deco desk lamps and paintings, refused to give Reno a $500 advance on the buffalo painting, complaining that he had only recently given him money to finance his girl-friend's abortion. Again, St. John hurls an elliptical line into the screenplay. Did Carol have an abortion? How did this affect Reno? In another scene, Pamela tells Reno that he'll get a better deal on the painting if he sleeps with the art dealer. She tells him to let the dealer have sex with him. Again, Reno is being asked to sell himself in order to sell his art in order to survive.

The scene in which the dealer rejects the buffalo painting is the final straw for Reno. The dealer stands before the painting. Reno sits in a shirt and tie (a concession to the world/society that is rejecting him) having tea with Carol who is elegantly dressed and made up. Reno and Carol have been transformed into a 'regular' couple.

The dealer, who they expect to propose a high fee for the painting, suddenly erupts into a torrent of violently critical statements saying, "This is shit! . . . Just a god-damned buffalo!". He storms out of their apartment in disgust. Reno sits astonished at the table. Carol smashes the teapot against the wall and then yells abuse at the departed dealer. The scene, whose composition is entirely different to any other in the film, looks more like a setting from a Godard film than *The Driller Killer*. This stark effect is used to show how much an artist has to compromise to realise his/her creative aspirations. Reno has to completely alter his appearance in order to play 'the game'. When the dealer criticises the painting as 'worthless', Reno gets his revenge by calling the dealer late at night and ambiguously inviting him over for the evening. The dealer becomes excited when he thinks that Reno is offering himself sexually to him and comes over with a bottle of wine. Reno appears in make-up with the drill (a far from subtle phallic symbol in this instance) and silently corners the dealer by the door. The screen turns completely red.

We next see Pamela arriving home, getting out of the old-fashioned lift (very much like the apartment block lift in *The Tenant*) and seeing the dealer nailed to the door. She freaks out; Reno appears with the drill on the landing. She thinks he is going to kill her but instead he tenderly says over and over, "It's me." He has become so unrecognisable to himself that he feels the need to introduce himself to her; she is unsure if it's him because of all the make-up he is wearing. The rapid cut makes it unclear if he kills her or not. Not a single critic has considered the possibility that he might have killed her. It is assumed that his tenderness makes this an impossible scenario. On the other hand, Pamela is his rival in love; he shared Carol with her. Remember that when he saw them together at the Roosters show, he fled the club and went on a violent killing spree.

The film ends where the theatrical tea-with-the-dealer scene left off. Carol is back at home with her husband. They hug and kiss in the kitchen. She says she's missed him; he says he'll make some tea and bring it to bed. She takes a shower. In this scene, we see the water driving down on her face, her eyes are closed, everything suggests safety and comfort. Meanwhile, her husband boils a kettle on the stove and fixes two mugs of tea. The accompanying soundtrack and the settings are straight out of a daytime TV show. It's the normal world. Carol shuts off the shower by turning two gold handles: the exact same shot is recreated in *King Of New York* when Frank White (played by Christopher Walken) shuts off his hotel shower by turning two gold handles. It's a typical Ferrara rhyming shot. She climbs out of the shower and dries off. Meanwhile in the kitchen, Reno breaks in and drills her husband to death, his twelfth victim. The film ends with a nice full circle. Carol enters her bedroom. A human shape is under the bedcovers. She thinks it's her husband. She starts talking to him, making comments. There is no response. She keeps talking: "Steven, come closer!" The screen then goes completely red again and she keeps talking to who she thinks is her husband. What she doesn't realise is that the human shape in the bed is Reno. The film fades to credits before she gets into bed and discovers that it's Reno.

The ending is a perfect full circle: we first see Reno in church, we last see Reno getting into bed like a child; symbolically, each environment offers peace and security. The irony of the situation is that he has just broken into Carol's home and killed her husband. Why? Because Carol's husband represented everything that Reno isn't and also everything that is oppressing him. Carol has a "normal" man to run back to when the pressure gets too intense; Reno has no one to run to. When the dealer rejects his painting, Carol, infuriated with the lack of support that Reno offers, leaves him. Her husband, the polar opposite of Reno in every respect, is the safety net that she has to save her from the plight that terrifies Reno.

The film therefore ends with a moment of tender release for Reno. He appears to have fled the city, fled the apartment and fled the slayings. Earlier, Carol had read a news piece in the newspaper about the murder of a down-and-out with a power drill. This tells us that Reno will be discovered at some point. He's in bed with a woman with whom he feels safe. Placed within the context of St. John's later, explicitly Catholic work, it's hard not to read a Catholic 'Virgin'/'Whore' dichotomy into the split between Carol ('the Virgin'), who Reno ends up with and Pamela ('the Whore'), who is portrayed throughout the film as Carol's promiscuous counterpart. When Ferrara brings the pair together in the sex scene in the shower, not only is it the first of many trademark shots of women having sex – it is also a moment where St. John fuses the dichotomy.

No women are harmed in the film which instantly separates *The Driller Killer* from the 'slasher' tag. All of Reno's victims are male. The art dealer, like the boss in *Ms. 45*, is a symbol of male oppression. The band are like a cartoon. Reno, interestingly, has no friends. His only companions are Pamela and Carol. His life as a painter is an isolated one. His killings are oddly choreographed. Before killing one down-and-out, he revs up the drill and poses like John Wayne. Ferrara adds a bleakly humorous edge to these scenes which critic Kim Newman saw as a light homage to the 'Western': "Ferrara constantly evokes the wide-open spaces of the Western, in the buffalo painting, the holstered drill, Reno's bucking bronco ride of a dying wino, to contrast with the urban hell his characters are trapped in." None of these killings are particularly frightening or shocking. Ferrara never uses any elements of the horror film genre, unless as a parody. The ringing bells that open and close the film may mildly allude to various horror clichés, but the drill slayings themselves are matter of fact. This numb result can be attributed to Ferrara's documentary style of filming. The only moral judgement on Reno's behaviour occurs late in the film when Carol criticises him for changing. She asks him what's wrong with him, what's happening to him. He says nothing. He is another of St. John/ Ferrara's urban victims, driven to extreme states of mind and action by an inability to communicate.

When the film got its original theatre release, a *Variety* review of the film noted that the audience "cheered every appearance of the drill", and there is undeniably some kind of B-movie cheer-along appeal to Reno. He's an unlikely 'hero' figure, but wild-eyed and armed with his 'dad' drill, he becomes a strange angel of mercy, putting down those he can't stand to see suffering. His killing spree is perhaps more rooted in euthanasia than mindless murder. In a sense, he kills those who scare him: when Reno drills a victim, he's trying to slay his own fears. He's at war with fear or, as in Fassbinder's *Fear Eats The Soul*, in fear of fear. If you've ever seen *The Driller Killer* in a cinema then you'll know how funny an audience tends to find the film. It's got spoofy elements and people laugh, although admittedly, much of the laughter is of the nervous kind. These B-movie moments lend weight to Ferrara's insistence that the film is a "comedy".

During the course of the film, Reno is gradually pushed towards the poverty line. His head is on society's chopping block. Society no longer values the artist. He or she is an outcast, an enemy of the government. The artist Reno, like the film *The Driller Killer*, is a threat to the white picket fence core of society. Ferrara and St. John collapse boundaries of meaning with *The Driller Killer*: the film offends the kind of middle-class 'philistines' who drove Reno to become a killer. When Reno sees a down-and-out, he at first sees the victims of an uncaring American society and government; then he sees himself. His compassion turns to fear. The more the bills stack up, the more the superintendent threatens them with eviction, the more Reno frets about whether his dealer will sell his painting, the more he starts to see himself as a victim. Ferrara drives this point home with sledgehammer subtlety by inter-cutting the narrative of the film with grainy footage of down-and-outs. For one scene, roof-top camerawork spies on a crime scene (in which a victim gets stabbed) from a high angle. The camera takes the place of Reno who is watching the scene through a pair of binoculars. Other, intensely disturbing and somehow moving grainy footage features down-and-outs slumped in doorways. As an artist, Reno feels a kinship with their total alienation. Society has forgotten them. It's a world where laws, rules, religion and government have broken down. When he is seen sketching a down-and-out in charcoal and talking with his subject, he seems at home, perfectly comfortable. This scene produces the same kind of effect as the opening scene in which Reno reaches for the down and out's hand in Church. Both scenes capture the essence of the film's subject: a fear of becoming what one fears the most. As if to leave no room for doubt, the film's closing credit reads: DEDICATED TO THE PEOPLE OF NYC – THE CITY OF HOPE. If that dedication doesn't make St. John/Ferrara's intentions clear, then one of the drill killings does. A down-and-out is seen lurking outside of Reno's apartment block. When Reno kills him, he nails first one hand to a wall and then the other, pinning the down-and-out in a crucifixion pose. The message is clear: those below the poverty line are being crucified by an uncaring government.

The grainy use of 16mm enhances the seediness of the milieu

and subject matter and combined with Kelsch's commanding 'rock'n'roll' camerawork, the result is powerful. Ferrara's rapid-fire attitude to editing means that there are plenty of edgy and rough cuts and the use of a red blank screen on three occasions is a nice touch, pseudo-Godard as executed by a 26-year-old first time film-maker. The film sets many blueprints for St. John/Ferrara's style: the alienated urban victim, the dimly lit nocturnal scenes, the spiritual/Catholic conflict lingering in the background, the violence, the blank relationships, the sheer threat inherent in an urban setting, the live band scenes, the sex scene between two women, the cold, detached male, the derelicts, the seedy bars and clubs, the religious imagery and iconography, Joe Delia's performance of both Bach and eerie atmospheric soundtrack music and most of all, the fiercely independent attitude to film-making.

Ms. 45 a.k.a *Angel Of Vengeance* 1981

"We were aiming at a cold sexuality, a violent tone. Roman Polanski is an influence on all my work. Thana isn't clearly defined. At times I think her sympathetic and at other times fascistic. It shook people up to see an innocent person like themselves suddenly become a wanton murderer" – Abel Ferrara to *Monthly Film Bulletin*.

"No one discussed the fact that she's (Thana) mute, ferchrissakes! It's about a lack of communication that will cause frustration and violence" – Nicholas St. John to *Film Comment*.

"Ferrara, aided by the presence of the extraordinary Zoë Tamerlis, gives a rigorously feminist reading of the always problematic revenge for rape genre" – *Monthly Film Bulletin*.

"It's a calculated attack on the male-dominated audience of exploitation films" – *TV Gen*.

"A film is a girl and a gun" – Jean-Luc Godard.

The leap from *The Driller Killer* to *Ms. 45* is a huge one and suggests that in the interim Ferrara had grasped how better to attain his vision. St. John's screenplay was inventive, James Morel's cinematography imaginative and constantly seeking out unusual angles and Joe Delia's chilling score veers from the eerie Bernard Hermann pastiche of the intro music to squalls of late Seventies No Wave New York noise and a nerve-jangling jazzy saxophone motif that weaves in and out of the narrative. The entire film is held together by an astonishing performance by Zoë Tamerlis who plays the central character, Thana, a mute seamstress.

It was a courageous move by Ferrara and St. John to make Thana mute. How many films have you seen where the lead character is unable to speak? By making Thana mute, Ferrara, Tamerlis and Morel were set the task of conveying Thana's emotions and personality without dialogue, without a voice-over, indeed without any kind of narratorial device. Other directors would probably have settled on a voice-over to flesh out the character. Instead, Ferrara and St. John make Thana mute and keep her mute. It's up to the viewer to read her mind, to decode Tamerlis's powerful facial expressions.

Although critics have compared *Ms. 45* to Brian De Palma's *Carrie*, Scorsese's *Taxi Driver* and Hitchcock, the general consensus is that *Ms. 45* borrows most heavily from Polanski's study of a schizophrenic woman's nervous breakdown, *Repulsion*. There are many similarities between the two films. The opening beauty parlour scenes in which Catherine Deneuve's character, Carol Ledoux (Carol the Quiet) is nagged by an overbearing boss are mirrored in the scenes throughout *Ms. 45* where Thana is hassled by her camp but lecherous employer.

The closest thing Carol has to a friend in *Repulsion* is a co-worker at the beauty salon. Likewise, the closest thing Thana has to a friend is her street-tough female co-worker, Laurie. Carol's home life is overshadowed by her overbearing sister (played by Deneuve's real-life sister). Thana's equivalent is her nosy, interfering landlady Mrs Nasone. Carol is frequently pestered by her neighbour's dog after she murders her lecherous victim with a candlestick: when the dog starts barking at the door, she is panicked into trying to hide the body. Thana is harassed by her landlady's dog after she kills a rapist/intruder with an iron and is panicked into dragging the corpse into her bathroom and dumping it in the bathtub. At one point in *Repulsion*, we see Deneuve ironing clothes without an iron. This is where St. John got the idea for the use of the iron as a weapon.

Men become sexual threats for both Carol and Thana. Carol lies in bed, a wardrobe blocking a door. She hallucinates the door being forced open despite the wardrobe blocking it and a man bursting in and raping her. As the man is abusing her, Polanksi captures a close-up of Carol's terrified eyes. Ferrara has his cameraman achieve the same effect while Thana is being raped in her apartment. During another hallucinatory scene, Carol sees a man in her mirror. The same thing happens to Thana: she hallucinates the first rapist in the mirror, standing behind her.

Near the end of *Repulsion*, Deneuve sits before a mirror and blankly applies lipstick with an almost somnambulistic disregard for the way it looks. Thana also sits before a mirror at her dresser in a similar scene and applies lipstick with the same numb expression. Finally, Carol barely speaks in Polanski's film; St. John took this haunting effect to its logical extreme and made Thana mute.

Ferrara and St. John have Thana completely transform herself throughout the film. Clothing is just one of many devices used to compensate for her muteness, and is used as a means to tell us what is going on inside Thana: a neat touch, since Thana works in the garment district. The designer she works for is in business to make women look beautiful, to package the external shell of the female body. When we first see Thana working away in the back-room of the designer's space, she is homey-looking, plain, a 'girl next door' in a white blouse, a bland skirt and jacket. She's not wearing any obvious make-up and she has regular shoulder-length hair. Everything about her mannerisms, the way she carries herself and the way she presents herself, is understated. As the film progresses, however, Thana is transformed. Ferrara's direction uses her appearance to tell us an emotional story. Each new outfit is like a silent monologue.

Thana, like Reno in *The Driller Killer*, is unable to communicate. Reno has to channel his feelings through painting; Thana has no way to channel them. Reno's only contact with the outside world is through his art dealer or through the two girlfriends he lives with. Thana's only contact with the outside world is through her workplace (and in particular her lecherous, fashion boss, played to superbly slimy effect by Albert Sinkys), her interfering, overbearing landlady (played with ghoulish relish by Editta Sherman) and the latter's suspicious dog, Phil. We never see Thana relaxed or at ease, just as we never see the hyperactive, fidgety Reno sit still for more than a second in *The Driller Killer*.

Like Reno, Thana is driven to a killing spree against the relentlessly imposing and threatening setting of New York City. In the film's second scene, Thana leaves work for the day and heads towards the subway. Scores of leering men make suggestive comments and gestures towards her. Ferrara would revisit this testosterone-driven vision of a New York City street in *The Addiction*, when he has Kathleen Conklin (Lili Taylor) walk past a similar succession of leering men. Like so many of Ferrara's characters, Thana is struggling with her vulnerability. She exits from that threatening street scene by going underground into the subway. She literally has to leave the 'street' to get away from those feelings.

The film begins with a shot of a busy Manhattan street. The sky is bright blue, the traffic chaotic. The title flashes up: 'Garment Center, Manhattan'. We then cut to a shot of something bright pink and emerald green. It moves. The camera draws back and we realise that we are looking at a woman modelling a pink and green dress in a fashion bureau. The model keeps spinning around. A camp, balding man tries to sell the piece to a stern looking female retail buyer, who Ferrara shoots sitting in her chair from such a low angle that she appears regal, her chair throne-like. She shakes her head when she is asked what she thinks of the dress – importantly, she doesn't say that she doesn't like it, she merely remains mute, non-committal. This aligns her with Thana, but only in so far as St. John and Ferrara want us to hone in on the very different natures of these two women. The fashion buyer doesn't speak when we first see her because this gives her power over the fashion boss trying to sell the line to her. Her silence is all about power. She appears strong, intimidating, confident, sexual. Everything about her screams 'strong woman'.

The boss says he has one other piece that he would like the buyer to see. We next see him scampering in a wildly camp manner down a corridor into the production space. He is waving a Kleenex around and acting in such an over-the-top way, that we are automatically invited to assume that Ferrara is telling us the man is gay. There are six or seven women working in the production space and

Thana is the farthest one, out of focus. She is at the rear of the room, anonymous, almost hiding. Her boss takes the other new dress and runs back to the buyer with it. He power-sells it to her and she now speaks, agreeing to see the piece. Her voice is sensuous and controlled. Another woman models the dress while the boss utters absurd sales lines such as, "when she moves, the material really seems to melt, it's like quicksilver." Each time the camera focuses on the buyer, low angles are used. The lens aligns itself with the grovelling and desperate boss who is trying to seal the deal.

Finally, in a cool, controlling tone, the buyer agrees to take the piece in various formats for "all the stores". The now deliriously happy boss sends all the workers home. They file out past him as he throws away insincere compliments. When Thana passes him – and she's the last to leave – he suddenly snaps out of his camp persona and becomes lecherous and threatening. He pats her on the head, strokes her shoulder and bids her goodnight in a suggestive tone. Ferrara now has us believe that the boss finds Thana attractive, although she is mouse-like, withdrawn and timid. She nods in reply. Morel lets the boss's gaze linger on Thana, as he watches her leave. This shot resurfaces in *Bad Lieutenant* when Ferrara has the camera observe the Lieutenant eyeing up the ass of a nurse as she walks away. In *Ms. 45*, the shot is executed with a subtlety of touch that still manages to drive the point home.

Once Thana has run the gauntlet of leering men and gone down into the subway, Morel holds the shot of the bustling street for longer than necessary, accentuating the chaos. An abrupt rough cut then jumps to a close-up of a window being smashed by an intruder. Glass shatters. We see a hand undo the safety latch and open the window. Wind chimes are shaking in the foreground. As the window is forced open, a plant drops onto the floor and a boot steps onto it. Every detail is shot to show domesticity being violated. As the intruder climbs in, Morel offers a close-up of the wind chimes which are attached to a small hanging mobile of a house. Typically, this kind of Eastern mobile is meant to ward off evil spirits. Ferrara and St. John are satirising the idea of safety and security here. Order has collapsed; nothing is sacred or protected.

The next cut is ingenious: a close-up of rack after rack of packaged meat in a supermarket. The camera draws back to a wide shot showing Thana shopping in a supermarket. It could be any regular movie scene: a very homey-looking woman in a white blouse and a dark work suit, looking bored and pushing her shopping cart around a colourful, brightly lit supermarket. It's standard sitcom stuff. Then we see that she's only got a piece of meat in her family-sized shopping cart. The message is loud and clear: for the two men who will shortly rape her, the leering men that Thana just passed on the street and also for the company she works for, a woman is a slab of meat. So, Ferrara is showing us two 'pieces of meat': one pushing the cart, one in the cart.

Another rapid cut takes us away from the shining light and artificial reality of the supermarket to a dimly lit scene where the intruder is snooping around Thana's apartment. The contrast in lighting takes us back to the darkness which permeated *The Driller Killer*. Ferrara creates further suspense with a long shot of a street scene. A couple and their child are walking along, all three of them hand in hand – a happy family. Then Thana comes around the corner carrying her grocery bag. She's alone. The contrast is arresting: after the easy contentment of the family shot, we see an unsmiling, miserable looking woman. At times, in these early shots, it's hard not to wonder if Ferrara is making reference to Dominique Sanda's performance in Robert Bresson's *A Gentle Woman*. Tamerlis and Sanda don't look that dissimilar and Tamerlis's moody, cold performance is very much like Sanda's in Bresson's film.

Then the film switches gear. First we hear children's voices; then, suddenly, a man wearing a mask leaps out of a doorway. The atmosphere abruptly changes from the happy mood created by the children's voices and the shot of the family. Ferrara stacks the scene for maximum shock. The rapist in the mask, leather jacket and jeans is Ferrara himself, although as in *The Driller Killer*, his role is credited to Jimmy Laine. He grabs Thana and drags her down a darkened alleyway at gunpoint, while Delia's ugly, pounding music erodes the peaceful picture that had been briefly set up. This is the second scene that Ferrara recreates in *The Addiction*. In that film he has Annabella Sciorra attack Lili Taylor in exactly the same way – she too is surprised, attacked and dragged down to the end of a dark alleyway.

The rapist throws Thana face down over some trash cans. While pointing the gun at her face, he hisses, "You make one sound, I'm gonna stick this thing in your mouth and then I'm gonna shoot it off." In light of her muteness, this is the first of many ironic comments made to Thana. Tamerlis's acting from this point on is remarkable. Her glazed-over, numb look of terror inevitably recalls Catherine Deneuve's performance in Polanski's *Repulsion*. The rapist pulls her underwear down (violently – in absolutely no way could this be perceived as 'sexy'), unzips his fly, mounts her from behind and rapes her. As he unzips his pants, Ferrara has the camera primarily focus on the gun, as a phallic symbol; the penis metaphor is also evident when the rapist sticks the gun in Thana's face and warns her to keep quiet. While he rapes her, we see her horrified face but mostly we see her tightly clenched fist. This is where Tamerlis's performance excels: she tells us everything we need to know about what Thana is thinking using only her right fist.

When the rape is over, the rapist hisses another threat and then flees. Again, with a powerfully clenched fist, Thana slides off the trash cans and falls onto the ground; she has been reduced to 'trash'. She has been dirtied by this vicious attack. The rapist is shown running down a corridor. Then we see Thana clutching her bag, shaking and traumatised. Morel fleshes out this disturbing image by switching to a high-angle shot. Thana is doubled over, hunched up, arms crossed, beside the trash cans. The extent to which she has been violated is captured in another rapid cut to the dark apartment where a drawer is violently pulled out by the intruder. It is Thana's drawer, Thana's apartment. He is violating her privacy, her possessions, her space, just as the rapist did.

The intruder is interrupted when Thana comes home, her clothes dishevelled and dirty. She looks a mess. She's in shock. He pulls out a gun and hides. Ferrara infuses this scene with a hint of Hitchcock's masterful suspense. Thana walks slowly into her apartment. We expect her to call the police or a doctor or even a friend. She keeps clutching her stomach: the rapist has badly hurt her. She has a blank look of shock on her face. The prim, 'girl next door' appearance has been soiled. Now everything looks wrong: the white blouse is grubby and hanging open, her tidy hair is messed up. She sits down on the sofa. Ferrara rides this tension for over 90 seconds. Then the camera (from Thana's perspective) zooms in on a pair of black boots. Squalls of saxophone blast out. Her facial expression struggles to react to yet another potential trauma. Morel gives us a shot of the intruder from the neck down, the anonymity adding to the terror (this is a man, rather than a male rapist). Only the cocking of a pointed gun is in focus.

Then we see the intruder's face as he puts his hand over her mouth and throws her back. He says that they're going to play a "little game": "You talk and I'll kill you." It's the same irony again: he, like the first rapist, warns her not to talk. They don't want their victim to be human in any way, in an extension of Ferrara's meat images in the supermarket. He asks Thana for money; she shakes her head. This is when we learn that she is mute. Her hair falls across her face. The rapist eyes her up and down, notes her dishevelled appearance and asks, "What happened to you?" His question makes us wonder if he might be willing to show her some leniency, that he might simply be a burglar who will take pity on her. Instead, he too rapes her, although this time by throwing her down and climbing on top of her rather than by raping her from behind. She is violated from all angles.

Once the intruder starts to gain sexual pleasure from the rape, he loosens his grip on the gun and repeatedly bangs the barrel onto the floor. Ferrara is again drawing links between the gun and the penis, as the rhythm of the gun being banged onto the floor matches the rhythm of his rape. Unseen by her attacker, Thana reaches out for a red glass apple paperweight (St. John is throwing Adam and Eve original sin connotations into the scene here) and takes it in her hand. The rapist's obscene breathing and attempts to kiss his victim contrast starkly with the icy, lifeless expression that Tamerlis gives Thana. Tamerlis's acting underlines with subtle brutality the complete detachment between Thana and the rapist. The rapist appears to be enjoying himself (his grunts and moans suggest this) but Thana is as detached as a lifeless doll. We feel her emotional withdrawal. It seems as though she has 'left' the situation mentally. It is only her body that he is violating.

The rapist then leers, "Do you think this might make you talk?" It's a sick moment that reinforces the gun imagery and the need for power and control that drives a rape. Just as the rapist is about to climax, he drops his gun, his eyes closed tightly. At this moment, Thana strikes him in the head with the paperweight, Delia's Bernard Hermann-style strings referencing a homage to Hitchcock in the background. Thana jumps up while the rapist reels from the blow. She strikes him a second time and then picks up an iron. She raises it with both hands over her head. Morel captures this shot from a very, very low angle, probably lying down, to lend the image overtones of *Psycho* (the iron replaces the knife). We don't see Thana strike the rapist; instead there is a brilliant rapid cut to two eggs frying in a pan. From constant male oppression, we don't get the final blow that kills the rapist but instead a cut to the overtly feminine image of two eggs.

The landlady, Mrs Nasone, is frying the eggs; her dog, Phil, suddenly starts barking, because he can smell death. We see a totally traumatised Thana sitting on the sofa, numb and in shock. Since leaving work, she has been brutally raped by a masked attacker, has come home to find a burglar in her apartment, has been raped by him too at gunpoint and has then killed him. Circumstance has completely altered her life in less than a few hours. Morel again opts for a low-slung camera angle to show Thana dragging the rapist's corpse into the bathroom. Once she has almost hauled him into the bathtub, she is disturbed by the yapping dog and nosy landlady. She rushes around her apartment, tidying up the mess and hiding the bloodied iron. It's an odd moment: Thana has gone from victim to criminal in a space of minutes. Suddenly, she has a corpse in her apartment and she has to get rid of it – it could be discovered by the landlady. She goes to the door, wrapped in the brightly coloured patchwork blanket that she was raped upon. We get a shot of a creepy old staircase, another reference to Polanski's *The Tenant*, which featured countless shots of an eerie Parisian stairwell. There is no one there. Thana shuts the door, leans back against it and slides to the floor. It's worth remembering at this stage that all of the above takes place in the first fifteen minutes of the film.

The next scene, which returns to the workplace, shows the boss shouting at a co-worker about some work on a neckline. The boss, who has previously been presented as overtly camp is now, like all men to come in the film, threatening and aggressive. Thana sees a man fixing up a trash can in the production space. She is reminded of the rape over the trash cans but is also given an idea. However, before she can act on it, Thana blanks out in what we assume is post-traumatic shock. Her co-workers huddle around her, concerned. Thana returns home and sees the dead rapist in her bath. Then she changes her clothes, a heavily symbolic moment in the film. We next see her barefoot at home in an untucked shirt and jeans – it's the most casually dressed we've seen her since the film began. She has some black bin liners, a large knife and puts newspapers on the bathroom floor. She presses the knife to the rapist's arm and starts to saw through it. The sound is sickening, the icy look of concentration on Thana's face chilling. Blood splatters onto the newspaper. We see the arm fall onto the floor and Thana wraps it in newspaper. Ferrara then has Morel execute a blatant homage to Scorsese's *Taxi Driver* by using a high-angle shot to show Thana dragging two bin liners of body parts through the hallway (recalling the shoot-out finale in Scorsese's film, where the arriving police are shot from overhead).

Then we see Thana in the kitchen. The contents of her refrigerator are spread out on the ledges. A bottle of tomato ketchup is to the fore, amusingly referencing the bloodbath (literally) that we have just seen. When she opens the refrigerator door, we see lots of bin liner-clad packages. Thana has cut the rapist up into small pieces and stuffed him into the refrigerator, a scenario which would later be copied in John McNaughton's *Henry: Portrait Of A Serial Killer*. Thana cleans the blood off the bathtub and bathroom walls. A close-up of the plughole shows blood trickling down it – this is solid *Psycho* meets Polanski fare. Then the prying, heavily made-up eye of the landlady (which looks scary in itself) is superimposed over the shot of the plughole.

Once the cleaning is done, Thana sits on the edge of the bathtub, ready to clean herself. She is wearing only the untucked shirt. She stands before the bathroom mirror, anticipating many similar shots in *The Addiction*. She unbuttons her shirt fully and prepares to take it off. A split second flash image of her breasts is interrupted by psychological hallucination: the first rapist reaches to grab her breasts. She crosses her arms over her breasts and Delia's violent, scuzzy music shocks you out of your seat. Ferrara is attacking the calculated relegation of women to sex object status in film. After asking the viewer to align with Thana's damaged status as a rape victim, St. John then has Thana apparently performing a kind of striptease in front of the mirror. This gear-change introduces the expectation of seeing Thana naked. As if to negate this expectation (and just as Thana's breasts are about to be exposed), Ferrara violently introduces the image of the leather gloved rapist's hand snatching at her. He follows this with another, even scarier shot: Thana sees not only herself in the mirror but also the masked rapist. She collapses to the floor. She hears noises from behind the shower curtain and looks: blood and human remains are being regurgitated by the plughole. It's a very Polanski-esque chain of images, each of which recalls the hallucinatory passages in *Repulsion*.

After this prolonged and horrific chain of events, Ferrara reverts to Hitchcock-esque suspense. Thana heads out to dump the first bin liner of remains, but the landlady becomes suspicious when Phil starts to bark at the bag and she repeatedly asks Thana what she is carrying out. Thana hurries past and dumps it in a public trash bin. (The landlady will eventually shop Thana to the police due to her dog's scenting the decaying flesh in Thana's apartment.) After the dumping of the body part in the bin, it's back to the work space, where the bright lighting, constant radio and bored humdrum of Thana's co-workers makes for a dull, downbeat environment. Thana drifts off into a daydream and burns a hole through the cloth she's ironing. We can safely assume that this mini-blackout is triggered by the fact that she's ironing: she killed the second rapist with her iron. The scene also alludes to the scene in *Repulsion* where Carol irons (without an iron) in a catatonic trance. The boss comes over and asks Thana what's wrong. He touches her and she flinches. Tamerlis delivers a facial grimace here that is perfect: this one contorted expression tells us all we need to know. Thana is traumatised. At this point, the elliptical nature of the screenplay raises some questions. Why didn't she call the police after the rapes? Why is she mute? Why is she mute but not deaf? Did an event turn her mute? Did some previous trauma turn her mute? Why doesn't she have anyone to call (friends, family)? The way that her meddlesome landlady smothers her suggests a long-term relationship. How long has Thana lived in the city? Was she a virgin before she was raped?

*

61

The next cut provides Ferrara's first blatant allusion on film to Jean-Luc Godard. After the commotion at work, we are faced with a blue background and to the fore, a close-up of an old man with dark sunglasses, a raincoat and a cloth cap. A flash of brilliant red passes by – a woman's red jacket. The camera draws back to reveal a rockabilly-styled punk trying to pick up girls who pass by. The old man sits silently behind him, holding a white stick. This bizarre image of the blind man coupled with the primary strength of the red and blue is pure Godard. Remember, this scene follows another in which Thana's muteness was acutely frustrating both for her, her boss and for us, the viewers. We wanted her to be able to tell somebody what had happened but she couldn't. Ferrara echoes this with the image of a blind man staring into a camera, which will create a film that he can never see.

A taxi pulls to the kerb and drops Thana off. She drops a bag by a wall on which a hand-painted sign reads 'No Dumping'. We see another change in Thana's outfit. Now she's wearing tight grey trousers, a scarf and a black jacket. The punk, who has followed her, picks up the bag and chases her across desolate urban landscapes, crying, "Hey baby you forgot your bag!" Clearly agitated, Thana runs down into an alleyway that turns out to be a dead end. Trash is everywhere. She runs straight up to the camera – hand-held camerawork flails frantically, flashing from each wall to the next, the whirling motion mirroring Thana's panic at the dead end. Then we see the punk coming into focus, running down the alleyway towards her, nearer and nearer. Thana pulls the rapist's gun from her bag and shoots her pursuer in the forehead. A close-up of the smoking gun shows her trembling hands and stunned expression. Curiously, with her red lipstick and trembling full lips, Thana has already transformed from the nondescript grey woman at the start of the film into a woman in bloom. In her book *Men, Women And Chain Saws: Gender In The Modern Horror Film*, Carol J. Clover said of this scene, "At this point, reactive murder turns to proactive murder. For the violence visited on Thana has caused her to notice, as the film has us notice, that in every corner of life, men take it as their due to dominate and abuse women."

We next see Thana come home, put the gun in a drawer (quite likely the drawer that we earlier saw the rapist rifling through while she was returning home after being raped for the first time) and then rush to the bathroom to vomit. The landlady (increasingly turning into a version of the religious fanatic mother in *Carrie*) starts pounding on her door until Thana answers. She says that she has heard Thana throwing up and wants to call a doctor. Meanwhile, her dog pads into Thana's apartment and sniffs around the refrigerator. Thana's nightmares that night of the two rapists, of children's voices, of the landlady's face seen through the front door peephole, cascade before us in a disturbing montage; again, Ferrara is acknowledging Polanski's influence here.

St. John puts the film back on the suspense track by having a down-and-out (and here we are returning to the poverty theme of *The Driller Killer*) discover one of the rapist's body parts (his hand) in a trash can that he's digging through for food. His discovery sets the police onto Thana's trail. A co-worker sits reading a newspaper whose headline reads: 'No Clues On Bizarre 45 Killing' while in the office next to her, the boss is talking to Thana. He says that her work has "not been up to par", that he's "concerned" about her and about the fact that she doesn't seem to be getting better. He acknowledges that she's mute (confirming what the viewer has guessed so far) saying that he understands that this means she's working under "a tremendous handicap". Then, her boss comes round from his chair and puts his hands lecherously on Thana's shoulders. He invites her to the office Halloween party on the 31st, adding, "There'll be boys your own age." Thana leaps up and writes a note saying, "I'll try." Once she's back on the production space floor, another co-worker asks Thana why she had to see the boss and she writes, "I just wish they would leave me alone." The most notable thing about this scene is that it marks another transformation in Thana's appearance: now she's wearing her hair tucked under a black beret with a bright red top, a black skirt and black knee-high boots. She is suddenly very beautiful, and has made a dramatic leap from conservative and anonymous to confident and mysteriously sensuous. The more Thana seems to physically 'stand out' in terms of appearance, the more she retreats psychologically into herself.

The next scene could come from any number of movies. Thana and her female co-workers are having lunch together. A cocky, lecherous guy sits at the next table making out with his female companion. When she leaves, he swaggers up to their table and tries it on with them. Thana's co-worker Laurie (Darlene Stuto) tells him to "fuck off", "get fucked" and "get bent". That is how *she* clears off unwelcome advances; Thana is unable to do this because she has no voice. Once the other girls have left, Thana trails behind. The creep follows her out of the diner and tries to pick her up with a variety of hackneyed lines such as, "When I see beauty, I gotta go after it." He mentions that he's a fashion photographer (yet another professional occupation which often treats the female body as a slab of meat) and reels off a list of magazines that he's supposedly shot fashion spreads for. He tells Thana that when he saw her in the restaurant, he thought she looked like a "Renoir or a Matisse" and then invites her to go back to his photographic studio where they'll smoke pot and he'll do a test shoot on her. Her indifference is total. After a spectacularly creepy line ("You're too beautiful to be a model"), he runs his little finger down her cheek (making us squirm on her behalf) and takes her silence as a 'yes' to his invitation. Never once does he notice that she's not said a word; St. John is satirising the male ego mercilessly here. Once inside, Ferrara and St. John deliver a killer slice of black humour. Thana and the photographer step out of the lift and into his studio. All the accessories of a photographic studio are in place but it's not to be the kind of fashion 'shoot' that he had in mind. Instead, Thana mows him down in a spray of bullets, all fired from the lift, the green walls of which perfectly frame her red and black outfit.

After killing the photographer, we see Thana perched at her dresser, applying lipstick before a mirror. Her hair is tied back and she's wearing a blue coat. She applies the lipstick in a deliberately excessive manner. It's as if she's sleepwalking; her eyes are glazed in a hypnotic stare. Her cheeks are scarlet with blusher and she has a lot of dark eye make-up on. As well as the shot from *Repulsion* discussed earlier on, this scene could also be compared with a scene near the end of Godard's *Hail Mary* (released three years after *Ms. 45* in 1984) in which Myriem Roussel (Mary) sits in her car and applies lipstick while looking in her rear-view mirror in an equally unsettling way.

Thana puts the gun in her bag and heads out. She is now dressed and made up so garishly that she's a walking poster girl for the stereotypical male concept of brazen female sexuality. Thana is dressed to court male advances. She's no longer shying away, she's setting the bait. The landlady is coming up the stairs with a young man when she sees Thana. She is shocked and comments on Thana's make-up (amusing considering how much make-up she wears). Thana hands her a note that says that she's going out to spend the night with a friend. Tellingly, the landlady's response is, "What friend?" as if it's an impossibility that Thana could have a friend.

We next see Thana disposing of more body parts in a locker. Her hair now has a reddish-orange tint to it. She drops the locker key into a cigarette ashtray before departing. Then we see a row between a pimp and his prostitute which is shot in a dimly lit doorway. The pimp accuses the prostitute of cheating him out of money and smacks her around. As if by magic, Thana appears and blows him away. By now, the Greek associations of her name (an abbreviation of Thanatos, the personification of death) are evident: she is the angel of death. An exquisite shot of a moodily lit stairway leads Thana into Central Park, where Morel lets the camera linger lovingly on a Manhattan skyline, rich with lights and blues and blacks. Thana deliberately goes there to seek out trouble. A menacing gang (heavily derivative of the type of gangs in the *Death Wish* series) surround her one by one, forming a circle. One gang member swings a set of nunchucks, implying the violence he has planned for her. Morel uses a variety of camera angles to reflect the degree to which the gang surrounds Thana and how vulnerable she seems, only to make the power shift more dramatic as she pulls the gun out and shoots each of the gang members in turn.

A cut takes us straight to a shot from the inside of a limousine. The camerawork of the rain-soaked, neon-drenched streets is taken through the car windscreen in a direct stylistic reference to Scorsese's *Taxi Driver*. There's the same hypnotic voyeurism at work, the same seedy rain-soaked romanticising of the urban landscape. The chauffeur-driven limo contains a wealthy Saudi Arabian businessman who asks his driver to pick up Thana, assuming that she is a prostitute. She gets in. The businessman offers her a cigarette and then money to spend the night with him. By now, Thana is no longer a victim. She sits smoking in the back of the car with a deadpan, 'fuck you' expression that comes straight from the retail buyer at the start of the film. She pockets his money while puffing on a cigarette that hangs from her mouth. (She has suddenly taken up smoking, just as Kathleen Conklin abruptly takes up smoking towards the end of *The Addiction*.) Thana is now sultry, powerful, sexy and in control – or so she thinks. We, of course, know that she has had some kind of nervous breakdown resulting from the trauma of the double rape. We know she was fragile and isolated in the first place. She pulls out her gun and shoots the businessman in the crotch and then shoots the driver in the head.

Next scene and it's daylight. Sun is bursting through Thana's windows. She wears a surly, defiant expression. She's standing at the kitchen sink, scrubbing the blood off her hands from the previous night's killing spree. This is a flat-out homage to Polanski's version of Shakespeare's *Macbeth* in which Lady Macbeth, slips into insanity and obsessively scrubs at the imaginary spots of blood that she thinks are visible on her hands. Tension is mounting because Phil the dog is again sniffing around at the door. Meanwhile, next door, the landlady has her radio on. The news announcer reports that the police are investigating "multiple murders" which have taken place during the night, all with a .45 calibre gun. Thana knocks on the landlady's door and hands Phil a bowl of meat. (Only she and we know that the meat is minced rapist.) Then she goes out with another bin liner of body parts. She has to dispose of the last of the remains to get the dog off her scent. The landlady, à la Polanski's *The Tenant*, stands at her window spying on Thana as she heads out with the bag. Thana spots the open trunk of a car which has Georgia licence plates: she dumps the bag in while the driver isn't looking. He comes back, closes the trunk and drives off. By this stage, she's wearing bright pink trousers and a black beret, boots, dark shirt and jacket combo.

From there, we cut to another tense office meeting between Thana and the boss. She's got her hair combed down again, rather than tied back or under the beret, and is wearing a pale pink sweater. But for the ill-fitting garish make-up, she would once again be the wholesome, nondescript Thana that we saw at the start of the film. The boss lectures her sternly: after the lunch with her co-workers (when she had gone off and killed the fashion photographer) she had not gone back to work. The boss tells Thana that people have been worrying about her, and adds that he's heard from the other girls that she isn't going to the Halloween party. She writes a note saying that she does want to go. He asks her if she has anyone to go with. She shakes her head. He asks her if she would like to go with him. She stares at him, first vulnerably and then coldly, suggesting that he has just set himself up for a date with the 'angel of death'. She then nods. He is pleased.

A cut takes us to a scene in the production space, probably later that day. Some of the girls are gathered around a window laughing because they can see a woman making love with a man whom they believe is her boss. One by one they flock to the window. Ferrara teases us for a while and then shows a couple making love on a desk in the building opposite. Their boss, and then Thana, join the voyeurs. Morel captures Thana in a moment of pure beauty: she looks like the young Nastassja Kinski (reinforcing that *Wrong Move* connection) as she glances seductively over her shoulder at the boss. The staging and pose are also reminiscent of some of Godard's shots of Isabelle Huppert in *Slow Motion* and *Passion*. There's something detached about the way in which Morel captures Tamerlis. It's a great shot: Morel watches Thana who watches her colleagues who watch two strangers making love. The purity of the shot is soiled when the boss turns to leer suggestively at Thana. He has turned from watching two people making love to stare at her after having invited her to be his date to the Halloween party, and the look she gives him incites him on. She is laying bait, just as she did with the Saudi Arabian businessman and the Central Park gang.

Ferrara drops in an explicit reference to *The Driller Killer* Super 8mm footage after this scene. It's not super 8mm this time but it is ill-fitting footage of a bag lady pushing her cart along the street and rambling on about women. It's a bizarre vignette that doesn't work or fit. Ferrara may have used this bag lady vignette to draw a line through the narrative because from here on, Thana snaps. She no longer shoots and kills men whom we feel she has some justification in wanting to kill. Her target ceases to be the kind of male scum that bothers women on a day-to-day basis. Audience sympathy, which up to now accounts for the film's strong cult feminist following, is suddenly called into question. It's as if St. John wanted to unsettle our perceptions. The change comes in Chinatown, where we see a pair of Chinese lovers kissing. We also see a very Godardian shot of Thana, dressed in a hooded black outfit, heavily made up, standing in a bright red phone booth holding a telephone in her hand. She suddenly looks plain evil. We know she can't be talking to anyone. She's glassily staring at the kissing lovers. The girl tells her lover that she has to go back to work. They break off and he heads back to his apartment. By this stage in the film, Thana has lost the ability to distinguish right from wrong, good from evil. She proceeds to chase the man through the street, her hooded outfit reinforcing her new role as a non-discriminatory angel of death. The Chinese guy can't get his keys into his apartment lock. Thana stands in the street, frightening in her hood. The squalls of saxophone start up, anticipating a killing. She goes for her gun just as he manages to open the door and vanish inside. She runs after him but the door is already shut. We know that she's now lost all touch with reality because she snarls angrily at having lost her victim. This man had no involvement with Thana; his crime in her eyes was that he exhibited his lust in a public place. She now sees all male sexuality as the enemy.

Ferrara then cuts to a dingy bar where a man pours out a typical boozy sob story to Thana. Why is Thana there? How did she get talking to him? Did he introduce himself or simply start rambling away to anyone who would listen to him? Did Thana go there to find a victim? St. John uses this scene as a counterpart to the fashion photographer scene. It's still a man trying to hit on Thana, but in a completely different manner. Unlike the photographer who projects his swollen ego onto her, this man is a down-in-the-mouth, broken-hearted individual. During the scene, he tells Thana that he's a travelling shoe salesman and knows that his wife is cheating on him; all the while he never once pauses to draw breath. Thana sips on her drink, listening to his monologue. He doesn't seem to notice that his companion never speaks, nor that she's wearing a hooded cape; it's another great St. John satire on male communication skills. Indeed, by this point, it's tempting to read St. John's screenplay as a condemnation of a male society that silences women. Ferrara cuts from the bar to a bench outside which is prettily framed by a bridge in the background. Thana now has her hood back up. There's a sense of confession at work here. The man is telling his darkest secrets to a stranger dressed in a pseudo-priestly outfit. He stares at the ground and continues his story, explaining how his jealousy grew bigger and bigger until he became certain that his wife was cheating on him. At the denouement, he says that he found her in bed with another woman. He then tells Thana (all in a blank tough guy drawl that doesn't even acknowledge Thana's presence) that he went home and strangled his wife's cat. This appals Thana and she pulls her gun out and points it at him. She pulls the trigger but the barrel isn't loaded: the trigger clicks but nothing happens. Only then does the man seem to notice her. He grabs the gun and after a dramatic pause, points it at his own head. He grimaces and Thana looks scared. We suspect that he will call the police, that her killing spree is over. Instead, he leans towards her and blows his own brains out. She no longer even has to pull the trigger: her presence alone is enough to bring about a man's death.

When Thana gets home, the landlady's dog barks as she comes up the staircase. Morel captures a beautiful shot of Thana against a white wall from a high angle. She waits for the landlady's door to open but it doesn't. When Thana gets into her own apartment, we see that she has been wearing yet another different outfit: we have seen the black cape, the red top and the black boots before, but now she is also wearing black leather trousers. To try and get the dog off the scent, Thana takes the last two bin liners out of the refrigerator. She sticks one in a cupboard and locks it and then heads out of the window and down the fire escape to dump the other. This completes a neat full circle, as Thana opens the window, brushes the wind-chimes and climbs out, performing an exact reversal of the intruder's break-in earlier. She is now breaking out of her own apartment – St. John may be suggesting here that the apartment and the remains of the rapist are imprisoning Thana. Predictably, the moment that she closes the window, the landlady knocks on the door, checks that Thana isn't in and then opens the door with a spare set of keys. She searches the apartment while Phil the dog heads straight to the bathtub and then to the locked cupboard. Discovering that the cupboard is locked, the landlady goes off to get a key. When she returns, she finds that Phil has knocked a vase of flowers over, leaving a purple stain on a white rug. "Now she'll know that we were here," complains the landlady in her eccentric drawl. She cleans up and flees without looking in the cupboard.

The next scene is the final scene at work. The boss is surrounded by the female workers who are laughing sycophantically at his jokes. He says that he is giving all of them the afternoon off because they've been working hard and because it's the day of the Halloween party. Thana is the only one who isn't smiling or laughing. She stands with a cold look on her face in front of a door bearing a plaque which reads MEN, in a touch of irresistible black humour from Ferrara and St. John. From there, Ferrara gives us a chilling shot of Thana in her leather trousers with her hair pulled back. It's her alter-ego. The camera starts with her boots and slowly works up her legs until we see that she's standing in her apartment, unsure what to do. The dog is barking at the door.

A close-up of a piece of paper follows, and the camera crawls along each word of a message written from Thana to the landlady, who is simultaneously reading it: "Can I take Phil For A Walk?" The landlady isn't sure. She says that Thana hasn't walked Phil in a "long time". This confirms that Thana has been one of the landlady's tenants for a while and also that she has become increasingly distant. Was she already cracking up when the rapes took place? Were they the final straw? In a chilling scene we then see Thana kicking Phil and dragging him through a maze of Manhattan traffic. After failing to get him run over by a truck or car, she takes him out to the ocean and ties him up. Thana gets out her gun and points it at Phil. Ferrara cuts before she pulls the trigger, leaving us to presume that she has killed the dog, and that Thana has completely lost her mind.

The film's most famous scene follows. We see a bullet on Thana's dressing table and then Thana herself, dressed as a nun. Delia's eerie piano music comes in. Thana in full habit, kisses each bullet that she is about to load. Her red lipstick clashes brutally with the nun's habit. Up to this point, we only see close-ups of her head and face and of her hands. The camera then pulls back to a wide shot showing Thana loading the gun. Her legs are wide apart. She's wearing stockings and suspenders. Then we see her full-on, but via a mirror's reflection (another of Ferrara's stylistic traits). She has her leather boots on. Her arms are bare. In a chilling homage to Robert De Niro's portrayal of Travis Bickle in *Taxi Driver*, she blows the end of the gun as if she has just fired it, blows kisses to invisible recipients and fires imaginary bullets (echoed on the soundtrack as if to tell us what she might be hearing in her head) in various directions. It's a feminised take on the notorious 'Are you talkin' to me?' scene in *Taxi Driver*. Morel then switches from the reflected mirror shot to a full-on shot. Thana sits, legs apart, bare thighs, firing her gun in all directions. The mix of sexuality, gunplay and nun's habit makes for a car crash between the sacred and the profane.

Then comes the Halloween party. A band are playing live, the music is blasting. Thana's boss is done up as Dracula. He introduces her to some people who ask if her name is Greek, driving home the mythical associations of her name that St. John doesn't want us to miss. The ghoulish costumes make for a Fellini-esque scene. Meanwhile, the nosy landlady goes back into Thana's room and unlocks the cupboard that has been interesting Phil the dog so much. In a surreal moment, as she is about to open the bin liner a gorilla appears at her door: it's a tenant who we saw earlier on the staircase, in a gorilla suit for Halloween. The landlady runs back to her apartment with the bag and opens it. It's the last of Thana's bags and, predictably, it's the one containing the decaying head of the rapist. As she's undoing the bag, the landlady calls Thana a "witch". She screams when she sees the head and Ferrara immediately cuts to the fashion house's Halloween party, focusing on the live band. (Band performances will surface in many of Ferrara's future films.) The camera moves from dancer to dancer. One of these dancers, wearing a mask and hat, is Ferrara himself which means that he plays two roles in the film. In the background, we see the boss (as Dracula) ushering Thana up a spiral staircase, away from the party. He wants to seduce her. With the finale in sight, St. John has Thana's symbolic 'parents', the boss and the landlady, turn on her. They are both figures who are potentially in positions to act as supports for Thana, though both have ultimately refused the role. We see the boss on his knees, his head between Thana's thighs, declaring, "Oh baby, the mound of Venus!" It's an absurd moment. Thana stands coolly above him, dressed as a nun, looking down as her boss moves down to kiss her boots. It's an inversion of their relationship and the sado-masochistic overtones that St. John lends this scene are almost certainly a comment on the boss/worker relationship. Here, though, it's inverted and he is powerless before her. He wants to fuck her and he'll do anything to make that happen. He grovels before her, uttering sweet nothings, kissing her feet.

Simultaneously, across town, the landlady has called the police. Two detectives are with her (the younger one played by St. John) as is the tenant in the gorilla suit. The rapist's scalp is on the table. The landlady says that Thana has killed her dog too. (Just before the first sighting of Thana dressed as a nun, a brief scene was dropped in showing a note from Thana saying that she was sorry but she had lost Phil on the walk.) Back at the party, the boss lifts Thana's robes and is confronted by a gun tucked into her suspender belt. He looks shocked, then Ferrara swiftly cuts back to the party where a loud gunshot rings out. There's panic and then a man runs up the staircase. As he does so, Thana appears and shoots him. He falls in slow motion. The slow motion film and slowed down soundtrack (complete with screaming children and what sound like roaring animals) gel precisely with the burning candles and ghoulish parade of costumed guests. It's like a head-on collision between Polanski, Warhol and David Lynch, as Thana stands in front of a giant spider's web backdrop (suggesting that she's like a fly trapped in the spider's web of her mental breakdown or her victims are like spiders trapped in her web of death) and shoots man after man after man in the crowd. It's a bad trip freakshow, a visual orgy of colour and menacing images.

Finally, Thana prepares to shoot a man dressed as a bride (yet another reference to the scenes of Polanski in drag from *The Tenant*). Behind her, Laurie runs over and grabs a knife from the buffet table. The terrified man in drag stares at Thana. Thana has her gun outstretched, ready to shoot him. Behind her, Laurie, with her skirt riding high so that her underwear shows, holds a knife outstretched from her crotch like a penis. It's a perverse collision of genders. Thana shoots the man dressed as the bride. He falls, his wig drops off and the blood pumps through his white dress against the white backdrop of the shuttered doors. Thana starts to turn around, sensing someone behind her or looking for a new victim. Morel shoots an intense close-up of the knife's blade as it heads towards the black cloth of Thana's habit. Laurie stabs Thana in the back. Thana turns to shoot her attacker only to find that it's not only not a man, it's her co-worker, Laurie. Her expression turns from angry to sad: like Reno, she can't bring herself to kill a woman. Instead, she speaks her only word in the entire film: "Sister." The fact that she cannot kill a woman and makes "sister" her only spoken word, has helped to earn the film its cult feminist following. Does Thana say "sister" as a feminist coding? A means of aligning herself with her gender against the scores of men that she killed?

Ferrara cuts to the landlady crying in her apartment, having first offered a shot of two photographs: one of either the landlady's dead husband or father and the other of Phil. The film ends with Phil the dog running up the staircase and pawing at the landlady's door. It's an odd ending, giving the whole film a heavily tongue-in-cheek, Lassie-style conclusion. More importantly though, Thana has spoken at last, which tells us that she had previously been struck dumb after a traumatic event or episode. Only when faced with death, was she able to find her voice again. Again, this sense of release from the prison of silence, lends the finale the spirit of a Robert Bresson ending. During the film, we can see several ways in which she is imprisoned: by being mute; by being female; by being socially isolated; by her job and boss; by her environment. Death has liberated her.

The Ferrara and St. John take on the rape-revenge genre (also the theme of Meir Zarchi's *I Spit On Your Grave*, Clint Eastwood's *Sudden Impact*, William Fruet's *Death Weekend* and Burt Kennedy's *Hannie Caulder*) is notable for a variety of reasons. After Thana's double rape, she avenges herself instead of turning to a powerful male figure (cop, judge, priest, friend or lover) to seek revenge for her. The male characters that appear throughout the film are all given the vilest and most base personalities. The two rapists are made as repulsive as possible. The boss see-saws from camp nonchalance to devious lechery. The fashion photographer is a perfect caricature of the strutting testosterone-fuelled male ego. The pimp is an abusive pig who beats women. The gang make it clear that they enjoy terrorising a lone woman and infer that they intend to rape her. The bar confessor is a twisted drunk who gets even with his unfaithful wife by strangling her cat. The street corner Romeo's idea of seduction is to chase a lone woman into a dead-end alley. The Saudi Arabian businessman treats Thana like a piece of meat that can be hired for a night for a few dollars. St. John couldn't make any of these nightmarish men any more repellent if he tried. In a piece about the film for *Velvet Light Trap*, Peter Lehman wrote, "All other rape-revenge films, with the notable exception of *I Spit On Your Grave*, include positive male characters with whom spectators can identify. Frequently, the avenging woman becomes involved with such a man and they form a couple at the film's conclusion. *Ms. 45* lacks any such men." Thana, like most of the female characters in the film, is portrayed favourably. *Ms. 45* couldn't be a clearer, well-aimed attack on male oppression of women if it tried.

Fear City 1983

"The theme of the film is 'thou shalt not kill' " – Nicholas St. John to *Film Comment*.

"Once again, Ferrara and St John have delivered an Eighties-style *film noir*, with the central metaphor of the City as hell: from the red glow of the strip joints through to the hard, metallic glint of the rain-washed streets, the atmosphere is quite simply infernal" – *Video Review*.

Fear City features Ferrara's most linear and conventional narrative. Nicholas St. John's screenplay puts a gripping plot first and his trademark spiritual-philosophical-psychological concerns second. The film is set in the sleazy world of New York's seedy strip clubs where a serial slasher (played by real-life black belt karate expert John Foster) is preying on the clubs' dancers. Nearly all of the victims are supplied to the clubs by a booking firm, the Starlite Agency, run by ex-boxer Matt Rossi (played by Tom Berenger) and his partner Nicky (played by Jack Scalia). When the slasher starts to ritualistically attack, maim and murder the Starlite girls, their business dries up. The club owners feel the knock-on effect too when the Starlite girls become too scared to work, causing club audiences to dwindle.

Matt Rossi is the third focal point of the urban victim trilogy. Unlike Reno and Thana, he is attacked third-hand. He never experiences the attacks: he isn't raped like Thana, nor is he driven to killing by his environment as Reno is. Ultimately, the film is all about Matt winning back his masculinity. We learn that he was once a successful boxer (via a series of flashbacks and also by the amount of memorabilia that is plastered on the Starlite office walls) and that he retired after accidentally killing an opponent (Kid Rio) in the ring. Thus, St. John pits an ex-boxer (who is tormented with guilt over the death) against a trained karate fighter who is attacking his dancers.

Ferrara's relentless use of mirrors as motifs make it clear that Matt's battle with the slasher is really a battle with himself. As if to reinforce the point, St. John has Matt punch a photograph of himself in a despairing moment of impotent rage. In a parallel scene, the slasher kickboxes his own reflection in a mirror. The more dancers that the slasher attacks, the more Matt feels his masculinity being stripped away from him. When he checks into a seedy motel near the end and goes into a rigorous training programme, he is symbolically attempting to reclaim his past. When he defeats the slasher in an alleyway battle, he reclaims his pride and his masculinity while simultaneously exorcising the guilt (over killing Rio) that has been eating him away.

There are clear parallels between Matt and Thana in *Ms. 45*. Like Thana, Matt is unable to communicate. The film's romantic subplot, which involves Matt's attempts to win back his ex-girlfriend Loretta (who is also one of Starlite's hottest dancers), runs parallel to his angry need to take the law into his own hands and bring the slasher to justice. At the start of the film, Loretta is dating another dancer, Leila (played by Rae Dawn Chong).

Early in the film, Matt and Nicky watch Loretta dance from a window in the club owner's office. The owner is Mike (played by *The Godfather II* veteran Rossano Brazzi) and his comments to Matt about Loretta lead us to understand that Matt is trying to get over breaking up with her. After her performance, Loretta goes to her dressing room. Leila is waiting for her. Matt heads towards Leila's dressing room with a birthday gift (a necklace that he gives her later). He is about to knock on the door when he hears Leila wishing Loretta a "happy birthday". He pushes the door open gently and we get a close-up of his peering eye in the gap of the door from inside the dressing room. (This shot is recreated when Harvey Keitel spies on the medical examination of the raped nun through a crack in the door in *Bad Lieutenant*.) He sees Leila giving Loretta a back massage. He leaves them and pulls the door closed. Shortly after, we see Matt and Nicky driving together (a confessional male moment rather like the driving scene between Mickey and Matty in *The Blackout*). Matt rebuffs Nicky's advice to forget Loretta by saying that he wants to give it another shot. In this scene, as in the rest of the film, Matt is introspective, sensitive and unable to express himself. This aligns him with Reno and Thana: all three characters are 'mute' in their own individual ways. In one key scene, Matt tells Loretta, "sometimes I can't find the right words", which sums him up perfectly: he's a man who favours action over words.

Lawlessness, a common theme in Ferrara's films, is again at the forefront of the action as more and more dancers are attacked. The police, as usual in Ferrara's films, are portrayed as inadequate. They repeatedly harass Matt and Nicky and other agency owners such as their rival, Goldstein, rather than focusing on finding the killer. The police believe that the attacks are the result of a mob feud, that a rival agency is trying to put Matt and Nicky out of business by attacking their girls. It's only after one of Goldstein's girls also gets attacked that the police realise they're dealing with a lone psychopath. Even then, we see the head of the homicide investigations, Lieutenant Wheeler, and his slimy partner, devote more time to trying to stop Goldstein and Matt and Nicky from turning vigilante with the aid of mob muscle (supplied by the super-smooth Mafia hood Carmine) than stopping the attacks. Just as in Ferrara's next feature, *The Gladiator*, the police are seen to be acting in opposition to the viewer's sense of justice. Police apathy, incompetence and laziness leads Matt Rossi, just as it will lead Rick Benton in *The Gladiator*, to take the law into his own hands.

Several key scenes in the film show the police treating Matt and Nicky like criminals. When Matt comes out of hospital after visiting one of the dancers who has been attacked, he finds the Lieutenant and his partner sitting on his car. Later on, they arrest Matt for beating up a man who they mistook for the slasher in their club, while Nicky is busy getting hospitalised by a slasher the police don't believe exists. Just as Thana found in *Ms. 45*, there is no law and no safety for the individual. The city, as the Lieutenant mutters at one point, is full of "suspects".

The first time that the slasher attacks a dancer (Honey), he grabs her suddenly from behind and drags her into an alleyway. He lays her face down and starts to strangle her and chop at her hair. Then he stabs her in the back. This inevitably recalls the first rape scene in *Ms. 45* and the first vampire attack in *The Addiction*. In all three scenes, a woman is abruptly attacked and dragged into a dark alleyway. The attack, like all of the attacks in the film, is horrific. We only learn the full details of the attack when Matt and Nicky visit Honey in hospital and she tells them that the attacker started to cut her fingers off one by one with a pair of scissors. A flashback of the slasher raising a pair of scissors towards her fingers is stomach-churning enough but Ferrara follows this with a shot of Honey's bandaged hand as it wraps around Nicky's shoulder. We see that several fingers are missing.

Unlike many other slasher films, Ferrara lets us see the attacker's face in the first alleyway attack. The point isn't to terrify the viewer by letting us imagine what this killer looks like, but instead to have us ponder why he's singling out these dancers for attack. Throughout the film, the slasher is seen to be clean-shaven, muscled and well-toned. His apartment is starkly furnished. Everything about this killer is pared down. He believes that he is a specimen of human perfection.

Twice we see the slasher hunched over his desk, writing up a new attack in a journal which has the words FEAR CITY crudely painted in red on the cover. Ferrara uses a Travis Bickle-style voice-over to accompany the writing scenes. These voice-overs reveal the Bickle-esque motives behind what the slasher is doing: "with the death of each criminal, each whore, each worthless life, man comes closer to purity." This man is a loner who can't stomach the filth and scum on the city streets anymore. The difference between this character (who is acting on feelings of urban alienation) and Travis Bickle, Reno Miller or Thana, is that there is nothing remotely believable about him. Paul Schrader made Bickle a credible character; we sympathise with Thana; we understand Reno, even if we don't like him. By contrast, the slasher is simply a cold, sadistic attacker who preys on women who dance in strip clubs. St. John never explains why the slasher singles these women out as victims. Why does he have such a strong hatred for these dancers? Does he have psycho-sexual problems? Does he have a past connection to a stripper? We are left in the dark as to his real motives and consequently he is a character that we can't understand. He attacks strippers, Thana attacks lecherous males, Reno attacks down-and-outs. Two of the three are human characters, the slasher as Honey tells Matt and Nicky in the hospital is "like an animal".

St. John was striving to create a slasher who re-constructs himself as an 'idea', a motif of purity. Towards the end of the film, when he kickboxes his own reflection, he destroys any notion of a soul/body separation. He believes that he is superhuman (hence St. John's original inclusion of Nietzsche's work in scenes of the slasher's room). His alter-ego and opponent Matt is, on the other hand, very human. He is a fallen man as we can tell when we see Nicky nostalgically flicking through a scrapbook at home that is full of clippings of Matt's boxing achievements. A key clipping reads ROSSI QUITS RING, CITES DEATH OF KID RIO AS PRIMARY REASON.

Matt is also a tender man, as we learn from his bid to win Loretta back from Leila. The fact she left him for a female lover is another broadside against Matt's masculinity. Throughout the film it seems as though Matt wants to relive his relationship with Loretta so that he can be more open, as much as he also wants to relive the boxing match so that he can turn back time and not kill Kid Rio. By the end of the film, he manages to find answers to both problems. In beating the killer, he solves his 'lost' masculinity; in winning back Loretta he solves his inability to communicate. When he finally gives Loretta his birthday gift, which turns out to be a pendant that says I LOVE YOU, she is touched and comments that when they were dating, he would never have done something so romantic. We can tell from this that he is a closed off, alienated man. For someone who spends his whole life working with women (albeit strippers), he is oddly unable to communicate with any of them.

Matt isn't able to communicate with his male friends either. A singularly ill-fitting flashback to his boyhood (a narratorial device that St. John revisits in *The Funeral*) shows him shining two Mafia gangsters' shoes. Halfway through the job, a car pulls up and a rival gangster mows the men down in a hail of machine gun bullets. Matt, who has curled up behind his shoe shine box, is spared by the gunman (but warned not to reveal what he saw to anyone). However, he is now mentally scarred for life. When he visits elderly mob boss Carmine for advice, we learn that Matt distanced himself from the 'neighbourhood' via boxing. His attempts to make something of himself rather than fall into the gangster role that we imagine awaited him as a young adult ironically resulted in his taking a man's life. After the guilt and shock at having killed Kid Rio, he reverts to type and runs a booking agency for strippers with Nicky who, we learn from the flashbacks, used to be his manager. Many aspects of the Matt/Nicky relationship seem to suggest that St. John is writing a thinly veiled portrait of his friendship with Ferrara.

The scene in which Matt takes Loretta back to their old dating haunt by the waterfront and gives her his birthday gift is very tender. A close-up of her hand pressing onto his is lifted straight out of the Robert Bresson stylebook. It's a touching image, but one that is soon tarnished. They go back to her place. Loretta appears in a vest and underwear and walks towards Matt on the sofa, passing a neon wall-fitting of a woman's head. It triggers a direct connection to all the neons that surround the strip club scenes and, hence, to the fact that Loretta is a stripper and that Matt sells her naked body to other men. St. John is reminding us that this isn't some cutesy Hollywood love scene. The club scenes are all colour-coded with the endless neon lights and signs that are a trademark of Ferrara's style. A touching moment follows as Loretta recognises that Matt has found a bottle of whiskey in her cupboards and she apologises that it's not his beloved bourbon. It's a classic lover's detail. Tellingly, she is already wearing the I LOVE YOU pendant. They kiss.

Ferrara cuts to Matt's nightmare. (A nightmare also follows a tender bedroom scene between Matty and Susan in *The Blackout*. Ferrara frequently follows a 'sacred' image with a 'profane' image.) We see one of the Starlite girls (Jorge) arrive back at her apartment. She thinks someone has followed her into the building and races to get into her apartment. Once inside, she peeps through the spyhole and finds that she was only being followed by an elderly neighbour.

We, the audience, also sigh because we had expected a clichéd scene in which she can't get her keys in the lock and the killer attacks her. Instead, she sighs a giant sigh, breaks into a nervous smile and flicks the lights on. When we least expect it, we suddenly see the slasher step out from the shadows and stab her. This scene dissolves into one where Matt, drenched in sweat, wakes up with a nosebleed in bed with Loretta (another souring of their romantic link that St. John would re-examine in a more poetic light in his screenplay for *Snake Eyes*). St. John takes a genuine romantic interlude and turns it into a nightmare. The nightmare scene dissolves into one of several aerial shots as a radio news broadcast announces that one of the victims of the "New York Knifer" died during the night.

Similarly, a tender scene of domestic romance between Leila and Loretta also turns sour. We see Leila going through what we assume to be her own handbag and bedside drawers. Then we see Loretta, naked in bed and just waking up. Leila says she is trying to find some cash. Loretta opens the drawers next to her side of the bed and points to some dollar bills. As Leila takes them, she sees some black and white photo-booth shots of Loretta and Matt. She mentions that she's working at the Latino club that night and makes an anti-men quip. Loretta distances herself by saying that she doesn't hate men, although Leila does. St. John feeds us the tension here: Leila is a politically minded, feminist and Loretta is torn between Leila and her ex-lover, Matt. Leila fixes Loretta some coffee, re-establishing a more romantic mood.

Later that night, Loretta lets Matt drive her home rather than meet Leila at the Latino Club. While Leila dances at the club (dressed in PVC), we see the slasher in the front row. Later that night, he attacks Leila in a subway station, in one of the most horrific scenes in the film. The station is deserted. Leila is out of her on-stage outfit and dressed in regular clothes. Just as she is about to light a cigarette, the killer grabs her from behind and makes a cut across her forehead. Blood from the wound runs into her eyes, blinding her. He then circles her like a tiger and slashes her on strategic points of her body. Ferrara's remarkable direction makes us not only experience Leila's terror but also 'feel' each slash. The doctors later tell Matt and Nicky that he believes that the killer is familiar with human anatomy because his cuts are designed to avoid major arteries, and therefore to delay death; he wants the victims to suffer. He also appears to want them to be able to identify him. After a lovers' scene between Leila and Loretta, it is typical that St. John has Leila attacked when Loretta fails to meet her after work. Leila, like many other victims, dies in hospital some time after the attack. The guilt and shock drives Loretta back to her heroin problem, which she had apparently beaten. Indeed, it is Loretta's snowballing drug habit that almost gets her killed. Once we have seen her return to her dealer, her increasingly wasted appearance (and inability to work or even answer the door to Matt) sets the groundwork for the anti-drugs theme that would also later lie behind *Bad Lieutenant*, *The Addiction* and *The Blackout*.

The film's final showdown takes place in a darkened alleyway. Loretta had come here earlier in the evening to plead with her drug dealer to let her have some heroin. He had slapped her and sent her away. When she returns with some money that she has borrowed from Nicky's girlfriend Ruby (played by Janet Julian, who would excel as Frank White's girlfriend in *King Of New York*), she finds that her drug dealer has been hanged. This is a telling moment. Just as Thana begins to kill any man, rather than the men who sexually threaten her, so this slasher begins to target anyone who fails to meet his standards of purity. St. John is inviting us to come up with hypotheses for the slasher's behaviour here. Why does he kill Loretta's dealer? To save Loretta from drugs? Or to make sure that no one interrupts him when he kills Loretta?

The ending of the film is very like the ending to *The Gladiator*. Matt, the vigilante figure, appears at the end of the alleyway. The killer, who has just been maced by Loretta, freezes. It's a show-down between the retired boxer and the trained martial arts expert. Loretta tries to crawl away in spite of a stab wound she has in her leg. Matt and the killer fight. We have to remember that when the killer's attack on Ruby went wrong, he briefly encountered Nicky. Ruby was waiting outside a club for Nicky to pick her up. Nicky was late. The killer leaped out on her and tried to drag her off into an alleyway. Nicky's car pulled up. He saw what was happening. The killer released Ruby and faced Nicky. There was no fight: Nicky swung a stick at the slasher who responded by kicking him so violently in the head that he had to be hospitalised. The recurring motif of Matt's lost masculinity or pride is restored when he defeats the killer; as he does so, he is driven on by flashbacks to the Kid Rio fight which haunts him so deeply. When the police arrive, they pronounce the killer dead. It's a three-way showdown between the criminal, the vigilante and the law, or in other words, law and lawlessness, its mirror image. The same triangle completes *The Gladiator*, though in *Fear City*, the Lieutenant begrudgingly tells Matt that he is a "hero". St. John makes the ending a rarity in a Ferrara film: not only is justice done but we also get a romantic closing shot of Matt and Loretta cuddling up together in the back of a squad car.

The camerawork, which revels in the rain-soaked *film noir* mood of the streets, reflects the subject matter perfectly. The film's opening aerial shots introduce us to the blurred neons that will weave in and out of the film. Ferrara intercuts footage of the streets with footage of girls dancing in the clubs. The third dancer that we see is Karen O'Shea, who played the fashion model at the start of *Ms. 45*. These brief scenes of the girls dancing (not unlike the scenes of the strippers in Scorsese's *Mean Streets*), like many of the other dancing scenes in the film, were brutally cut by the British censors when the film hit both cinemas and home video, as Ferrara complained to *City Limits* back in 1985: "It's (*Fear City*) been banned (in Britain). The cut they sent over is very botched up. It's an abomination man, when they start cutting, but just fuck 'em."

The majority of scenes are set at night and more than once, we see Matt restlessly pacing the streets, his office, his apartment or the deserted waterfront as the dawn rises. Matt is a night owl, partly because of his business and partly because of the things that haunt him. Many of the scenes between Matt and Nicky and club owners or Mob bosses are lit and shot to suggest a subtle homage to *Mean Streets*. The strip club footage itself, and in particular the sleazy almost-nude shots of Melanie Griffith, is not glossy and airbrushed but depressingly seedy. Many scenes are bathed in a red diabolical glow. At one point, Matt enters one of the clubs and is drenched in a red haze that originates from a neon flashing GIRLS GIRLS. He might as well be entering the gates of hell.

St. John adds a series of layers to the film that perhaps pick up the feminist themes touched on in *Ms. 45*. When the first attack takes place, Ferrara interweaves scenes of leering, cheering men watching Loretta strip, with the brutal attack. It seems he is implying that the men in the audience are degrading the dancer as much as the killer in the alleyway behind the club. The scene is also a calculated critique of films that portray sexual violence in a titillating manner. In *Fear City*, any strip club scene that might arouse the viewer is rapidly cut with a scene of violence or threat towards women. There are other scenes that attack the exploitation of women more explicitly. When we first see the offices of the Starlite Agency in full flow, Nicky is snapping at Jorge because she did a 'bottomless gig' and didn't remove her g-string. When she says that this was because she was having her period, he gets mad at her. The phone interrupts his complaining and a policeman tells him that Honey has been attacked.

When the girls are all too scared to work, club owner Mike calls Nicky and complains that the girl that they sent as a replacement is getting booed offstage. Mike comments that she's so "ugly it hurts my eyes" and that "she couldn't give a rapist a hard-on" before saying he wants another girl sent to the club or "I'll kill that fat sow!" Again, this demonstrates intense (verbal) violence directed towards women. The male cops are no better, referring to the dancers as "pussy". The assaults are brutal attacks on women too: the way in which the killer immobilises his victims by strategically wounding them suggests that he is terrified of women. He doesn't steal from them or rape them, he only wants to maim and injure. When his victims start to die from their wounds, the slasher's attacks become sicker. He kills the Goldstein girl with nunchucks and a razor. He attacks another girl with a huge sword. Mostly though, he attacks the anatomy of their work: their faces, their hands, their arms and in particular, the anatomy most used for dancing: legs and back. It's as if he wants to stop them from dancing and stripping; these girls make him feel impure, so he kills them. Each one of the attack scenes is stomach-churning in its horrific portrayal of a sadistic, control freak attacking and maiming women who are shown to be unable to protect themselves. Only Loretta fights back and this is only possible after Nicky's girlfriend Ruby has given her a can of Mace to use.

The Robert Bresson influence surfaces thematically when Matt is first interrogated in a police station jail cell by Lieutenant Wheeler and then when he tries to confess to a priest in a church. On both occasions, he is imprisoned: first literally, then subsequently by his soul. St. John would go on to take this small scene and develop it into an essential part of his writing style. Ferrara garnishes the church scene with shots of a statue of the Madonna and also a crucifix. Matt asks the priest for forgiveness for a sin he hasn't yet committed. The priest says this isn't possible and after making Matt recite the act of contrition with him, sends him away to say 25 'Hail Marys', '25 Our Fathers' and also to ask God for guidance. We see Matt praying before dozens of blazing candles at the altar in the church, in a scene loosely evocative of the church scene at the start of *The Driller Killer*, certain scenes in *Bad Lieutenant* and also the scene in which Harvey Keitel prays in *Mean Streets*. Again, only Ferrara would be able to include a scene like this and make it work. The incorporation of such spiritual disquiet into this genre displays key themes and stylistic traits that would soon form part of Ferrara's auteur signature.

3

THE TV YEARS 1985–1986

Miami Vice: 'The Home Invaders' 1985

It's hardly surprising that Ferrara ended up directing two episodes of *Miami Vice*. The drugs, the prostitution, the humid city, the girls in bikinis and the slimy low-life dealers and pimps are more or less constant elements of his work anyway. The plot of this first episode revolves around a gang of 'home invaders' who have made six attacks on occupied Miami homes, stolen $2 million worth of goods, tortured and brutalised their victims and put five of them in hospital. The gang, who wear hockey masks or stockings are a high-profile case, so Lieutenant Castillo (Edward James Olmos, significant to Keitel's performance in *Bad Lieutenant* later on) is asked to draft some of his vice team onto this robbery case. To add a twist, the head of the robbery case is Lieutenant Malone, former mentor of designer-stubbled, gravel-voiced vice detective Sonny Crockett (Don Johnson). Castillo, who works diligently and quickly, soon shows up Malone with his detective work. When he and Crockett interview the wife and mother who is part of the family that we see attacked before the opening credits, the familiar Ferrara theme of lawlessness creeps in. The woman calls one of the attackers (who burned their maid with an electrical device, probably a cattle prod) an "animal". The line recalls the hospital bed scene in *Fear City* where Honey describes her attacker to Matt and Nicky using the same word. If this was the opening of a Ferrara film, the police would prove useless, the crime would pass by unpunished and uninvestigated and either the woman or her husband would start to

85

crack up and take the law into their own hands. But it's *Miami Vice* and piece by piece, Castillo and Crockett (working as a double act because Ricardo Tubbs – Philip Michael Thomas – is on leave in New York) set out to solve the case.

We see Castillo thumbing through paperwork. Crockett is seen smoking and driving around Miami, Ferrara intercutting flashy slow-motion footage (possibly a homage to Godard's bleakly beautiful footage of Nathalie Baye in *Slow Motion*) of his car with very Ferrara-esque footage of the city's neon-lit night life. The filming shows that whether Ferrara is directing scenes in New York or Miami, the fascination with a city's nocturnal landscape remains at the forefront of his style.

Castillo figures out that the gang had been working similar burglaries in the Chicago area. He accesses paperwork from the Chicago Police department and talks with a detective. From this he learns that during the spate of Chicago burglaries, a number of prostitutes were badly beaten by 'johns' (clients). He sends Trudy and Gina out to investigate any prostitutes who get beaten up. One such girl quickly turns up and after an initial shot of her sitting on a bed in a very sleazy, low-rent motel or apartment room, nursing a black eye and testing Trudy, Gina, Crockett and Castillo with her wise-talking chit-chat, she goes to the station to try to ID the 'john' who beat her up. The entire motel scene (and especially the fact that the character is a prostitute) is the most explicit incidence of the Ferrara style in this episode.

After another attack, this time on an elderly couple, Malone and Castillo clash again, their specialities making for an almost gang-like rivalry. As with the tension between gang lords in the later *China Girl*, there is an odd mix of competition and mutual respect between the two. Castillo solves the case when the questionnaires that he has asked each female victim to fill out throws up a common thread: that they all have their hair cut at a beauty salon called the Hair Emporium. Gina goes undercover as a flashy, rich customer and smokes out the parking lot attendant, who asks far too many questions. The team put him under surveillance and watch him at work when a middle-aged woman drops her car off. He checks her licence in the glove compartment, memorises her address, copies her keys and then calls the gang from a payphone. Gina then takes the prostitute to the beauty salon car park and has her I.D. the attendant as the 'john' who attacked her.

Crockett and Castillo follow the woman so they can stop her, explain the situation and stake her house out. She thinks they are attackers and a vaguely comic car chase ensues, with camerawork and vehicle choreography that could come straight from *The Gladiator*. Once the situation is explained, the woman, a kooky divorcee, is glad to help. The team tail the gang (one of whom is played by Paul Calderon who would go on to work with Ferrara on *King Of New York*, *Bad Lieutenant* and *The Addiction*) but lose them. Crockett and Castillo sit at the house waiting for the gang, but they don't arrive. Crockett calls the station where Gina and Trudy are sitting with the divorcee. He asks her questions about her routine to see if they've missed anything obvious which would alert the gang's suspicions. He asks about the blue Corvette and she tells him that it's her daughter's car. Crockett and Castillo then realise that the gang are at her daughter's house – it was her car, licence and keys that the attendant checked out.

Once they have the address, the two race over and ambush the driver. Then we see the gang torturing the woman's daughter and her husband, who are facing each other and tied up. It's the kind of mental torture and physical cruelty that Ferrara would re-examine in *Cat Chaser*. These very brief torture scenes, along with the earlier references to other tortures, especially the burning of the maid, were all cut by the BBC due to the media furore when the episode aired on British TV. Newspapers billed the episode as one which the BBC had especially cut because it was directed by Abel Ferrara, the maker of *The Driller Killer*. Even when working on a household TV show like *Miami Vice*, Ferrara still clashed with the censors.

Ferrara sets up the final bust nicely. Light reflects off the still waters of a swimming pool, throwing patterns onto Castillo, Crockett and the house. Crockett's reflection appears in the patio door glass, the next best thing to a mirror shot. Castillo throws a chair through the glass and in the confrontation which ensues the duo shoot and kill all of the gang members. The closing scene has pupil usurp mentor as Malone turns up to party with the victorious team and the woman. He tells Crockett that he has quit because Castillo and the case proved to him that he no longer had the talent he once had. Crockett outgrows his teacher and mentor and becomes his own man, in a rather corny ending.

The episode features many distinct Ferrara touches: the neon-drenched streets, the prostitute's motel room, her beaten face, the torture scenes, some of the car scenes and in particular, some clever visual puns. In one scene, Ferrara has the camera watch Crockett who is watching the suspect through a pair of binoculars. In another, he has a gang member photograph a potential victim's house (marking where the alarms are, where the doors are and so on). A girl in a bikini comes roller-blading out of the house. The camera clings to her body like a wet swimsuit. Then we see her out of focus through the gang member's camera. Ferrara then has a rapid close-up of the gang member re-setting the focus of his camera lens. An out of focus shot follows (as seen through the gang member's binoculars) which then finds focus on the girl who is bending over and fastening her roller-blade boots. It's an almost Godardian trick: a possibly exploitative shot of this fleshy woman is turned into a neat essay on the impossibility of capturing a woman's beauty on film.

Miami Vice: 'The Dutch Oven' 1985

'The Dutch Oven' revolves around issues of guilt, love and betrayal. Crockett's partner, Trudy Joplin (Olivia Brown), bungles an undercover drug bust when she shoots the key suspect four times and kills him. Ferrara opens the episode with shots of Trudy applying garish make-up. She goes to a club and hangs around outside, posing as a prostitute. The drug deal goes wrong when Tubbs is held up inside the club. Trudy and Crockett pursue the suspect through Miami traffic in an energetic car chase. When they head him off in an alleyway, the suspect opens fire on them and Trudy blows him away.

After a tense scene at the vice headquarters, where Trudy is wracked with guilt at having killed the suspect, Ferrara slips in a beautifully staged scene of her playing piano at her home later that night. She's just taken a shower and all her make-up has gone. A series of exquisite shots of her hands (including their shadows on the keys) recalls the harbour-side scene in *Fear City* where Loretta places her hand on Matt's. Both of these shots are Ferrara paying homage to Robert Bresson's extraordinarily poetic framing of the human body. Trudy is then framed, playing the piano, with a rain-drenched window to her left. To drive the introspective mood home, Ferrara then offers a shot of her staring out of the window, picking up the beautifully melancholic air omnipresent in Jean-Luc Godard's *Passion, First Name Carmen* and *Hail Mary* trilogy.

The reason for the piano scene is explained as the plot unfolds. Trudy goes to a nightclub where a band are playing (another of Ferrara's live band performances). The singer, David, is her ex-boyfriend and it is implied that she once played keyboards in his band. They broke up but clearly still miss each other. David's oldest friend is a coke dealer called Adonis, who introduces himself to Trudy as a big time "Candyman". He's actually a small fry dealer but likes to play the part of a major player.

After the show, Ferrara has the camera pick up a trail of discarded clothes on the silk sheets of a bed. Predictably, the trail ends with Trudy and David in bed together, vowing to give their relationship another go. The rest of the episode revolves around Trudy's struggle: does she bust Adonis and his Colombian drug connection and risk losing David forever or does she turn a blind eye and keep her working and personal life separate? Crockett advises her to do what she feels most comfortable with; Tubbs tails Adonis and is hungrier for the bust. After a montage of flashbacks to her love affair with David and some lonesome pounding of Miami's streets, Trudy sets up an undercover deal in which Crockett will buy coke from Adonis. The deal goes down in a nightclub, they bust Adonis and the episode ends with the band arriving and David accusing her of using and deceiving him before cutting her dead with the pay-off line, "You've got no soul, no damn honour."

Although this was a paid TV job, there is still evidence of Ferrara's style in the episode. The closing line of dialogue could easily come from a St. John screenplay. Trudy's introspective wrestling with guilt at having killed a man and at shopping her lover also makes her something of a Ferrara-esque character. Crockett lectures her in his car afterwards when she starts pondering aloud if she followed procedure accurately enough. She is at war with her identity. When David takes her to a party and she sees open drug use as well as a bartender dealing, she is torn between the urge to do her job and her loyalties to David. Interestingly, ex-New York Doll David Johansen performs at this party. (He had also sung the opening and closing song on the *Fear City* soundtrack.) The three live band scenes in this episode also recall the nightclub scenes in the later *China Girl*.

Other distinctly Ferrara-esque touches include the use of a lengthy, lascivious shot of two bikini-clad girls crossing a street to introduce a scene in which Crockett is playing cards outside a hotel. For a TV show, the shot is excessively long and breaks up the momentum of the narrative. The other slice of pure Ferrara is when we see Trudy and her colleague, Gina, working undercover as prostitutes. A car pulls up and an old guy solicits them. As the scene unfolds, it becomes clear that he's offering Trudy $50 to sleep with the two brace-wearing geeky boys in the back of the car, who can't be older than 12 or 13. He then adds that he'll pay $60 if he can watch. The close-up of the grinning boys (a collision of innocence and budding pubescent sexuality) that follows his request is shot in such a way as to provide a genuinely obscene image.

This moment also recalls the scene in *Bad Lieutenant* where Harvey Keitel pulls over two teenage girls and masturbates in front of them. The way Ferrara uses the camera to capture the faces of the father and the boys recalls Pasolini's fascination with physiognomy. Needless to say, Trudy and Gina lure the man into an alleyway and bust him. Elsewhere, Ferrara makes an early shot of a graffiti-strewn nightclub passageway stink of sweat and smoke. He has the scene filmed so that its stench almost seems to filter out of the TV screen. Another scene, in which Adonis does a deal with a slimy customer outside a cheap liquor store, also reeks of the kind of authentic sleaze that only Ferrara can capture.

The Gladiator 1986

"It's just this little car crash movie I made in two weeks to get some money to write a screenplay" – Abel Ferrara.

"Rick Benton is another of the director's urban victims, turning to violence as a way of striking back at his own personal problems" – *Monthly Film Bulletin*.

The Gladiator is a small-budget telemovie about a mechanic, Rick Benton, (played by Ken Wahl) who turns vigilante after his kid brother, Jeff, is killed by a drink driver who plagues the Los Angeles city area by preying on victims in his black death machine of a car. *The Gladiator* is a predictable, often extremely boring film, which apart from some of the Ferrara traits mentioned earlier, is nothing more than a slice of bad B-movie action. The rock soundtrack grates, the acting is wooden, the plot lacks any refinement and subtlety and only James Lemmo's cinematography rescues it from complete disaster. It's interesting to see how Ferrara copes with a screenplay, cast and crew that he clearly has no interest in. He doesn't bother attempting to get any performance out of the cast and the editing is sloppy and obvious. The film was apparently shot in two weeks, and it looks like it. Ultimately, it's mass-market made-for-TV entertainment and nothing else.

The only point of interest is Rick Benton, who is a West Coast Matt Rossi. Like Matt, an outside force disrupts his life. Rick is first seen pulling up at his modest house in a red sports car. The sun is shining and we immediately fix him as a wealthy young man. However, the vehicle turns out to be a car that he's servicing for a radio DJ called Susan Neville (played by Nancy Allen). When we see him in his own vehicle, a beaten up old blue pick-up truck, the weather is grey and grimy and he's driving along a muddy path. We learn early on that Rick and Jeff's parents are dead. Rick has had to raise Jeff himself and early scenes of them bonding under the hood of the sports car, show how paternal Rick is in the way he deals with Jeff.

Jeff dies after pestering Rick into taking him out for a driving lesson in the pick-up. After a series of quips from Rick – he can't believe his brother is old enough to start learning to drive; he asks Jeff if he has his learner's permit with him and tells him how dangerous drink-driving is – they go out driving. Jeff accidentally shoots a crossing. A black car races after them and starts ramming them from behind. Eventually, due to inexperience, Jeff loses control of the pick-up and they plough into an oncoming truck.

The film had begun with a shot of a bearded man in a bar, having his demand for another beer turned down by the bartender. When the waitress leaves for the night, a mysterious black car with black tinted windows, tails her and drives her off the road. The driver of this black car (presumably the drunk in the bar) becomes Rick's adversary, the slasher to Rick's Matt Rossi.

After scenes of Rick recovering in hospital and struggling to accept that his brother died in the accident, he has a flashback to the night of the crash. In response to the memories that the flashback jogs, a police lieutenant (played by Robert Culp) arrives to take Rick's statement but says that without a description of the driver or the car, the police are unable to do anything. This scene is revisited in *The Addiction* when Kathleen Conklin is told (also at a hospital, though this time after being bitten by the vampire) by a policeman that there is nothing that the police can do. Again, the theme of lawlessness surfaces: if the police can't do anything, then who can? Rick is faced with the same set of emotions that so many of Ferrara's characters are faced with: impotence, anger, fear, vulnerability and guilt.

Rick checks out of hospital and goes home. Like most other TV movies, a soft rock soundtrack lazily accompanies Rick as he walks around his empty home, telling us that he's grieving his brother's death. He is sitting smoking a cigarette when his only friend, Joe (a parts worker), brings back the blue crash truck, reconstructed and repaired. We then see Rick at a group meeting (Citizens For Highway Safety) that a hospital counsellor referred him to, where victims of drink drivers sit around and discuss their horror stories. The theme of the meeting is how to stop drink drivers from killing any more victims.

Just as Alcoholics Anonymous fails to keep Matty sober in *The Blackout*, this self-help group doesn't comfort Rick. Instead, it gives him the idea to turn vigilante and stop drink-driving himself. The driver of the black car continues to prey on victims. In each of these scenes, the black car pursues any driver who appears to be driving drunk. The more these random car accidents happen in the Los Angeles area, the more Rick realises that they are all connected. Every time he hears or reads about one of these accidents in the news, he sticks a pin in a wall map indicating where the accident took place.

The rest of the film, like *Fear City*, has a central plot (Rick trying to avenge his brother's death and stop the driver of the black car) and a sub-plot (a blossoming romance between Rick and Susan Neville). Rick, unlike Matt, doesn't have a Nicky (Joe is more a work colleague than a friend) or a Carmine or even an established lover like Loretta. He is totally alone. He drives around at night against a backdrop of neon-drenched streets, hunting for the murderous driver, just as Matt patrols his city looking for the slasher. Like Reno, Thana and Matt, Rick is one of Ferrara's silent, introspective victims. We have no idea at this stage what he's thinking or feeling.

The turning point in the film comes when Matt pulls into Danny's Dogs, a fast food drive-thru, to find two drunken young kids throwing stuff around. The restaurant manager comes out to warn them. Again, the theme of lawlessness is highlighted as the restaurant manager struggles to control the two young troublemakers. The two kids get into their car and try to cut in line in front of Rick's truck. They hoot at him, jeer and then ram his pick-up. He snaps (reminded of his brother's death), backs up and smashes into them three times. They drive off. The police arrive and at first try to accuse Rick of starting the trouble. The restaurant manager, who called the police, tells them that Rick was acting in self-defence. Rick tells the cops that the kids were "drunk" while the manager tells the police that Rick should get a "medal" for what he did. To reinforce the lawlessness theme, Rick ends up with an aggressive threat from one of the officers who tells him he'll find "trouble" if he takes the law into his own hands.

When Travis Bickle reaches this degree of angry isolation in *Taxi Driver*, he effectively turned himself into a walking arsenal. In *The Gladiator*, Rick does the Los Angeles equivalent and turns his pick-up truck into a tank. We see him weld reinforced steel around the wheels of the truck, add a huge bumper guard and a more powerful engine, and re-spray the vehicle gun grey. Once that is done, he returns to his nocturnal search for the black car as a vigilante.

The rest of the film follows a pattern: the driver of the black car rams a driver who he believes to be drunk off the road; Rick rams a driver who he believes to be drunk off the road. Rick apprehends his drink drivers by first warning them via a loud speaker system fitted onto his truck and then via a steel harpoon device that he fits on the back of his truck like a rocket launcher. Meanwhile the death car driver runs victims off the road with a tyre-shredding device that he has fitted to his wheel-caps. The media catch on to the story after Rick contacts the police by CB radio after each 'citizen's inter-vention' and says that 'The Gladiator' has once again immobilised drink-drivers. He has been driven to take the law into his own hands because he sees no law and order. His mission to avenge his brother's death is no different to Thana's reactive killing spree.

The police investigation (headed by the lieutenant who visited Rick in hospital) wrongly connects Rick's vigilante activities with the death car driver's attacks. The Lieutenant thinks that The Gladiator is "both Jekyll and Hyde". As the police get closer to catching Rick (whom they publicly tag as a dangerous vigilante), Susan Neville seduces him by pretending that there is something wrong with her red sports car. The twist here is that she devotes a great deal of her radio show to The Gladiator who has become something of a public hero. A series of cold romantic scenes between Rick and Susan explains that Rick is separated from a wife who left him because he insisted on taking care of Jeff. We learn that Rick sacrificed his marriage for his brother.

In one scene, their kissing is interrupted by a TV news report on which the Lieutenant aggressively condemns The Gladiator, calling him a "vigilante" and commenting, "Nobody is above the law!" Susan complains that the media are turning The Gladiator into a "hero" and says that he is all her radio show callers want to talk about. Rick says that maybe The Gladiator *is* a hero because he's "fighting something worth fighting against". Susan disagrees, saying that The Gladiator is more dangerous than the drivers he rams off the road: "he's the worst kind of criminal, making himself out to be some kind of crusader, breaking every law in the book." Rick angrily replies that The Gladiator is saving lives and that he wishes The Gladiator had been around to save Jeff on the night he got killed.

By the time Susan Neville is presenting a special live show on The Gladiator, Rick is out driving around Los Angeles. This is the moral turning point of the film. Just as Reno and Thana both end up blindly killing any man who gets in their way and the slasher kills a drug dealer after previously targeting strippers, Rick realises that he has lost all perspective on reality when he runs what he assumes to be a drink driver off the road. The speeding driver isn't drunk, he's trying to get his pregnant wife to a hospital. Later, he gives a full description of Rick and his pick-up truck (two details that started Rick's vigilante mission) to the police who issue an all-points bulletin to officers. Rick hears the bulletin on his CB radio.

Unlike Reno or Thana, Rick is made aware of the wrong he is doing by his environment. He calls Susan from a pay phone. They meet at a diner. Rick says he's been driving around all night thinking about Jeff. Then he offers a coded explanation as to what he's been doing: "Sometimes you think you're doing the right thing and it screws up. Everything goes wrong and you get in so deep that you can't get yourself out of it. You just can't stop." This is closed-off Rick at his most articulate, trying to pour his heart out to Susan. She tells him to deal with his anger and he says he has been dealing with his anger and that it's "scaring the hell" out of him. Ferrara's characters are all forced to deal with their anger, always with disastrous consequences. The scene also works as a veiled confession, providing a tentative connection with Ferrara's later, overtly Catholic work with St. John.

Rick, wracked with despair and grief, phones the Lieutenant and gives himself up. On the way to the station, he sees the black car. He radios in to the police and pursues the black car to a deserted junkyard where the two have a head to head as Matt and the slasher did in *Fear City*. They drive directly at one another and on impact both cars explode into flames. Rick staggers from the truck into the smoke, at which point the police arrive. The Lieutenant stares at Rick who points at the driver of the black car, who is lying on the ground, and explains, "This is the guy who killed my brother," before adding, "The Gladiator is finished." He is cuffed and led away, the smoky, moody crime scene fading to black. Unlike the end of *Fear City*, there is no endorsement of Rick's behaviour, only disapproval from the Lieutenant and his team. However, through this assertion of Rick's conscience, the ending carries a strong moral overtone.

Crime Story: The Pilot 1986

When Ferrara accepted an offer to direct the pilot feature for Michael Mann's TV series, *Crime Story*, it gave him his first taste of period film-making (something he would revisit with *The Funeral*). The pilot, like the series, is based around Lieutenant Mike Torello (played by Dennis Farina), a rough and rugged tough guy, recently assigned to the MCU (Major Crime Unit) of the Chicago Police Department and his bid to bring down rising mob star, Ray Luca. This polarity establishes the familiar Ferrara theme of good versus evil. The show is set in 1963 Chicago and consequently period detail is omnipresent: cue quiffs, sharp suits, cars, jukeboxes, diners, bars and a pumping rock'n'roll soundtrack. Although Torello is another of Ferrara's lonely, alienated characters, the pilot is mostly of interest because it signifies the degree to which Ferrara's grasp on the spectrum of film-making technique had tightened. Everything from the considered pace and the dazzling cinematography to the deceptively simple *mise en scène* announced Ferrara's arrival as a major director.

The film's centrepiece, a lengthy shoot-out that erupts out of the mob gang's bungled attempts to rob a department store, is choreographed and executed with frantic style; on two occasions, the shots become so chaotic and intense that it feels as though a rabid dog might be running around and filming the scenes with a hand-held camera strapped to its head. Apparently a device called a 'Pogo Camera' was used for these scenes, as Ferrara explained to Gavin Smith: "It was just a stick you hold with a little bash box, one of those little cameras you use for a chase, stuck on the bottom. It was like running around with a broomstick with a camera stuck on the bottom."

After an action-packed hold-up that dominates the first ten minutes of the film and then a further museum heist, Torello's pursuit of Ray Luca leads to moral discomfort, when he finds that the son of family friends, Johnny O'Donnell (played by David Caruso), is also on Luca's pay-roll. When Torello's colleague Conley is murdered by Luca, he starts to crack up. In one scene, an apparition of the dead Conley appears in Torello's office and talks to him. It's obvious that this isn't a regular hard-nosed cop.

When Johnny double-crosses a major mobster, first his parents get beaten up and then Luca kills him. Torello, who doesn't play by the rulebook, personally responds to the beating of O'Donnell's parents, by going with two other masked men and roughing up the mobster. In another scene, we see an attorney accuse Torello of trying to secure a conviction by using an illegal wire tap. He talks his way out of this, again bending the rules.

Torello, like Gilley (another cop), in *King Of New York*, believes that the criminal justice system favours the criminal and provides an obstacle rather than an aid to police work. In a court scene, Torello attacks an attorney for defending mobsters. He believes that he is right and that if rule-bending helps him to achieve his goals, then so be it. As usual, Ferrara blanket-bombs his lead character with a taste for the lawless life. Torello complains that, as a cop, he only gets paid $12,000-a-year to risk his life, while the criminals he pursues get richer and richer.

Torello also has another side to his personality. At home, he's consumed with sexual jealousy (believing at one point that his wife is having an affair) and plagued by nightmares of the latest day's work that nearly got him killed. He greets a bloodthirsty crime scene not by following police procedure but by quipping that it looks: "like a Jackson Pollock". If Torello wasn't a cop, then he would inevitably turn up in another Ferrara film. He's got the perfect Ferrara character cocktail: a hard, uncommunicative shell with a soft vulnerable centre.

4

THE TERRITORIAL TRILOGY

China Girl 1987

"It's a story about a racist society. The neighbourhood is changing, more Italians are leaving and more Chinese are moving in, and you're bound to have a volatile situation. There's something very beautiful about tradition but there is also something very ugly about it" – Nicholas St. John.

"Stylish, assured update of Romeo And Juliet" – *Sight and Sound.*

China Girl is Ferrara's personal favourite of all of his films. It's basically a violent reworking of *West Side Story* (itself based on Shakespeare's *Romeo And Juliet*). Italian-American teenager Tony (played by Richard Panebianco), a poor kid who works in a pizzeria, falls for a Chinese-American teenager Tye (played by Sari Chang), who is virtually kept house prisoner by her gang leader brother, Yung Gan (played by Russell Wong). All three names are coded: Yung Gan sounds like 'young 'un' as in 'young one', Tye sounds like 'tie' referring to the cultural and traditional ties that she is trying to break away from and Tony is a loose play on 'tone' as in skin tone. The film is the first of what I have dubbed Ferrara's Territorial Trilogy.

Ferrara opens the film with a series of shots that serve as a neighbourhood tour guide: a Catholic display, a shot of sun-drenched fire escapes, a building with a Latin inscription dating the building's conception as 1926 and an amusing sign for a pastry store called 'La Bella Ferrara'. This, one can't help but feel, suggests a certain amount of ethnic bias on the director's part, since he's of Italian-American descent. From these introductory shots, which explain that we're seeing selective images of Little Italy, Ferrara has Director Of Photography, Bojan Bazelli focus on a series of Italian-American faces as they observe the dismantling of a sign for what was once the 'D'Onofrio Bakery'.

The bakery is being replaced by a Chinese restaurant called the 'Canton Garden'. It is situated opposite the pizzeria where Tony, his older brother Alby (James Russo) and Alby's friend Mercury (David Caruso) work. Both places sit on the edge of Canal Street, a street which serves as a border between Chinese and Italian territories. Time and time again, characters in Nicholas St. John's screenplay make quips about how Canal Street divides Little Italy and Chinatown. The Chinese Triad gangs, headed in this film by the 'old man' Mr Tang (played by Stephen Chen), are shown to be involved with the Italian Mafia for the mutual benefit of both camps. The elders of both organisations accept that peace is necessary for mutual growth and profit. Gang wars attract too much police attention, as Mr Tang tells Mafia hood, Nino: "We must never allow ourselves to be divided by war or to be interfered with by police investigation all because a few reckless children cannot live within the traditions of our society."

Much of St. John's focus is on the difficulties of elders enforcing tradition onto their youngsters. Early on in the film, after Tye has been lectured by her brother for dancing with Tony at the nightclub, her friend snaps, "This ain't China!" Later, her brother comes home from a difficult meeting with a Triad member during which he has been told to kill his cousin, Tsu Shin (played by Joey Chin); he creeps in on his sleeping sister and tucks her up in bed. Then he surveys her room, noting American magazines by her bed, a Bruce Springsteen poster on the wall, make-up products littering the floor and then old black-and-white photographs of their relatives in China. Tye, like Yung Gan, chooses to break from tradition. Yung Gan spares his cousin and instead of killing him as ordered, plans to return to Hong Kong with him. The consequence of this is that Tsu Shin ends up shooting both Tony and Tye on a crowded Chinatown street. Tye chooses love to escape her cultural prison, he chooses violence and disobedience.

Throughout the film, Mercury (aptly named for both his red hair and his volcanic temper which we see to full effect when he stands on top of an apartment block and machine-guns the surrounding buildings) and Alby challenge the cultural orders and identity handed down to them by the Italian Mafia bosses. Likewise, Tsu Shin constantly takes the 'law' into his own hands and ignores Yung Gan's orders (which come from the 'old man' and the uncles).

The plot revolves around the 'Canton Garden', a symbolic encapsulation of all of the film's themes. The Italian neighbourhood (as represented by Mercury and Alby) is angry that a Chinese restaurant has opened in the locality. Tsu Shin and his gang ignore orders which state that the restaurant is now under Mafia control, and storm in one night, slap a waitress, cut the owner's chin with a knife and demand to be paid protection money. This breaks the arrangement that has been made between the Triads and the Mafia. The elders have peacefully come to an arrangement about the 'Canton Garden' but the young gangs will not abide by it.

The first time the Chinese gang hits the restaurant, Alby and Mercury attack them at the Canal Street traffic lights. Next time round, Tsu Shin fire-bombs the restaurant because the owners don't pay his protection money. The explosion also succeeds in blowing out the pizzeria windows. Alby, Mercury and a fellow gang member go to Chinatown to seek revenge for the act. They interrupt a one-on-one fight between Yung Gan and Tsu Shin. Outside of the gangs' hierarchy, dissension and greed is omnipresent. The subsequent gang battle between young Italian and Chinese gang members results in a major Triad-Mafia meeting at the pizzeria and the subsequent knifing to death of one Chinese gang member and the hanging of another. These murders are set as examples by the gang leaders who want peace.

The romantic sub-plot, a symbolic encapsulation of the film's themes, is poorly developed and somewhat passionless. Tony and Tye meet in a smoky nightclub and start dancing together; they are immediately attracted to one another. When the song ends, the crowd parts and Tsu Chin and his gang chase Tony out of the club. For the rest of the film, the two lovers have to rendezvous secretly in order to avoid being punished or excommunicated by their immediate elders. When we see them together for a second time, à la *Romeo And Juliet*, Tye is leaning out on the balcony of her apartment, looking out on a rain-soaked night. Tony appears below and calls up to her; they fix a date. When the date comes around, Tye arrives late as she has had to wait for her brother and his gang to go out before leaving. As soon as they are inside a nightclub, Tye goes to a toilet cubicle and changes out of her everyday outfit and into a slinky black dress. This transformation represents the symbolic shedding of a cultural and ethnic identity; Tye leaves her 'Chinese-ness' in the ladies room. Tony, who is constantly checked up on by Alby and Mercury, leaves his 'Italian-ness' at the pizzeria.

Tony and Tye's blossoming relationship echoes the relationship between the Triad and the Mafia elders. Mercury's constant racist attacks on the Chinese set him up for a surprise when he finds the Mafia boss sitting in the pizzeria with the Triads after the gun battle in Chinatown. He cannot accept that the Chinese and the Italians can work together. When Tony and Tye make love in a deserted apartment building, it is a symbolic union of both sides of Canal Street. They are the link between the two cultures. The fact that everybody refers to them throughout the film as 'children' or 'kids' is perhaps St. John's way of illustrating how youthful naiveté is sometimes purer than adult logic. Tony and Tye are the product of a gradually integrating society. When Tony attacks Mercury for shouting out racist slurs at a Chinese stall-holder, he is representative of a new generation and a new set of attitudes.

At his brother Alby's funeral, Tony arrives late and collapses onto his brother's corpse, crying. This scene, composed in golds, yellows, whites and blacks, is in many ways a dress rehearsal for *The Funeral*. The mob boss, Nino (just like Christopher Walken's Ray in *The Funeral*), thinks he knows who committed the murder and tells Tony and his mother that things will be "taken care of". Tony explodes at the boss, saying that Alby won't be brought back by the murder of a rival gang member. He is attacking the way the whole of his neighbourhood operates, the 'eye for an eye' mentality. Tony wants peace. His sensitive outburst here inflames his elders who take his rage against circumstance and tradition to be disrespectful.

One scene in *China Girl* offers a rare break from Ferrara's thematic fixation with the inadequacy of traditional law-enforcement groups: two mounted police officers save Tony from being attacked by Tsu

Shin and Yung Gan. Tony and Tye have a rendezvous in a deserted alleyway, but they are discovered there by Tsu Shin and Yung Gan who seem set to teach Tony a lesson (one he was spared at the start of the film when Mercury, Alby and the rest of the gang came to his aid). Two mounted policemen appear and force the two parties to go their separate ways. When they've gone, Yung Gan strikes Tye and splits her lip.

A brilliant piece of editing cuts straight from a close-up of Tye's shocked face and bleeding lip to a close-up of a statue of the Madonna being carried by bearers in a Catholic procession. This procession forms part of a Catholic street festival. When Tsu Shin and Yung Gan have stabbed Alby to death, they flee into the Catholic street festival and bang into the bearers carrying the Madonna. The statue falls (a shot which would be recreated in *Bad Lieutenant*), breaks and the decapitated head of the Madonna spins on the wet street. The Catholic festival scenes are included as a loving tip of the hat to the appearance of the same festival in Scorsese's *Mean Streets*.

It is no surprise that Tony and Tye are gunned down at the end of the film. St. John is arguing here that racial harmony, even if possible between two lovers from different races, cannot work unless society alters its views; a racist society won't allow Tony and Tye to be together. The way in which Ferrara films their tragic end captures this point perfectly. Tony, fresh from Alby's funeral, goes to Tye's apartment building. Prior to this we see him lying on his bed, dressed in black, the room almost in darkness. Earlier, we saw him lying on his bed, white walls, bright lighting and a dark crucifix hung over his bed (a recurring motif in Ferrara's bedroom shots). The lighting alone in these two scenes offers us all the insight we need into Tony's psychological transformation. He calls up to Tye, whereupon Yung Gan and his gang surround him. Tye runs out and throws her arms around Tony, preventing her brother from shooting him. Then, Mercury and a bunch of Italians appear from the other side of the street.

Again, just as in *Fear City* and *The Gladiator*, the film ends with a showdown. Tony and Tye stand in each others' arms. They have the Italians behind them, the Chinese in front of them. Their love has become a symbolic 'Canal Street'. They divide two races and communities. Earlier we see other scenes of cultural exchange between the gang bosses: the Mafia boss has dinner with the Triads at a Chinese restaurant, the Triad boss has the meeting with the Mafia boss at the pizzeria. There is willingness to compromise at the top, and in the young lovers (though for very different reasons), but nowhere in the middle. Yung Gan tells his sister that she is "no longer Chinese" before leaving for Hong Kong. The lovers are next seen kissing and canoodling on a busy Chinatown street. Tsu Shin steps out of a doorway and moves towards the couple with a gun. Tye sees him and steps in front of Tony. He shoots her and the bullet goes through her heart and then through Tony's. They fall to the ground, each with blood soaking their clothes around the heart. They lie dead on the wet street, holding hands. It's a powerful closing statement. The film ends with an overhead shot of the dead lovers, perhaps suggesting a freeing of their souls. Certainly, the only way that they are able to be free is through death.

Although Ferrara regards *China Girl* as his finest accomplishment, there are evident flaws in the film. Tony's character is very poorly fleshed out and Panebianco is often left to silently mug like an extra from Coppola's *The Outsiders*. Chang, whose role *Variety* referred to as "idealised porcelain beauty", is given very little character to work with. This may be intentional – she is repeatedly portrayed as a submissive victim of her brother's traditions (note the scene where her three punk rock girlfriends call by to take her out to a club and she says she has to stay home to please her brother) and, therefore, something of a blank. When she and Tye make love in a deserted building, their acting is self-conscious and awkward though, again, this may have been Ferrara's intention, suggesting two nervous teenagers making love for the first time. On the plus side, Ferrara was clearly very comfortable directing David Caruso, Russell Wong and Joey Chin. All three deliver powerhouse performances, especially Caruso who embellishes his street-tough, racist thug role with a high-pitched energy throughout. However, some of the characterisation remains distressingly vague: what happened to Alby and Tony's father? Was he a mob guy? What happened to Yung Gan and Tye's family? Did they abandon them for the American dream? Or are they dead?

If these were indeed flaws then their presence would unquestionably be due to the fact that Ferrara's main focus must have been on Bojan Bazelli's breathtaking cinematography. The streets, as they were in *Fear City*, are mostly rain-soaked and illuminated with the glare of neon signs. Many scenes are washed over with blue lighting. Shadow play is a constant motif throughout. We see Tony's shadow against a wall before we see him. The violent fight scenes (mostly with sticks, knives, chains and bats as opposed to guns) are regularly played out in a web of shadows. In the first major gang fight scene, Ferrara even lets the shadows of the fighting gang members take centre stage as we see a silhouette of a bat striking someone's body.

The recurring shots of steam rising from the streets, fire escapes and tenement buildings, dimly lit alleyways, fences and gates, traffic lights and the contrasting neons of Chinatown and Little Italy provide a *noir*-ish backdrop to another of Ferrara's visual interpretations of New York as a kind of hell on earth. When Alby has been stabbed and crawls up a staircase, back to the apartment he shares with Tony and their mother, he manages to rap on the door. His mother opens the door and a veil of red light pours out. It's typical of Ferrara that Alby's mother, who should represent safety and comfort, is instead re-cast for a split second as the keeper at the gates of hell, ready to receive her son.

Cat Chaser 1988

"*Cat Chaser* is another example of how difficult it is to transform a sharp and racy novel into a classy movie. Despite a fine cast and atmospheric production by Abel Ferrara, the pic doesn't quite make the grade" – *Variety*.

Like *China Girl*, *Cat Chaser* is concerned with territory – both geographical and interpersonal. The film revolves around a love triangle between ex-Marine George Moran (played by Peter Weller), former Dominican Republic General and Head Of Secret Police Andres DeBoya (played by Tomas Milian) and their mutual love interest, Mary DeBoya (played by Kelly McGillis). Mary DeBoya is married to the General, an extremely wealthy Miami-based real estate player, while Moran runs and owns a hotel on a strip of Miami coastline. There are two twists: he and Mary were youthful sweethearts in their mutual hometown Detroit and Moran was one of the Marines who served in the American intervention in the Dominican Republic revolution of 1965 (as an adversary of DeBoya).

Moran and DeBoya spend *Cat Chaser* fighting over Mary, who in turn, represents a symbolic recreation of Moran (symbolising the American Marines) fighting against DeBoya (symbolising the Dominican Republic military dictatorship). This makes *Cat Chaser* the second part of Ferrara's Territorial Trilogy. The film concerns Andres DeBoya's immense wealth. We learn that he keeps a stash of money somewhere in his home in case he has to flee unexpectedly. The lure of this cash forms a web of deceit and greed around George 'Cat Chaser' Moran, a lonely, introspective man haunted by his experiences in the Dominican Republic intervention when he fell into enemy hands. Instead of being killed by the young girl who was ordered to shoot him, she brought him "first aid and a beer". Her name, Luci Palma, and his memory of her ("sixteen, skinny, beautiful") haunts Moran. Moran's voice-over explains his need to revisit Santo Domingo to try to track down this girl, years after the war. He's a prisoner of his various memories: old flame Mary, the soldier girl Luci Palma and his experiences as a Marine. By the end of the film, he has successfully exorcised all three memories and re-shaped his associations with all three 'territories', either literally or symbolically.

The film opens with black-and-white newsreel footage of the 1965 intervention, a stylistic trait that Ferrara would return to in *The Addiction*. The first time we see Moran, he is fishing an empty cigarette packet out of the hotel pool with a net. This sets things off nicely because Moran will spend the rest of the film trying to remove something dirty from what seems to be an otherwise clear picture. The blue skies, the blue waters of the swimming pool, the white hotel and beach and Moran's frequently white or blue clothing, set the neutral colour scheme that surrounds him.

As the plot unfolds, various characters worm their way into Moran's life, each looking for a way to double-cross DeBoya and steal his secret cash nest. The first is the heavy-drinking, fellow ex-marine and Dominican Republic veteran Nolan Tyner (played by Frederic Forrest) who turns up early on in the film looking for a hotel room. Moran instantly recognises his army tattoos and the pair bond by the poolside. Tyner and Moran discuss the Dominican Republic and Tyner deviously steers the conversation onto DeBoya. Here, Moran reveals that he knows DeBoya and also that he was romantically involved with Mary in his younger days in Detroit. Tyner quickly reveals himself to be working for DeBoya, who has hired him to spy on Moran and to see if he is either seeing the General's wife, Mary or involved with the General's sister Emilia DeBoya (a guest at Moran's hotel and the person responsible for throwing the cigarette pack into the pool).

The General's sister turns out to be a decoy by which to introduce Jiggs Scully (Charles Durning) into Moran's life. Initially masquerading as a consultant and private detective, Scully soon reveals himself, like Tyner, to also be working for DeBoya. He too has been assigned to tail Moran and find out if he has any interest in the General's wife. Scully sets up an impromptu meeting between Moran and DeBoya on the beach. Again he reiterates his disinterest in Mary to DeBoya who offers him $2,200,000 for the hotel (and an unspoken clause that Moran won't pursue Mary in any form as part of the package), a figure that will later have tremendous significance. Here, the hotel becomes inextricably linked with Mary and also the former intervention. DeBoya wants to buy American land and, in the bargain, Moran's pride, as well as his potential interest in Mary.

It is an assault on Moran's territory, just as Moran and the American military intervention of the Dominican Republic was an assault on DeBoya's territory. Moran rejects the offer and the games begin. After insisting to DeBoya that he hasn't made any moves on his wife, Moran's voice-over confesses, "Funny how you can tell the truth and still feel guilty. I guess it has to do with sins committed in the mind being sins just the same." This could be a line fed to a Ferrara character from a Nicholas St. John screenplay and instantly establishes Moran as another Ferrara protagonist tormented by the struggle to remain pure in an impure world.

This coded building of tension is diffused when Moran returns to Santa Domingo with a view to finding Luci Palma and laying old ghosts to rest. Ferrara shoots the streets of Santa Domingo as he shoots the streets of Miami and New York – drenched with urban realism. He captures a low-life feel, a seedy mood, graffiti-covered buildings and begging kids instead of New York's down-and-outs; poverty is omnipresent. In spite of this slum-like landscape, the palette is still very colourful and Ferrara juxtaposes this bright visual depiction of contemporary Santa Domingo with more black-and-white newsreel footage of the intervention. Footage of Moran being captured by the Dominican army and being spared by Luci Palma, also shot in black and white, gives us a taste of Moran's recurring nightmare. Even an early shot of him in a taxi in Santa Domingo underscores how tormented he is by this flirtation with death. He talks about the intervention with the driver and then pays him to place an English advertisement in a newspaper reading, "Cat Chaser is looking for the girl who ran over rooftops and tried to kill him." The advertisement doesn't lead Luci Palma to him but it does lead Mary DeBoya to him, who is ostensibly there to see a Polo match with girlfriends.

Ferrara first shows us Mary DeBoya in a darkly lit scene, her back to the camera, smoking a cigarette, lending her a *noir*-ish femme fatale overtone. There is no protracted reunion scene. She and Moran immediately make love in his hotel room in a scene so dimly lit that it harks back to the murky depths of *The Driller Killer*. After a wonderfully composed shot of Mary smoking on the balcony with blue bedsheets wrapped around her (recalling a similar shot of Brigitte Bardot draped in a red towel in Godard's *Contempt*), we see her wearing a bright red dress as they walk the streets and discuss her marriage to DeBoya. She admits that she has no interest in DeBoya. When Moran asks her why she simply doesn't leave him, she says that she's reluctant to do that in case he thinks she's only divorcing him to get the $2,000,000 promised in a pre-nuptial agreement. Already it is obvious that she too is interested in finding a way to double-cross her husband in order to get some of his money.

Back in Miami, Tyner sniffs around Moran's trip, trying to find out if he ran into Mary (because he knows from DeBoya that she was on the island). Ferrara cuts to a terse scene at the enormous DeBoya mansion where the couple are having dinner together. Maids and servants wait on them. The scene, like most of those between the husband and wife, is composed of browns, blacks and greys: a funereal coding that mirrors the slow death of their marriage. DeBoya says that he had seen one of her friends (whom she was meant to have been with in Santo Domingo) the day before. Mary tries to lie, explaining that she had decided to stay on for an extra day. Her husband asks her if she saw Moran. Their dialogue makes it clear that DeBoya knows she has seen Moran but we don't get any insight into what he knows about their past.

We learn nothing about Mary's past with Moran either. Were they high school sweethearts? Lovers in their early twenties? Nothing is made clear: all we know is that she suddenly showed up at Moran's hotel in Santo Domingo and they resumed a passionate love affair. The Santa Domingo scenes contrast strongly with the dinner scene. The colour codings of the two settings (dark at home, bright colour in Santa Domingo) is mirrored by the colour codings of the two couples (the DeBoyas dark, Moran and Mary red, white, blue and a combination of other bright colours).

The third peripheral character thrown into Moran's life is a sleazy Santa Domingo pimp called Raf. He had introduced himself to Moran and Mary in Santa Moringo, claiming that he knew where to find Luci Palma. In a connecting bar scene where we learn that Raf is a pimp, Ferrara can't resist opening the scene with a shot of two women kissing, yet another of his trademark shots of two women kissing or having sex.

Raf shows up in Miami with a prostitute who claims to have known Luci Palma. She is introduced as a bit of exploitative fluff and lingers around in her bikini across several scenes. Raf is in league with Scully, who is in league with Tyner, and all three are after a slice of DeBoya's money. Scully captures Moran as he's leaving a hotel room rendezvous with Mary, takes him to a bar and explains about DeBoya's secret stash of cash. In this scene, Ferrara employs a 360-degree tracking shot around the table at which the two men are sitting, to underline the extent to which Moran is surrounded at that point. Scully proposes that if Moran can get Mary to tell him where the emergency cash is hidden then he'll kill DeBoya, freeing the lovers to be together. Moran suggests that they create a situation where DeBoya panics and flees with the cash, whereupon they can rob him.

In a rhyming shot which perfectly recreates the first shot of Mary in the film, we see her on the balcony at the home she shares with DeBoya. DeBoya tries to kiss her, but she pulls away, disgusted. Clearly he knows what she is thinking and they start to talk, in cold tones, about the pre-nuptial agreement. He says that it is now optional and that it is up to him if he decides to 'honour' it. Their cold break-up is interrupted by the sound of an explosion in the marina – a bomb planted by Raf and Tyner at Scully's suggestion.

The next morning, Mary sneaks out and sees Moran. He tells her about Jiggs' plan. In true femme fatale style, she doesn't trust Scully's pledge to kill her husband. Meanwhile Scully and DeBoya are talking in his office. Scully is trying to convince him that the bomb was planted by a political organisation out to get him. This is intended to make DeBoya try to flee with the emergency stash. DeBoya's past as head of secret police comes up. He explains his former interrogation and torture methods: strip the victim and do something horrific to them. As he icily relays this information while smoking a cigar, Ferrara tries to hone in on DeBoya's reputation as a torturer. Throughout the film, there are attempts to make us feel how much people fear DeBoya, but somehow we never latch onto the terror that Ferrara wants us to feel. Even when Raf tells Moran about some of DeBoya's most feared torture methods – sewing eyelids to eyebrows, cutting off womens' nipples, castrating men – it still fails to push the terror button in the viewer. Scully then drags Moran and Raf to see DeBoya. Tyner is already there. In a show of power, DeBoya has Moran badly beaten and Tyner drowned. Raf hands DeBoya a photograph of Mary and Moran together in Santo Domingo. In return for his help, he is shot dead.

The next scene is one of several which have contributed to Ferrara's reputation as a film-maker who revels in exploitative sleaze. DeBoya wakes Mary up. He points a gun at her. The bedroom is partly in darkness and partly bathed in blue light, to suggest a bruise. He tells her to get out of bed. He makes her undress. He tells her to lie down on the bed. Then he tells her that he knows she slept with Moran on her trip. He presses the gun to her mouth. She cries and whimpers. Then he strokes the gun barrel down her neck and down her chest. There is confusion before she slaps him and tries to escape. DeBoya grabs her, smacks her across the face, calls her a "fucking bitch" and forces her to her knees, by way of a stranglehold grip. All of this happens while Mary is naked, mirroring the recent scene where DeBoya had told Scully that he always stripped his victims before torturing them. He kneels his wife down before documents that relinquish her rights to any settlement and makes her sign them. He then throws a suitcase at her and yells, "Pack your stuff and get the fuck out of here!" It's a disturbing scene. McGillis, naked and vulnerable, is pummelled and terrorised by DeBoya. After all the talk of his past as a brutal General, it is only in this scene that we get a taste of what kind of man he is and why he is feared so much.

After this scene of brutal abuse directed at his wife, DeBoya sends two of his hoods to castrate Moran. They chase him around the hotel swimming pool, one of them menacingly brandishing a pair of garden shears. Moran overpowers them and gets to go and collect his reward: Mary. When he picks her up, she has two suitcases which she is able to smuggle out due to the bomb hoax engineered by Scully.

It quickly becomes clear to DeBoya that Scully is after his money. DeBoya, a hood and Scully take off with an identical pair of suitcases for a hide-out. Here, a second scene of abusive torture takes place. Scully goes to the bathroom holding a beer, knowing that DeBoya is planning to kill him. DeBoya and his hood pump the closed door full of bullets after hearing what they assume to be the sound of Scully urinating. They enter the bathroom, the shower curtain goes back and Scully reclaims his power by pointing the gun at them. His beercan is positioned on the toilet seat, the pouring beer mimicking the sound of urination. In a truly horrific scene, he then inverts DeBoya's torture techniques back onto him, using torture on the torturer. In light of the fact that we had earlier seen DeBoya explain the fundamental psychology behind his torture methods, this is a cunning invasion of DeBoya's territory.

Scully makes DeBoya and his hood undress, the camera never straying to crotch level. The bathroom setting is seedy; again, like the club in the 'Dutch Oven' *Miami Vice* episode, Ferrara makes the seaminess of the scene almost tangible. Scully makes the two men get into the shower and turn the water on. The camera pulls to a wide shot, revealing the men's genitals. Peter Lehman, in an essay on this scene in *The Velvet Light Trap*, wrote, "The scene is the most aberrant instance I know of whereby male violence against the male body is given explicitly sexual connotations, a result of Charles Durning (Scully) ordering the men to strip and then creating a protracted sadistic scenario for their deaths." Lehman also highlighted the unparalleled ugliness of the men's bodies: "When Sylvester Stallone is sadistically tortured in Rambo: First Blood Part II for example, his nearly naked body is displayed as an erotic object which transforms to an ideal of masculine strength, power and beauty. The bodies of the Latino characters in *Cat Chaser* are granted no such erotic connotations; they are in all regards, in the terms of conventional judgements of masculinity, 'unimpressive'. If anything, their nakedness makes them appear pitiable both as they are about to die and even in death."

The scene is obscene mostly because all three men, torturer and tortured, are so vile-looking and shapeless. This ugly image, combined with the sordid setting of the dirty bathroom, makes for an unsettling scene when Scully shoots them both dead. Their blood splatters against the bathroom walls, and they lie slumped together as if killed in the middle of a homosexual encounter.

Now that Raf and Tyner are dead, Scully opens the suitcases to find that Mary has switched them, taking the money and filling the bogus set with women's magazines. He heads to the hotel and confronts the lovers, who are sunbathing and reading a letter that has arrived from Luci Palma. It turns out that Mary had deliberately duped DeBoya after he had beaten her. The total cash comes to $2,200,000, the figure that DeBoya offered Moran for his hotel at the start of the film. Scully pulls his gun and tries to get the money but Moran shoots him. By getting the letter from Luci Palma, winning back Mary, landing $2,200,000, burying old ghosts in Santa Domingo and settling scores with DeBoya, Moran is finally free from the memories that have been haunting him. The final scene, which almost seems like an afterthought, shows the lovers on a balcony. It could be at Moran's Coconut Palms hotel or somewhere else. Either way, it feels as though it was hastily added on to make it clear that Moran wasn't charged with the murder of Scully.

At the end of the film, we see that Moran has conquered his memories and reclaimed his various 'territories'. He has made peace with his past army experiences by returning to Santa Domingo.

Although Ferrara didn't plan on having Moran narrate via a voice-over, it does help the viewer to unravel a hopelessly labyrinthine plot. Ferrara would also return to the intercutting of black-and-white historical footage and a voice-over narratorial technique in *The Addiction*, indicating that he gained invaluable experience from the *Cat Chaser* shoot.

King Of New York 1990

"The gangster environment is a bourgeois setting turned on its head, so to speak. My gangsters do the same things that capitalists do except they do them as criminals. The gangsters' goals are just as bourgeois as the capitalists' " – Rainer Werner Fassbinder.

"Abel Ferrara's flashy story of an underworld king who loses his crown is executed with the mix of splatter and gallows humour that Ferrara has made his own, but without the roots in a personal or ethnic history which characterise Scorsese's *Goodfellas* or Coppola's *Godfathers*" – *Sight and Sound*.

Everything gelled with *King Of New York*. There is Ferrara's command of a powerful cast, the haunting soundtrack which interweaves classical music and hip hop, immaculate *mise en scène*, seamless editing, the alternately seedy and sophisticated settings, the word-perfect dialogue, the gently simmering narrative, the confident almost boastful cinematography and the eerie 'silence' that Ferrara plucks from the setting. The immaculate fusion of European art movie and American gangster movie makes this one of Ferrara's most distinctive pieces.

King Of New York opens with a gangster, Frank White (played by Christopher Walken), being released from jail and checking into an elegant suite at the Plaza Hotel (an early indication of how wealthy and powerful White is). During his jail sentence, rival gangs have moved onto his territory. His release from jail is accompanied by a series of violent episodes in which White's gang re-claims his former territories. First we see his gang double-cross and kill a Colombian gang. Then we see White shoot Italian Mafia boss Arty Clay in front of his own gang. Finally, he double-crosses Larry

Wong and his Triad drug cartel, killing them and stealing their massive supply of cocaine. This scorched earth policy stems from White's territorial hunger, his need to win back his territory. In this respect, as the title suggests, he's a king fighting over land.

The twist to his character is that, in his own words, he wants to "do something good" for the city. He sets his sights on preserving the Community General Hospital in the South Bronx, which is going to be closed as a result of fiscal cuts. White tells the officials responsible for the closure that he will personally raise the $16 million needed to keep it open. Although he sets up a fund-raiser (which features a live number by Freddie Jackson – Ferrara's fondness for a musical performance in his work is demonstrated once more), he intends to raise the bulk of the money from drug sales. Most of the money from the drug sales will come from poor neighbourhoods like the Bronx, hence White will take from the poor (those who would benefit from the hospital) to impress the rich (politicians and city officials).

When we first see White he is in his jail cell where, for the only time in the film, we see him wearing prison clothes and glasses. The brief tracking shot shows him huddled up in his cage over a desk either reading or writing. After watching him exit through countless doors, the prison bars throwing reflections and shadows over each scene, we see a series of shots from the outside: the bars on the prison windows, the barbed wire fences, the iron gates. Every one of these shots snowballs into giving us a taste of White's captivity.

He gets into the black limousine that will ferry him around for the rest of the film. This isn't a just-out-of-jail scene where the convict walks through the gates with a bundle of clothes, it's a scene where a major criminal leaves jail in a symbol of his wealth. The sky is a bluish black. This establishes the blue colour-coded lighting that will track White for most of the film – it matches his icy, cold personality and his detached, faraway emotional make-up. Ferrara cuts from this cold scene to a warmly lit, very Godardian close-up of a woman's face. She looks sad, her gaze far away.

Then we see a Latino gangster with three prostitutes. One is wearing a PVC police cap and is too wasted to stand up straight; the gangster fondles her ass. Once he leaves this brothel-like scene, he goes outside and makes a phone call from a phone booth, whereupon three gangsters gun him down and shove a newspaper in his face with a photo of White and the headline: 'Frank White Released From Prison'. This establishes a powerful aura around White, showing us by way of this perfectly choreographed brief flash of violence how much he is to be feared. By contrast, similar attempts in *Cat Chaser* to give this kind of aura of intimidation to DeBoya completely fell flat.

The operatic music that runs throughout the film accompanies our first clear view of White in the back of the limo. His face is deathly pale. The bags beneath his eyes are pronounced, he looks drawn; the blue lighting gives him the hue of a dead man. He has a haunted, distracted stare. It is the face of a man who has just been released from imprisonment. He has two women in the limo with him: one blonde, one Afro-Caribbean. He smokes a cigarette that one of them gives him. A series of beautiful shots of the city lights tumble before us one after the other. One shot straight out of Howard Hawks' *Scarface* creates a sign of the cross. A shot of blurry golden street lights forms an initial, vertical, line down the frame. Then a train, its windows lit up, passes through the street and the frame horizontally; the two form a sign of the cross.

After some equally exquisite shots of misty, wet street scenes, the moody keyboard music starts to compete with a Schoolly D hip hop track. The limo drives through a poor neighbourhood. Prostitutes come up to the limo and down-and-outs stand around fires lit in garbage cans. One prostitute lifts her skirt to show her ass. Another series of close-ups of White, bathed in blue light, shows him detached and stony faced.

Ferrara cuts to the famous drug deal that Jimmy Jump (played by Wesley Snipes) and his gang do with Colombian King Tito. Jump tests the coke and then hands Tito a suitcase. Tito opens the suitcase to find it full of tampax. When he asks what they are for, Jump shouts back that they're for plugging the bulletholes, and shoots him. Blood sprays against a yellow wall beside a painting. The same shot is recreated later when White guns down Arty Clay (his blood splatters against a green wall, beside a painting). As the Tito gang get shot one by one, we see three bulletholes spray through a door. In a reverse slow motion shot, we see a Colombian gang member (who was on the other side of the door and the three bullets) fall through the collapsed door. In stomps another of White's men who shouts, "Room service, motherfucker!" It's the kind of scene that explains Quentin Tarantino's fondness for the film, and why he has repeatedly sung the praises of *King Of New York*.

The next scene shows White in the shower. We see first a shower head and then water pouring out of it. We feel that it is White's first private shower in a long time. Although this is also a stereotypical just-out-of-jail film scene, Walken plays it with an odd twist. This is one of the very few scenes in the entire film where we see White alone. As if aware of this and desperately looking for company, White stares straight into the camera, a peculiar expression on his face, part old man, part little boy; it's a superb piece of haunted acting from Walken. Meanwhile the camera shows us the paraphernalia of White's hotel room: a 'welcome back card', a bottle of champagne, a gold lighter and some flowers. The camera cuts back to White in the shower, observing as he turns off the shower using two handles. This shot echoes another in the Tito shoot-out where Jump waves around a pair of handguns at exactly the same angle. Jump is shooting guns, White is trying to 'wash' away his sins.

The camera then crawls up the foot, leg, ass, back and finally head of the blonde woman who was in the limo. She's loading a handgun. Ferrara then cuts to a shot of the Afro-Caribbean woman from the limo fastening a black suspender belt before a mirror (yet another of Ferrara's trademark mirror shots). For many viewers, both shots will set the 'exploitation' alarm bell ringing. The next shot is the key to the film. White stands at his hotel window and stares out across the nocturnal skyline. The lights of a skyscraper are superimposed onto his chest. It's as if his soul is floating in front of him and the city is his soul. It is then that we realise that White is in love with the city, despite all its chaos and contradictions.

In every scene we see White portrayed as the epitome of respectability. He is always impeccably dressed and is represented by a 'Park Avenue' lawyer – his attractive, intelligent lawyer girlfriend (Jennifer, played with perfect understatement by Janet Julian). He has connections in high places and visits art performance shows (the one in the film features a cop getting shot by black criminals and thus reminds White of his incarceration) and expensive restaurants. He is an eloquent spokesperson and fund-raiser extraordinaire.

The irony of White wanting to keep the hospital open (at one point he says that "privileged districts shouldn't be the only ones with hospitals") is heavy. White is a poster boy for a privileged lifestyle: luxurious hotel suite, huge black limousine, a band of employees (at one point we see his entourage working at their computers in a makeshift office in his hotel suite), big money circuit social life and dinners at the finest restaurants. His world, as Fassbinder's quotation suggests, is "a bourgeois setting turned on its head." White is no different to any of the wealthy people that he mixes with (on both sides of the law). Moreover, as Fassbinder commented, White's goals, "are just as bourgeois as the capitalists'." Even when we see White taking Larry Wong around the hospital, he talks over the details of the drug deal with Wong while a small girl is in a hospital bed next to him. He even plays with a fluffy toy and hands it to the child while concluding his offer for the drugs. It's a scene as demonstrative of corruption as any in *Bad Lieutenant*.

St. John again creates a good and evil dichotomy by setting White against his cop adversary, Bishop (played by Victor Argo), a sickly, pill-popping detective, who still believes in honest, old-fashioned justice. His colleagues, Gilley (played by David Caruso) and Thomas Flanigan (played by Laurence Fishburne) are young hot-headed detectives who favour rule-bending to bring criminals to justice.

Bishop tracks White throughout the film, climaxing with a head-to-head showdown, first in Bishop's apartment (where White ambushes him) and then on the subway, where Bishop shoots White and White shoots Bishop. No one wins. When Bishop comes home to find White sitting in his lounge, he finds himself subjected to a monologue from White in which he tries to justify his actions. White tells him (and this scene works as a confession) that he has never killed anyone who didn't deserve to die. He argues that Larry Wong was a slum lord who exploited those who fell below the poverty line, that Arty Clay, a man whose front was an Italian restaurant (whose window statue of the Madonna is twice shot in close-up, each time recalling *Mean Streets*) left behind a fortune of $13 million and that King Tito was using 13-year-old girls as prostitutes. By the film's end, White is a confused moralist. As Bishop puts it, "Who made you judge and jury?" When he asks this

Abel Ferrara promoting *Snake Eyes* in 1993. (*Rex Features*)

Abel Ferrara as Reno Miller in The Driller Killer, 1979. (*Kobal Collection*)

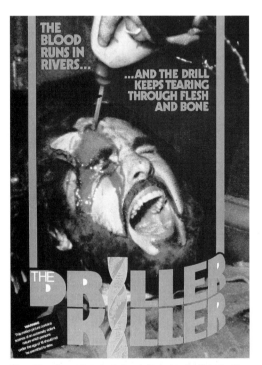

The video sleeve that single-handedly led to the introduction of the British Video Recordings Act in 1984.
(*Ronald Grant Archives*)

One of the Driller Killer's victims.
(*Ronald Grant Archives*)

Zöe Tamerlis in *Ms. 45*. (*Ronald Grant Archives*)

The original promotional poster for *Ms. 45*.
(*Ronald Grant Archives*)

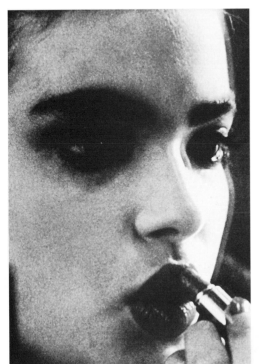

Zöe Tamerlis becoming the Angel of Vengeance.
(*Ronald Grant Archives*)

Abel Ferrara as the first rapist in *Ms 45*.
(*Ronald Grant Archives*)

Melanie Griffith in *Fear City*. (*Ronald Grant Archives*)

Sari Chang and Richard Panebianco in *China Girl*.
(*Kobal Collection*)

Kelly McGillis and Peter Weller in *Cat Chaser*.
(*Ronald Grant Archives*)

Christopher Walken in *King Of New York*.
(*Ronald Grant Archives*)

Janet Julian and Christopher Walken in *King Of New York*.
(*Ronald Grant Archives*)

Frankie Thorn and Harvey Keitel in *Bad Lieutenant*.
(*Kobal Collection*)

Zöe Lund and Harvey Keitel in *Bad Lieutenant*.
(*Kobal Collection*)

Harvey Keitel and Madonna in *Snake Eyes*.
(*Ronald Grant Archives*)

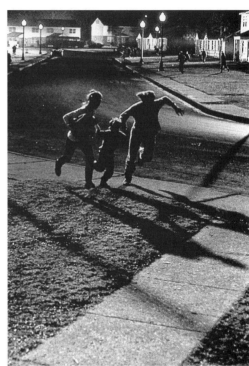

Madonna in *Snake Eyes*. (*Ronald Grant Archives*)

Ferrara's remake of Don Siegel's *Invasion Of The Body Snatchers*. (*Kobal Collection*)

Lili Taylor in *The Addiction*. (*Ronald Grant Archives*)

Annabella Sciorra in *The Addiction*. (*Ronald Grant Archives*)

Christopher Walken, Chris Penn and Vincent Gallo in *The Funeral*. (*Kobal Collection*)

Abel Ferrara at the Cannes Film Festival, 1997. (*Kobal Collection*)

Claudia Schiffer and Béatrice Dalle, stars of *The Blackout*, at Cannes in 1997. (*Ronald Grant Archives*)

Abel Ferrara in 1998. (*Rex Features*)

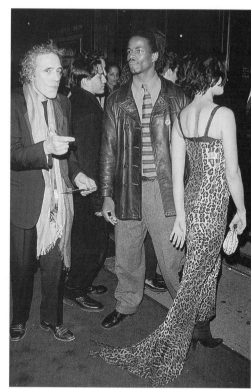

Abel Ferrara – The King Of New York. (*Rex Features*).

of White, we see tears in White's eyes. He's corrupted and damned, in spite of his wish to "do something good".

The scene also contains another very subtle homage to Howard Hawks' *Scarface*. As Bishop enters his dimly lit apartment, we see a light shade hanging from the ceiling. The fitting from the lampshade to the ceiling forms a tiny cross. It's difficult to pick up on but, as in *Scarface*, it's one of a handful of ominous shots of everyday objects that are cut and framed to form the sign of the cross. This detail serves as a backdrop to White's confession to Bishop. Once his confession is over, he takes Bishop's gun and makes him handcuff himself to the chair. He tells him that he wants him to feel like a criminal. In response to the $50,000 reward out on White's head, White tells Bishop that he has put out a $250,000 contract on "anyone involved with this case". He tells Bishop that he wants him to feel hunted. It's like Scully turning DeBoya's torture methods back onto him, an inversion of roles.

White is hunted throughout the film – by rival gangs, by his conscience, by his past and by the police. Gilley and Bishop are determined to nail him, and when Gilley clashes with Bishop about how to deal with White, it is a clash of young and old. This illuminates the division even in the police force: Bishop, an older, sickly detective, wants to bring White to justice, Gilley, a charismatic young detective simply wants to kill White because he is frustrated with the failings of the legal system. This theme recalls the inter-generational wars between gang youngsters and elders in *China Girl*. In both cases, fiery youth favours rule-bending over the elders' need to play it by the book.

There is also a parallel between the police in this film and Mike Torello and his Major Crime Unit in *Crime Story*. When Gilley says that the criminal justice system "favours scumbags", it could be Torello talking. When Torello moans to a lawyer that he only earns $12,000 a year, it mirrors a scene in which Gilley complains to his colleagues that they only get $36,500 for risking their lives day in, day out. This line comes after they've seen Frank White at a fundraiser on TV and Gilley observes disbelievingly that White's turned into a "fuckin' movie star". St. John is keen to point out that crime pays while justice doesn't. Again, as in so many of Ferrara's films, the police are not portrayed in a favourable light. Shortly after White's release from jail, Gilley, Bishop and Flanigan forcibly pick him up, drive him off in an unmarked car, take him to a derelict area and rough him up. It's a form of warning as much as it is an admission from these detectives that the legal system doesn't work. White is already out of jail; trouble is already starting up. They are as hungry to bust him as he is to take over all the business of the other drug cartels. This rough harassment again sets a scene of lawlessness – as in *Bad Lieutenant*, the police are not there to do justice, they are as corrupt as those they pursue.

Although Bishop does kill White by shooting him on the subway, he is also killed by White. After shooting off the handcuffs that White made him put on, he follows White to the subway station. Once on the train, he runs through each carriage, lending the scene an instant familiarity because we've seen this kind of action in so many films, until he finds White, staring catatonically into space. It's one of many shots of White deep in thought, eaten up by his demons. White takes a woman hostage and explains to Bishop that he is the stronger man because he could blow her brains out whereas he knows Bishop couldn't.

Interestingly, White and Bishop's clothing is identical and colour-coded. For the first half of the film, we see White only wear all black – almost always a black suit, a black shirt and black shoes. For the second part of the film he wears a black suit, black shoes and a white shirt. In this final scene (as in its predecessor at Bishop's apartment), Bishop is also wearing black shoes, a black suit and a white shirt. Ferrara is using costume to play with ideas of good and evil, right and wrong, criminal and police officer – from their outward appearance, cop and criminal seem almost reflections of each other. This doubling also recalls White forcing Bishop to handcuff himself to a chair so that he knows what it feels like to be treated like a criminal. At the film's denouement, White and Bishop engage in a gun-fight in the subway, during which both are shot, and from which White walks away. The colour red – frequently associated with hell in Ferrara's work – also stands for the police in this film. Thus, when White gets out of the train carriage, red is omnipresent: the carriages are red, as are the pillars in the subway station. After he has gone through a crowd and got into a taxi, we see White's bleeding stomach: red blood on a 'white' shirt. Prior to that, it appears that he's got away with yet another cop killing, but when the red of his blood contrasts with the blue lighting in which he is usually seen, we know that he is dying.

During the film, White kills a lot of people, but as he says, no one who doesn't deserve to be killed. When he kills Gilley at a policeman's funeral, in one of the most intense scenes in the film, the viewer is left with a perverse sense of justice being done. Gilley might have been a cop, but he was a bad one. In the middle of the burial scene, Gilley runs off to his car, plagued by guilt at having caused his colleague's death (earlier we saw Gilley clowning it up as best man at the dead cop's wedding reception – clearly they were friends). He gets into his car and, à la Keitel in *Bad Lieutenant*, gives vent to an emotional outburst. Instead of shooting his radio, as Keitel does, he punches the dashboard while shouting. Then we see a black limo sweeping around the cemetery driveway, the burial party framed in the background. The limo pulls up beside Gilley's car, the electric window rolls down; we get a shot of Gilley, then a reverse shot of White sticking a shotgun out and blasting Gilley in the face. The sheer audacity of such a murder tells us that White is hell-bent on self-destruction. When we first see him reunited with his (mostly black) gang, he half-jokes that being in jail has made him feel as if his "feelings are dead". When he shoots Gilley, it's as if he wants to be dead. It's a kamikaze act by a man convinced that he is bigger than anyone and anything.

When Gilley and his gang (less Bishop, who doesn't approve of their actions) make a hit on White and his gang, Joey (Paul Calderon) tips them off and betrays White. Later, White stands at the top of a stone staircase and asks him why he betrayed him. Piling on biblical allusions (and mirroring Judas's act of betraying Jesus) Joey says that he did it for the money. White issues orders for him to be shot and buried with the money that he received for his betrayal.

Gilley's attack is the operatic centrepiece of the film. This is the first scene in which we see White in his white shirt and black suit. The setting is a nightclub, bathed in blue lighting. A top-less woman is dancing. One of White's gang is kissing a woman.

Another woman leans over, pushes him aside and starts kissing the first woman herself. Two women trade blow-backs on a joint. The camera slowly crawls up the legs of a dancing woman, and we see the topless woman dancing again. We see people taking drugs. A hip hop track is pumping. Gold light filters from lights on the walls. When Joey arrives, with a supposed connection interested in buying the drugs that White has stolen from Wong, his entrance is bathed in red light. The three sit together. Light from a burning candle and from a wall light create a red glow on White's face. This colour-coded red light tells us that it is a police set-up.

After agreeing a price, we see the buyer's tester making out with another woman; she puts a line of coke on his chest and starts licking it. White and his black female colleague pass by, watching the scene, with a cold lack of response, through beaded curtains. A hooded gunman appears on the stairs and the black woman throws herself in front of White, taking the bullets. White shoots the attacker. The dynamic shoot-out that follows recalls John Woo's stylised violence and is yet another example of Ferrara's immaculate directing of gun-play. As one gang member gets hit, he spins 360 degrees, reminding us that seconds earlier the same people were spinning 360 degrees but because they were dancing, not in death throes.

The drug tester shoots the blonde who was licking coke from his belly and her blood splatters across the white bags of the drug. Outside the club, Jump and White flee in a limousine, but one of the attackers is hanging onto the limo door. Jump unmasks him. They realise it's a cop (the same one who was married earlier in the film) and smash him against a water hydrant. After a car chase (the fluid execution of which stems from what Ferrara learned on *The Gladiator*), Jump and Flanigan end up having a showdown in a derelict rain-soaked wasteland where down and outs are standing around trashcans. As always, Ferrara is conscious of those who have fallen below the poverty line – this is what *King Of New York* was ultimately attacking, an American society crippled by Reaganomics. This showdown is also familiar Ferrara stuff and having shot Flanigan, Jump is in turn shot by Gilley. While Gilley tries to comfort Flanigan, Fishburne delivers a deranged deathbed performance, whooping, wailing and flailing like a hyena. After shooting him in the head – a mercy killing – Gilley returns to Flanigan, kisses him on the cheek and tells him he loves him.

There are four other individual scenes that merit specific attention. The first is a sex scene on the subway between White and his lawyer girlfriend Jennifer. It has the concentrated iciness of a Robert Bresson shot. The icy blues and greys of the scene back up the coldness of their union. White repeatedly gropes her breast and Ferrara twice squeezes in shots of one of her nipples, a familiar Ferrara trademark. Walken plays White with pale understatement. He gives White the sense of being a deeply emotional man behind his steely shell. When he 'confesses' to Bishop elsewhere in the film, there are tears in his eyes. He isn't the dead man that he appears to be.

Another scene between Jennifer and White, set on a balcony, has him confess to her his need to "do something good" before time runs out. He speaks of lost time (in jail and as a criminal) and almost as if he knows his time is up, desperately focuses on the hospital to have somewhere to hang all of his confused and buried feelings. However, he never once expresses anything close to love to Jennifer – he seems able only to relate to an idea, not a person.

The third scene also relates to Jennifer. After Jump has been bailed, he, Jennifer and the rest of White's gang run into the detectives. Bishop stares at Jennifer and says, "Proud of yourself?" As in a similar scene between Morello and Luca's lawyer in *Crime Story*, Bishop is asking Jennifer how someone who has studied law can use it to defend someone like White. Gilley spits into Jump's face. Jump wipes the spit from his face and then sucks it from each finger in a sexual manner. It is a vile scene that inverts the violence implied by Gilley's gesture. It is also a scene that would be revisited in *The Addiction* when Annabella Sciorra licks blood dripping from her lips with her fingers.

The fourth scene occurs once the lights have gone up on an art performance show. We see White and Jennifer talking. We see the man behind them talking to Jennifer. Finally we see a city official talking to his black girlfriend, Alicia. Each of these three brief snippets of dialogue has no sound, an idea that Jean-Luc Godard has used in many of his films. It quite brilliantly mimics a lack of

121

communication. When the dialogue sound returns, White is talking to the city official and learns about the fiscal cuts that will close the hospital. Ferrara cuts back and forth from the official's black girl-friend (who played Raf's prostitute in *Cat Chaser*), preying on her unusual beauty as he did when she lay around in her bikini in *Cat Chaser*. In another reappearance, Sari Chang (who played Tye in *China Girl*) plays a TV reporter reporting on the fund-raiser for the hospital.

Every scene in *King Of New York* is colour-coded to indicate the different camps in the plot. Every scene involving Frank White is bathed in blues and blue-blacks. Every scene featuring the cops is bathed in reds and oranges. Indeed, Gilley – White's most dangerous threat – has bright red hair. And at the centre of every scene is Frank White, his surname a colour (the name itself suggesting purity and also 'china white', a type of heroin). Put these three colours together and you have red, white and blue. The intention behind this incredibly complex and faultlessly executed colour-coded lighting is to bring all the elements together as a damning visual indictment of the red, white and blue of the American flag, and consequently a damning indictment of the government's economic and social policy under Reagan.

For the final death scene, where White has come out of the sub-way by a staircase (which is shot in a manner reminiscent of the staircase in *The Addiction*) and then climbed into a cab, his features, lit with a blue-ish light, contrast with the increasing numbers of red flashing lights on the police cars surrounding him; the red has overpowered the blue. Ferrara mounts the tension in the closing scene by having the traffic and police surround White so that he's trapped like Tony Carmonte at the end of Hawks' *Scarface*. However, instead of having White gunned down like Carmonte, Ferrara has him fade into death, his head falling to one side and his gun cocked in his hand. It's an anti-climactic death and finale but accompanied by the shots of the winged angel on the taxi driver's dashboard, the cross swinging from his rear-view mirror and the haunting, operatic music playing in the background, a mood of crucifixion is implied. White has rushed towards death. Wiping out the Tito, Clay and Wong gangs was suicidal enough but shooting Gilley at a police funeral was insanity. As his speech to Jennifer on the balcony hinted, he wanted to make himself a martyr and keeping the hospital open was his cause. It gave him an excuse to escape himself, to run from a world that he couldn't live in, a system that couldn't contain him and a conscience that was eating away at him. His territorial urges became a hunger that ultimately killed him.

5

TRUE CONFESSIONS

Bad Lieutenant 1992

"The extreme religious orthodoxy of such a narrative may give Ferrara fans cause for concern, for despite the on-screen depravity, *Bad Lieutenant* is ultimately a paean to the virtues of true Catholicism" – *Sight and Sound*.

"The script is cut to the bone, the set-ups have a *vérité* feel, while the editing mimics real time in long, nearly unwatchable sequences" – *The Time Out Film Guide*.

"I was very proud when someone said that it was the best anti-drugs film they had ever seen, because there was no moralising in it . . . I believe it's a religious film, because hell is here now and so is the opportunity to know heaven" – Harvey Keitel talking to *Sight and Sound*.

"We all intended to go all the way with the movie and unlike many directors he (Ferrara) went all the way with it, and didn't censor or self-censor in any way" – Zoë Lund talking to *Empire*.

Redemption. *n.* 1. Buy back 2. Pay off 3. Turn in for a prize 4. Free, as from sin 5. To atone for.

Bad Lieutenant is one of five films that question the existence of God by stretching a 'cord between the sacred and the profane'. The other four are Pier Paolo Pasolini's *Theorem*, Jean-Luc Godard's *Hail Mary*,

Pasolini's *Salò* and Robert Bresson's *The Devil, Probably*. Each of these four films deals with a world where God is absent. Each of these four films stays with you. Each of these four films combines beautiful images of the sacred and horrific images of profanity. In *Salò*, a statue of the Madonna watches over some of the most unspeakably horrific images ever seen in cinema. In *Hail Mary*, Godard's revisionist modernisation of the Virgin Birth, Mary (Myriem Roussel) pumps gas for a living and struggles to restrain her sexuality after being blessed with a virgin pregnancy. In *Theorem*, a maid becomes a saint after a passionate bout of casual sex with a stranger (Terence Stamp). She, like the family she works for, is corrupted and violated by a mysterious man who might be God or the Devil and whose past is as elliptical as the Lieutenant's. In *The Devil, Probably*, a severely depressed young man, struggles to find God in a contemporary French society where Catholicism has lost its significance and power. In a bid to find something more than living itself, the young man explores meaningless casual sex, befriends a junkie who steals money from the contribution boxes in Church and obsesses about suicide. Bresson elegantly and chillingly addresses what it means to be a young man in a society where God has been replaced by materialism. Bresson's comments on the film in an interview with Paul Schrader, parallel with the Lieutenant's need to fill himself with material and carnal pleasures to compensate for an absence of God: "When people become so materialistic, religion is not possible, because every religion is poverty and poverty is the way of having contact with mystery and with God. When Catholicism wants to be materialistic, God is not there."

In *Bad Lieutenant*, Harvey Keitel plays a nameless New York Lieutenant (known only as 'Lt.') whose relentless appetite for personal degradation finds an escape route to redemption when a nun is raped in Spanish Harlem. Just as the Madonna overlooks torture scenes, murder and graphic sexual acts in *Salò*, so a statue of the Madonna also watches over the Lieutenant's descent into hell. The stifling mood which pervades *Salò* is also present in *Bad Lieutenant*. The scene in which the Lieutenant pulls over two teenage girls and then forces one to show him her ass and the other to mimic giving a blowjob, is a Manhattan-isation of certain scenes in *Salò*, in which Pasolini adapted De Sade's novel, *120 Days In Sodom*, to illustrate the relationship between fascism and sexual desire. *Salò* asks us what happens when all moral and social laws and bonds are removed. What happens if four fascists are allowed to act out their wildest sexual fantasies? The boys and girls who are rounded up and imprisoned at the country house in *Salò* are held captive by the power of the fascistic climate just as the two girls are held captive by the Lieutenant's badge in *Bad Lieutenant*.

The Lieutenant's journey into hell involves unfathomable scenes of degradation, all intensified by Ferrara's use of the real time narrative device. His indulgences, seemingly the acts of a man devoid of conscience, form a catalogue of depravities. He tries to steal drugs from a crime scene,' he has sex with whores, he is an alcoholic, he steals from thieves and he is an addict. He eyes up a pair of dead girls in a crime scene at the start of the film, he pulls two girls over and subjects them to a horrific bout of sexual cruelty and he voyeuristically peeps on a naked nun during a medical examination after she has been raped. Even family is not consecrated ground to him. At one point in the film he snorts cocaine off photographs of his daughter's first communion. He gambles, playing Russian roulette with both his own life and the lives of his family. He tells his bookie that he hates his home life and litters a conversation with his sons on the way to school with expletives; after dropping them off, he snorts a line of coke the second they get out of the car. The estrangement from his family seems absolute.

The Lieutenant is as much of a corrupting influence on those around him as the mysterious stranger is in *Theorem*. His relentless pursuit of ways to 'get high' mirrors the increasing scenes of degradation and abuse in *Salò*. In that film, each sub-section of the narrative introduces a more extreme scene. By the end, when a series of tortures cascades before our eyes, Pasolini has numbed us with the possibilities of human cruelty and yet, despite the relentless depiction of an immoral world, there is a moral element to the film. A lone woman, mostly seen playing the piano, is the moral touchstone in the film. When she commits suicide by hurling herself out of a window, having witnessed the catalogue of horrors that Pasolini is about to inflict upon us, her split second act is the sole moral commentary. In the same way, the Lieutenant's redemption is also the viewer's redemption.

When Jesus Christ appears to the Lieutenant in a church, Ferrara and Lund offer the viewer the same pause for breath that Pasolini offers with the woman's suicide. Jesus Christ (complete with crucifixion wounds) stands before the Lieutenant. This crucified image of Christ directly relates to the preceding scene in which the raped nun asks the Lieutenant if he believes that Jesus died for his sins. In this scene, a man who has committed all manner of sins, is confronted with the silent image of the crucified Christ. It is a juxtaposition of the sacred and the profane, just as in an earlier scene when the Lieutenant first stumbled into Church (having peeped at the naked nun and masturbated before the two girls during the night) and struggled drunkenly to pick up the fallen Madonna.

When the Lieutenant spies on the naked nun and gets so turned on that he goes out and enforces the masturbation scene, the effect is no different to Godard's agonised shots of Mary trying to suppress the urge to masturbate in *Hail Mary*. Painful close-ups of her fingers caressing her belly and moving down through her pubic hair only to draw back as if scolded, are as equally riddled with the tension between a belief in the sacred and a desire for the profane.

Aside from the obvious Pasolini and Godard influence, *Bad Lieutenant* also features many quotations from Martin Scorsese's *Mean Streets*. The closest thing to a 'plot' in Scorsese's film revolves around the money that Johnny Boy (Robert De Niro) owes Mike. Part of *Bad Lieutenant*'s 'plot' revolves around the Lieutenant's increasing gambling debt. At the end of *Mean Streets*, Johnny Boy gets shot in a car because of his debts. At the end of *Bad Lieutenant*, the Lieutenant gets shot in his car, also because of his gambling debts. The gambling acts as the thread in both films, weaving the whole together.

The two films share many other similarities. *Mean Streets* starred Harvey Keitel as Charlie; *Bad Lieutenant* also stars Keitel, this time as the Lieutenant. Of the many songs that Scorsese uses on the *Mean Streets* soundtrack, one of them, Johnny Ace's 'Pledging My Love' is also used by Ferrara in *Bad Lieutenant*. One of the Mafia bosses (Mario) in *Mean Streets* is played by Victor Argo, who plays one of the Lieutenant's cop buddies in *Bad Lieutenant*. Early on in *Mean Streets* we see Charlie in Church. Due to the rape of the nun, we frequently see the Lieutenant in Church. Domestic scenes of different characters' homes in both films feature Catholic iconography, such as crucifixes, statues and statuettes, prominently. *Mean Streets* opens with a shot of a Catholic feast and street festival (an image of the sacred) and cuts to a scene of a junkie shooting up in the toilets of the bar where most of the film is set (an image of the profane). *Bad Lieutenant* constantly see-saws between these two states.

After a long-haired hoodlum shoots a guy dead in some toilets in *Mean Streets*, Charlie goes to see the 'big man' and ends up eavesdropping on a table full of mob bosses (including the one played by Argo) from behind the men's room door. He discovers from their conversation why the shooting happened. In *Bad Lieutenant*, the Lieutenant accidentally eavesdrops on the raped nun's confession to a priest where she recounts the details of the rape. She tells the priest that she knows who her rapists were but will not give their names.

In *Mean Streets*, Charlie, after staying up all night with Johnny Boy (who has crashed in his bed), peeps through the blinds at a woman undressing from her night clothes and then getting dressed in her day clothes. We later find out that it's his girlfriend Teresa (played by Amy Robinson). In *Bad Lieutenant*, Ferrara recreates exactly the same camera angle to capture the Lieutenant spying on the medical examination of the nun after her rape. In both scenes, Keitel plays his characters with eye-popping, voyeuristic Catholic guilt. Both Charlie and the Lieutenant are wrestling with their faith. Charlie often talks to God and is seen in several scenes holding a finger in a candle's flame: he is trying to feel what 'hell' would be like. He has yet to shake off all the ideas that priests have bombarded him with since he was a child. The Lieutenant, on the other hand, has lost his faith, or is at least estranged from it. He rediscovers his belief when he hallucinates the image of Jesus Christ, but prior to that he is a walking sin machine, crashing from one episode of hellish degradation to another.

A scene from *Mean Streets* shows Charlie and his buddies getting stinking drunk in a bar room, during which Scorsese offers a surreal image of Keitel, drunk out of his mind, laid out on the floor. The giddy, dizzy camerawork perfectly captures the state of drunkenness. In *Bad Lieutenant*, Ferrara takes this one stage further and has the Lieutenant, drunk out of his mind, guzzling from a vodka bottle, the liquor splashing down his chin and onto his chest. The point here is that *Bad Lieutenant*, at least stylistically, takes its cues from *Mean Streets*. They are very different films but there are plenty of quotations from Scorsese's masterpiece in *Bad Lieutenant*.

Bad Lieutenant opens with stark black titles rolling over a blank, white background. This is how Pasolini's *Salò* begins: black titles on a white screen. There is no soundtrack (Pasolini does use a soundtrack). A baseball commentary is taking place on a radio station. By allowing the sound of radio (which, we soon discover, is playing inside the house shown in the opening shot) to open the film, Ferrara is subscribing to Robert Bresson's maxim that sometimes real life is the only soundtrack needed. We then see an image – a regular house with trees outside and bushes around the front. There's a car in the garage and a car parked out front in the street. There's even a satellite dish on the roof. It seems to be a fairly typical American house on a fairly typical American street.

A man comes out of the house, wearing a black suit and a white shirt. Two small boys are with him. All three of them get into the car parked out front. We quickly conclude that a father is driving his two sons to school. The boys complain that they're late because their Aunt Wendy was hogging the bathroom. So far, everything's normal. The father is scowling, stony faced. Then he erupts, telling them that he's boss, and that when it's time for them to go to the bathroom they are to tell Aunt Wendy to "get the fuck out of the bathroom".

Suddenly, everything has changed. The boys fight, the father turns the radio on and listens to baseball. He drops them off at school and they kiss him goodbye. A cross swings from his rearview mirror, providing a clear link to the closing scene of *King Of New York*. He watches his sons cross the zebra crossing, then snorts some cocaine and immediately relaxes, his agitated mood vanishing. Ferrara set up the scene to make us think that this man was pissed because they were late for school. Instead it was because he needed some cocaine. Already, Ferrara has changed gears. This isn't a regular American dad. He swears in front of his sons, snorts coke the minute they get out of the car and encourages them to disrespect his wife's sister.

The next scene sets the mood. This coke-snorting, bad-tempered dad is a Lieutenant in the New York City Police Department. He arrives at a murder scene where two girls have been shot. One is wearing a white blouse which is splattered with blood. The camera lingers just a second too long on this shot, further building on the feeling of unease that we have about this man: the Lieutenant is not above checking out the dead woman's breasts. Instead of investigating the crime scene, he stands fidgeting with his nose (reminding us that he has just snorted some coke) and then goes over to talk with some detectives about their collective gambling on the Mets vs Dodgers baseball games. Already, then, we place him as a drug user, bad dad and gambler.

The Lieutenant's once-muscular physique has gone to the dogs, a huge middle-age paunch arcs over his trousers. His face is constantly scrunched up and tense. We next see him going into a diner, where he asks for a cup of coffee. The woman who serves him looks suspiciously like Zoë Lund in a blonde wig (due to budgetary restrictions, it probably was). He sees a black guy taking something out of the trunk across the street. This shot invites us to think that the Lieutenant has seen something suspicious, that he will now at least do his job well. He heads to a payphone. A scene in Don Siegel's *Dirty Harry* springs to mind, where Harry Callahan (Clint Eastwood) sees a bank robbery in progress, calls for back-up and then goes back to his snack before blowing the bank-robbers away. Instead, the Lieutenant calls his bookie to place a $6,000 bet on the Mets and $4,000 on the Dodgers for his colleagues. It is established that he already owes $15,000, but that he now wants to double his bet on the next game. If he loses, he'll owe $30,000. By now, we are starting to grasp just how self-destructive the Lieutenant is, how quickly he is running headlong towards a demise of his own making.

Ferrara keeps the shocks coming by once more duping us into thinking that we're going to see the Lieutenant come to his senses and do his job. We see a car pull up to the kerb; one of a bunch of dealers goes up to the car and does a drug deal. The Lieutenant appears from down the street and breaks into a run. The dealers run off but one runs into a building. The Lieutenant follows him up the stairs, seemingly in pursuit of a suspect. We sit back, relieved that at last he's acting as he should, that our preconceptions of what a policeman should be are about to be confirmed. Ferrara is inviting us to believe that we'll see car chases, villains, urban shoot-outs, a lieutenant at war with his rule-playing police commissioner – *Dirty Harry* kind of stuff. Instead, he greets the dealer as if he knows him and gives him a bag of coke to sell. First, he smokes some crack and then snorts some coke. When the dealer warns him that he'll end up in trouble, he snaps, "Who are you? A fuckin' drug counsellor?" In a moment of black comedy, some voices are heard on the stairs and the Lieutenant calls out, "Get back! Police activity!" It is now clear that he not only swears in front of his kids, advocates their disrespecting of Aunt Wendy, is hooked on coke, has a dangerous taste for dancing and smokes crack but is also hopelessly corrupt. To add icing on the sordid cake, Ferrara has him ask the dealer to get the bag of coke back out so he can take a little wrap to tide him over.

There are three more scenes that are intended to shock us. They are also intended to set the Lieutenant's journey towards redemption on course. We see a boudoir scene, not unlike the one in *King Of New York* where a blonde girl licked coke off a drug tester's stomach. A naked blonde is on the bed on all fours. A skinny woman with short dark hair and wearing all black is positioned behind her. She binds a black gag in the blonde woman's mouth and pulls her up towards her. Once she has done this, she starts to grind and thrust her crotch up against the blonde woman's ass. All the while, Johnny Ace's 'Pledging My Love' plays in the background. The song was used in Scorsese's *Mean Streets* in a scene where a Vietnam war vet goes berserk in the bar and attacks a woman dancing with a man. This scene may have aroused Ferrara's initial interest in the song but the background behind the song makes it an even more appropriate choice for *Bad Lieutenant*. Johnny Ace recorded the song towards the end of 1954. Shortly after the sessions, he committed suicide playing a game of Russian roulette backstage after a show; he gambled everything and lost his life. This is exactly what happens to the Lieutenant, and also what happens to Johnny Boy (Robert de Niro) in *Mean Streets*.

Then we see the Lieutenant slumped in a chair, topless, a bottle of vodka raised to his lips. Has he been watching the women make love? Or is this a later scene in the same boudoir? He guzzles on the bottle so violently that the vodka dribbles down his chin and chest. Then we see him dancing with the blonde girl we have just seen, though now she has underwear on. It's another throwback to a Scorsese film, this time to a scene in *Taxi Driver*, where Keitel danced with Jodie Foster. The girl who was dressed all in black (and who played the dominant sexual role) appears in a black kimono and joins them. She puts her arms around both of them and the three of them stand wasted, dancing.

The next scene is unforgettable. The Lieutenant stands naked, a rare moment of full frontal male nudity, a rear view of him captured in a mirror. He is out of his mind. He whines, groans, cries, stands with his arms outstretched in a crucifixion pose. When he starts rolling from one side to the other like a drunken wind-up doll, it makes for a chilling portrayal of a soul in torment. Ferrara told *Sight and Sound* that initially he felt that the crucifixion imagery seemed too obvious: "We almost didn't use it because of that, but then again, who knows what he was doing, that's not something you plan out . . . That shot was a nine- or ten-minute piece and we only used a little bit of it." It's an astonishingly raw piece of acting, disarming and also profoundly affecting.

The next scene shows the Lieutenant arriving at another crime scene. This time it's a grocery store. A cop is standing with the Korean store owner and two black kids. The owner says that the kids stole $500 from him. The Lieutenant, wired, drunk and menacing, tells the cop to go and get him an iced beer. When the kids and the owner start arguing about whether or not a crime was committed, the Lieutenant pulls out his gun, aims it at one of the kids and fires, though he does not hit him. He then tells the cop to take the owner to the precinct. He then gets the hoods to hand over the $500, sends them on their way and pockets the cash. In an odd extension of this scene, Ferrara then has the Lieutenant wander aimlessly around the store. This sense of the camera lingering on after the scene is complete recalls Antonioni's method of trying to capture the space between the end of a scene and the point at which the actor becomes himself once again. Antonioni has spoken of these moments of run-on camerawork as work within a 'margin'. It is a no man's land. The scene is complete, the narrative suddenly obsolete. Keitel/the Lieutenant wanders around the store and the camera follows, enveloped by dead air and nothingness. What is Ferrara trying to tell/show us? It's like a tiny break in the film's unrelenting pressure. We see the Lieutenant deep in thought, lost perhaps. What is he thinking? A reverse shot from the rear of the store shows him looting some cigarettes. A small girl (the owner's daughter) stands by the back door watching him. It is her appearance that instils the scene with a sudden profundity and intensity. She is the all seeing eye, an implement of God, a symbol of the Lieutenant's lost purity and innocence.

The third scene to 'set the scene' kicks off with Zoë Lund playing 'Zoe', a drug connection. She looks nothing like she did in *Ms. 45*. She has orangey red hair stacked up, wears black, and is ghostly pale and intensely skinny. Whereas in *Ms. 45* she looked, as many people commented at the time, like a cross between Bianca Jagger and Nastassja Kinski, here she looks like a wasted Audrey Hepburn. She calls out in a husky voice that the door is stuck. When she gets it open, the Lieutenant comes into the seedy apartment. He's guzzling the beer that he just picked up from the store. She greets him with the kind of familiarity that suggests that his visits are frequent and tells him that she's got some "brown shit" that he'll like. She prepares his hit on some tin foil, holds it for him and heats it from underneath. He gets high, looks consumed with pleasure and then combs his hair back. She smokes a cigarette. She fixes him up with a second round. A close-up reveals sweat on his forehead. He closes his eyes, holds the smoke, utters a slight cough and then his eyes droop. She then smokes a hit too, eagerly hoovering up the smoke. She holds the smoke. The sound of falling rain is audible outside. Her eyelids briefly open to reveal her whacked-out, drowsy eyes. She stares at him and the scene cuts. Everything up to this point is designed to build up a clear character portrait. Every scene features the Lieutenant – he's never off camera. The use of real time renders each scene irrelevant outside of the context of its neighbouring scenes and the 'action' has a documentary feel to it. The Lieutenant is constantly pursuing a more complete method of self-degradation, he's going further and further down into his own private hell. The next scene opens the path to his redemption.

Bad Lieutenant is essentially about a Lieutenant who is so corrupt and so consumed with vice, that he becomes a walking symbol of all of mankind's sins. Ferrara reminds us of this by frequently having the Lieutenant appear in a scene which is bathed in red lighting, signifying hell. When he first learns about the nun's rape from the detectives in a car park, the lights in the underground car park are red. As if to underline the allusion to hell, he almost gets into a full-blown argument with one of the detectives when he mentions all the other women who get raped and questions why the rape of a nun is so much worse. The detective gets riled and asks the Lieutenant if he's a Catholic. He smiles and says that he is, but only after having referred to the Church as a "racket". This tells us that the Lieutenant, like Ferrara himself, is still surrounded by the iconography of the Catholic Church but has lost his faith. He changes the discussion from the detectives' collective shock at how someone could dare to rape a nun to the next Mets and Dodgers game. This recalls the first crime scene that we saw the Lieutenant attend, in which his preference for talking about gambling instead of investigating the crime scene in front of him immediately subverted any possibility that this was a 'maverick cop doing things his way' genre flick.

The nun's rape is also shot in a sea of red, linking the Lieutenant's soul and his descent into hell with the rape itself. When the Lieutenant has doubled his bet to $60,000, after a quick conversation with his bookie at – of all places – his daughter's first communion in Church, he watches the game, high and drunk, in a bar. Ferrara has Keitel filmed so that a red neon beer sign from behind the bar reflects onto him. After watching the game on the bar TV, he walks around the streets. A guy greets him. He takes him into a club. Techno music is pounding. The Lieutenant goes through the crowd. At one point, a woman grabs his sleeve and he hurries past. Was this an extra trying to get Keitel's attention? If so, it's a brilliant mistake to leave in and obviously the utilisation of a natural moment that Cassavetes would have endorsed. The guy, who turns out to be a dealer, takes the Lieutenant to the back of the club, where he gives him some coke. He takes it, bathed in the red glow of a large red EXIT sign hanging over his head.

He then goes to see the kid to whom he gave the bag of coke on the stairs at the beginning of the film. The kid has the Lieutenant's share of the drug money: $30,000. The kid lives with his mother in an apartment whose walls are blood red. When the mother gives him some rocks of crack, he might as well be in hell. To drive this home,

Ferrara has the Lieutenant linger on the staircase, paranoid from smoking too much crack. Someone opens their front door and he pulls his gun on them. He's a sweaty, jittery, dishevelled wreck. He's almost too high to walk. His descent down the staircase is painful and loaded with the implication that he is going 'down' into hell. When he reaches the front door, Ferrara has him filmed from outside, emerging from a dark doorway. He then offers a reverse shot, filmed on a hand-held camera which weaves wildly about, taken from the Lieutenant's vantage point. Ferrara wants us to feel that the Lieutenant is jumping out of his skin. He wants us to feel how unbearable it is to be that high and paranoid. He wants us to taste the Lieutenant's despair.

From there, Ferrara deposits us back at the brothel-style apartment where the girl who wore all black during the Johnny Ace scene is sprawled out on a mattress. The mood of the room is dark and scarlet. From here, the Lieutenant calls the bookie's boss. He says he wants his $60,000 debt doubled and placed on the final Mets vs Dodgers game. The big man doesn't want this. The Lieutenant shouts at him and tells him to take the debt. Thus, in the hell of this apartment, the Lieutenant sells his soul to the bookie boss.

The rape scene itself makes for difficult viewing: bathed in red, we see a statue of the Madonna pushed over, the nun screams and cries out. She is thrown down and stripped, we see a flash of her pubic hair (unthinkably sexualising her). One of the boys then turns her onto her front, the other pulls her hair, and the first boy rapes her. Shots of Christ being crucified (Scorsese's *Last Temptation Of Christ* meets Pasolini's *The Gospel According To St. Matthew*) flash across the screen to underline the horror of the crime. Christ himself is present as a moral commentator. When I saw the original cut of the film, Schoolly D's explicit hip hop track 'Signifying Rapper' hammered over the scene, articulating another dichotomy between the secular and the non-secular. The track (which was featured throughout the film) had to be removed from the film after rock band Led Zeppelin took legal action, citing the track's similarity to their own song 'Kashmir' as a motive. Subsequently, Schoolly D's rap was replaced by some terrible church organ music, the play-out replaced by Ferrara and Paul Hipp singing 'The Bad Lieutenant' and the hospital scene where the nun is examined left silent.

One of the most disturbing scenes in the film comes when the Lieutenant enters a hospital. He finds the room in which the nun is being given a medical examination after her rape. A nurse stops him and he shows her his I.D. When she walks off, Ferrara has the Lieutenant leer at her ass. It's a chilling moment. He then hears voices through a door and goes to open it. Ferrara immediately offers a reverse shot of the Lieutenant's voyeuristic eye peeping through the crack in the door. A nurse stands by the raped nun's bed and strips the nun's gown away. She lies naked on the bed. Ferrara cuts back and forth between the Lieutenant's eye and the naked nun. She turns her head towards the door and sees the Lieutenant watching her. She is then covered, and she sits up; we then hear descriptions of her injuries. Finally, we hear that the attackers broke her hymen (and therefore violated her sacred virginity) using a crucifix. It's a blunt and horrific moment designed to deflate any sexual thrill that the Lieutenant has experienced through his voyeurism. His sexualisation of the nun is suddenly equated with the image of a crucifix being used as a phallic rape object. When we see an investigating officer bagging the bloodied crucifix as evidence in the church, Lund and Ferrara have effectively driven us to feel real shock at what these two boys have done.

However, this scene is followed by one of the most infamous sections of the film, and seems to imply that the Lieutenant has indeed been sexually aroused by the sight of the raped nun. He pulls over two Jersey girls (apparently sisters) and finds that they're driving not only with a tail-light out but also with no driving licence. We discover that they've come in from New Jersey in their father's car without his permission. Kent Jones, in a piece on the film in *The Hard Press*, described this scene as unfolding like a "materialising photograph". In a horrific abuse of his badge and power, the Lieutenant plays a psychological game with them. He threatens to take them to the precinct and call their father unless they do something for him. His conditions turn out to be that the passenger lifts her skirt and flashes her ass at him, and that the driver shows him how she would give a blow job, while he masturbates. In the eight-minute long scene, the girl driver wears a silver cross as a ring on one of her fingers. Every time she grips the steering wheel (while mimicking on order how she gives a blow job), we see the cross flashing in the light.

An endless tracking shot that switches back and forth between the Lieutenant standing in the rain-soaked street and the young girls in the car (poised between total freak-out and shock) has most audiences squirming in their seats. Ferrara told *Sight and Sound* why he thought the scene has such impact: "It comes after the scene where he's seen a nun naked and for a boy who grew up in a Catholic school, that's a wild thing to walk in on. It's like, 'How far down can a guy go? What does he need to get his rocks off?'" Most disturbing is the driver's face as she tries to do what the Lieutenant asks of her. It's possible that this scene was improvised because it feels so edgy and restless. Keitel is grimacing and gritting his teeth like a maniac and she is hesitant, as if we can feel her wondering if she has any choice but to do something that she doesn't want to do. When she does start mimicking the way that she would give head, as Kent Jones says, "like a porn queen", there's an uncomfortable innocence in her eyes. The Lieutenant keeps masturbating, face contorted, off-loading an avalanche of degrading obscenities onto the girls. When he first starts masturbating, the driver watches what he's doing with a look of bewilderment.

When the Lieutenant finally comes, he seems ashamed and stunned at what he has just done, zips up his fly and vanishes. Ferrara, who had switched to a wide shot to show both the Lieutenant and the driver towards the end of the masturbation, lets the camera linger on the girls. It's an anti-climactic moment. We see the passenger pull her skirt back down, the driver sit astonished. We can feel how traumatised they are. The Lieutenant has 'raped' them too. Ferrara has also described the scene where Zoe shoots the Lieutenant up as a form of "self rape", saying that, "the act of putting a needle in your arm is like a rape." Moreover, the Lieutenant's sexual cruelty and abuse of power is a form of rape. He has exploited his position to pull these two girls over and terrorise them on a New York street. Like the out-of-towner who gets beaten up in the strip club in *Fear City* or the out of towner in *Ms. 45* who drives off back to Georgia with one of Thana's body part bags in his trunk, these girls are violated by New York City. In so far as each of the three has a role to play in helping the Lieutenant get off,

137

the scene recalls another in Godard's *Slow Motion* in which a businessman creates a De Sadean erotic chain in his office involving two prostitutes and a business employee, each of which has a role to play in his getting off.

After this shocking scene, the Lieutenant goes to the church where the rape was actually committed. We see him outside, dawn breaking, a grey-black light accompanying him as he swigs from a bottle and climbs the steps of the church. Then, shot from the inside, we see him enter, bathed in a brilliant white light. This is a sign that God is working out the Lieutenant's redemption. Why has he come to the crime scene alone? He later says that he's head of the investigation but the investigation doesn't start until the morning, when the flash of a police photographer's camera wakes him – he has fallen asleep in one of the pews.

He climbs over the crime scene tape and sees FUCK sprayed on the altar. He is high and drunk. He takes the fallen statue of the Madonna by the hands and tries to lift her. She's too heavy for him. Instead he lies down on his back on the altar, the crucifix above him. This is one of the most important scenes in the film, because the Lieutenant is symbolically offering himself as a sacrifice.

Throughout the film, Catholic iconography haunts the Lieutenant. The scene where we see his daughter receiving her first Communion is introduced with a close-up of Christ on the crucifix. The Lieutenant is wearing a white tie (the first time we see him in a tie). He looks the symbol of purity. As the children receive communion, we repeatedly hear the Priest saying, "the body of Christ". At the same time, the Lieutenant is making a deal with his bookie, in the church. Later, in one of the film's many shocking scenes, he tips out a line of coke onto a spread of photographs of his daughter's communion. After snorting a line off a photograph of her dressed up and receiving communion, his mother-in-law appears in the doorway and catches him in the act. She says nothing. It parallels the scene where the nun notices him peeping in on her naked body.

After snorting this coke, he goes into his daughters' bedroom (and this is in the middle of the night) to look at them. As he does so, we see a cross hanging on the wall. Even if he has lost his faith, we can tell that his wife is still a believer. When he goes to collect his share of the drug money from the Latino kid, he sits down on a kitschy Jesus Christ sofa with the boy's mother. The boy hands him the box of money. It is covered in stickers and pictures that typify the Catholic iconography in the film. When the Lieutenant struggles to get out of the sofa, the camera angle makes it seem as though Jesus Christ is holding him back, drawing him towards Him. After the paranoid descent of the staircase and the hand-held camera shot, he heads for his car. Up the street, we see a huge cross hanging from the side of what looks like a Church.

Earlier the Lieutenant had eavesdropped on the nun's confession. He heard her say that she knew the boys who raped her, that they went to the school (presumably a Catholic school) that she teaches at. He asks for their names but she says she can't say, explaining that she must forgive their actions and turn "bitter semen into fertile sperm, hate into love." The Lieutenant cannot understand how she can forgive such an unspeakable act. After a second meeting with Zoe, in which she shoots him up in graphic detail, a brief montage passes by: a figure cloaked in black lying face down on an altar, a nun's hand clutching a rosary, a crucifix.

This cuts to the nun getting up from lying face down on the altar. Here, the camera has become God, watching over first the nun and then the Lieutenant. She kneels before God and prays. The Lieutenant sits down beside her and begs her to tell him who raped her. By this point though, his motives are ambiguous. He has $30,000 under his arm in a box that the street kid gave him. There is a reward for $50,000 (as the bookie tells him) for anyone who can bring the rapists to justice. Is the Lieutenant trying to make the nun name names so that he can get the reward and clear most of his debts? Or is he trying to make her act of forgiveness (which to him is inhuman and incomprehensible) human by cracking her belief system? She doesn't budge and instead gives him the rosary, asks him if he believes in God and tells him to pray to Jesus.

Ferrara repeatedly frames the Lieutenant with signs of the cross in the same way that Howard Hawks framed Tony Carmone with the same image in *Scarface*. The Lieutenant is constantly surrounded by Catholic iconography. His car has a cross dangling from the rear-view mirror, which we see as he snorts coke after dropping his sons off at school. When he stands naked in the apartment with the two girls that we assume are prostitutes, he raises his arms in a crucifixion pose.

The climax to the religious imagery in the film comes in the scene where the nun leaves the Lieutenant on his knees in the church (with her rosary) and he is visited by a vision of Christ. This extraordinary piece of acting from Keitel, a deranged succession of howls and high pitched whines, reveals the Lieutenant confronting a Christ who, he feels, makes him do everything. He confesses all of his sins to this apparition. Prior to this scene, he's been to see Zoe who has shot him up with heroin; the bookies are going to kill him and his family if he loses the $120,000 bet that he's placed; he's slumped beside the nun in the Church, a box of drug money under his arm and begs the nun to reveal the identity of her killers. He's almost sworn in front of the nun. Now he fingers the rosary she has left him and cries tears of spiritual torment. Ferrara interweaves shots of the Lieutenant howling at Christ and then reverse shots of a stony-faced Christ on the cross, looking down on him. The Lieutenant's pleas are desperate: "I'm so fuckin' weak! Help me!", "Where the hell were you?", "I did so many bad things, I'm sorry!" and finally, "Forgive me!" He goes from being consumed with rage at Christ for letting him become what he is, to begging for mercy and pleading for redemption. He kisses Christ's bloodied feet and the apparition dissolves.

When the Lieutenant cuffs the rapists and takes them out to his car, the entrance to the den has red light flooding out of it. All of these colour-coded red scenes reflect the Lieutenant's journey into hell. The final scenes after he has led the rapists from the den feature no red lighting at all. He has found redemption for his sins.

In a surreal sequence, the Lieutenant's vision of Christ turns into an image of the black woman who is returning the chalice that the rapists stole, and who knows their identity. The Lieutenant has got down on his knees and begged for Christ's mercy and he gets it. Following up her information, he goes to a crack den where he finds the rapists watching the Mets vs Dodgers game on TV. Predictably, the crack den is bathed in red. A crackhead, wearing a pinkish-red shawl, is high and dancing. As the Lieutenant smokes crack with the rapists (symbolic of Jesus and the two robbers on Calvary), the televised game ends. The Mets won – the Lieutenant's $120,000 bet on the Dodgers is lost. He now has nothing left to lose. Was Christ's visitation a drug-induced hallucination? Maybe. Was it real or imagined? This doesn't matter. All that matters is that the Lieutenant believes that he was visited by Christ.

Seated in his car towards the end of the film, the Lieutenant struggles once more with the concept of forgiveness, again returning to the nun ("how could she forgive that?") and her example. He decides, literally, to sacrifice himself so that the rapists can go free. He practises the nun's code of forgiveness and gives the $30,000 to the rapists, puts them on a bus and sends them away to start a new life, though this means that he has no money left with which to pay his gambling debts. He has to forgive them because that is what Christ wants him to do. He has to sacrifice himself to free them. The accompanying howling and whining at the bus station as he slaps one of the rapists and grips him by the throat, mirrors a scene on the way to the Port Authority Bus Terminal where he pointed a gun in their faces to show them what it's like to feel as defenceless as the nun did. He wants revenge, he told the nun this, he wants to bring them to man-made justice, but instead he hands them over to God's justice.

He returns to his car and, beneath a billboard that reads IT ALL HAPPENS HERE, is shot dead. Ferrara films this death scene in one long shot from the opposite side of the street. A grey car pulls up beside the Lieutenant's vehicle. A voice, probably that of the bookie's big man boss, shouts, "Hey Cop!" and shots ring out. The cry vaguely recalls the "Hey You!" that Frank White shouts from his limo before he blows away Gilley at the cop funeral in *King Of New York*. A crowd starts to gather around the car. A truck pulls across the frame in a very Cassavetes-esque moment of reality interfering with film. Ferrara had set up the camera across the street in a van. When the time came for the Lieutenant to get shot, Ferrara had jumped out of the van and was running up to passers-by on the street and telling them that someone had been shot. You can see people's curiosity get the better of them, as a crowd starts to gather around the car. Another truck pulls across, obscuring the view and the film ends. Kent Jones has called this finale "one of the greatest endings I've seen in a movie, modern or otherwise."

The Lieutenant's death, which he had been pursuing for the entire film, liberates him. This ending is very much in the vein of Robert Bresson's films. When his bookie warns him that the big guy will kill his family and blow his home up, the Lieutenant says he'll pay him $10,000 for his troubles, noting, "I hate that fuckin' house." He also jokes that he's a Catholic and that therefore, "No one can kill me, I'm blessed." It's a moment of dark humour, rather like the scene in which the Lieutenant drives around drunk, listening to the game on his car radio; the Dodgers strike out and he pulls out his gun and shoots the radio. This scene, darkly humorous, is Lund's homage to Hawks' *Scarface*. In Hawks' film, Tony Carmonte's male secretary answers a phone to someone who starts messing him around. He pulls out his gun, ready to shoot the person down the phone receiver. In both cases, frustration leads to an act of senseless destruction which, nevertheless, carries humour.

There are many things that we never see the Lieutenant do: talk with his bosses at work, go to the precinct, do any police work (the closest he gets is trying to steal a bag of coke from the back of a car at a crime scene), talk with his wife (from the coldness of the two brief scenes of them together we can barely tell that they're married) or show any affection to his family. The list could go on. There are only four family scenes in the film: the opening shot of the Lieutenant leaving the house and taking the kids to school; the Lieutenant waking up from the sofa, turning the TV on and in the process ignoring his wife, Aunt Wendy and his mother-in-law; the Communion scene and finally the scene where he snorts coke from the Communion photographs and then goes up to his daughters' bedroom. There is no love in his life. When he visits his drug connection, Zoe, he does not speak. He doesn't speak with the two prostitutes either. He doesn't speak with his wife. The nun, the nurse and the diner waitress (who he buys the coffee from) are the only female adults he speaks to.

We see the Lieutenant go to prostitutes, masturbate over girls in cars and spy on a naked nun for sexual pleasure but we never see any private scene with his wife. He appears to hate his home life: it's sterile and can't satisfy him. When he was asked by Gavin Smith why the film gives us no sense of the Lieutenant's past, Ferrara said he wasn't interested in the past: "Who cares? That's just the way he woke up that morning."

Smith also cornered Ferrara on the way in which women are used as 'sexual objects and props' in *King Of New York* and *Bad Lieutenant*.

Indeed, Zoe and the nun are the only women who have substantial (compared to other female characters in the film) speaking parts; one is a wasted junkie and the other the subject of a vile rape. Ferrara explained why the women seem to be decoration: "That's what women are to those people. The *Bad Lieutenant* doesn't own Germaine Greer's body of work to study in his car between cases." Ferrara is right: the Lieutenant is a cop. He degrades women, he is racist (when he shoots his radio he also screams racist abuse), he is a junkie, an alcoholic, a gambler – in short, a corrupt cop, a total scumbag. It is an acutely moral film, from the title, which tells the viewer straight from the word go that the main character is thoroughly reprehensible, to the nun's act of forgiveness and the religious imagery that constantly stalks the Lieutenant like his conscience unravelling. Shot in real time, the film gives the viewer no escape, no breaks in the narrative to provide light relief. Apart from the nun's rape and the interludes with Zoe and the nun, the Lieutenant is constantly in our faces, rubbing our noses in his degradation. Peter Lehman wrote the following of the structure: "the film's use of space, sound, editing and pacing is as unusual as the definition of its central character." The Lieutenant's personality is reflected back in the way in which Ferrara presents the film.

The Lieutenant's redemption comes from trying to bring a nun's rapists to justice. The Bad Lieutenant becomes Good Samaritan, trying to help his fellow human and failing. He wants to rescue the nun and see justice done; she wants God to do justice, not a corrupt police officer. His redemption only comes when he can begin to understand the strength and faith that lies behind her decision to forgive her attackers. Prior to arriving at the spiritual crossroads that leads him to redemption and then death, the Lieutenant is shot up with heroin by Zoe who lulls him into a trance with a monologue comparing addiction to vampirism. It is from this scene that *The Addiction* grew. This character, as Zoë Lund explains in the interview that concludes this critique, understands the Lieutenant. She knows where he is coming from, what makes him tick. Zoe, like the Lieutenant, is trying to regulate life's pains with narcotics. Her search for an absence of pain mirrors his. When she says, "We gotta' eat away at ourselves 'til there's nothing left but appetite", she's talking about the journey the Lieutenant is on.

Only when he has confronted ultimate degradation, pure horror, pure evil, complete annihilation of self, is he ready to accept God. He has to find redemption from darkness, where others find redemption from purity. Zoe knows that suffering will eventually lead to salvation.

Bad Lieutenant closes with a beautiful, moral ending, loaded with issues of redemption and forgiveness, as the Lieutenant sacrifices himself to free other sinners. The nun points out to him that Jesus died for his sins just before he sees Christ. The Lieutenant dies for the rapists' sins, his sins washing theirs clean. It is this moral leap that he struggled with, and it is this same issue that we as viewers struggle with after the film has finished. The Lieutenant constantly asks himself (and the nun and rapists) how the nun could forgive such an act. When the film ends, we also ask ourselves how he could forgive the rapists and sacrifice himself to save them. The film is an essay on the complexities of Christian faith.

AN INTERVIEW WITH ZOË LUND

Josh Long, *Exploitation Retrospect* (ER): *Bad Lieutenant* is a fine achievement. Being the writer, you obviously have a firm grasp on the film's main theme of religious redemption. Did you experience the same enlightenment?

Zoë Lund (ZL): I never went through a similar experience within the religious context. Although, any sort of knowledge regarding religion is a personal journey quite resembling any sort of quest for truth.

ER: Well, let's go to the other side of the spectrum. Is *Bad Lieutenant* the most personal film you've acted in?

ZL: Yes. What I was trying to say is that I never lost my religion. I have always had a certain increasing awareness of religion, but have never put myself in the shoes of the Lieutenant. I do believe that the Gospel is the ultimate story. What is amazing about the book is that over the millennia, the gospel has become so refined to the point where the Christ story does present a very refined and highly charged model for the search for truth. We can use the book as a basis for our own path to spirituality and grace.

ER: Why did you have the search for redemption flow through a corrupt policeman as opposed to a mill worker or letter carrier?

ZL: In some way his corruption is entirely irrelevant, and in other ways it's really important. To the irrelevancy, in no way did I want it implied that were he not corrupt he would have been OK. That whole attitude of the film, him being corrupt, I think allows him to be closer to humility. And in his own strange way, perhaps what a policeman ought to be. For example, there are communities, especially here in New York, that have been totally corrupted by police bureaucracy. On the other hand, even after their death, officers who were corrupt are remembered in their community, even though they did drugs and hung out with whores. They know their surroundings and if someone was getting mugged, goddammit, that cop would be there! That type of corruption seems to be preferred, whereas here in the Lower East Side, dozens and dozens of cops stand about waiting to bust busloads of junkies who just want to get their fix and go home. At the same time, a murder could happen two blocks away. Out of their own cowardice and misplaced sense of duty, they will stay on the corner and stalk the junkies.

ER: So everything is not what it seems.

ZL: Yes, sometimes when people are corrupt they are in touch with their own humanity and will know their community better, be closer to their community and will know the priorities of the community better. If someone has a more humane sense of justice and the priorities of justice, I think that person could be judged corrupt. Corruption does not make the Lieutenant a sinner. I always like to point out that Christ himself hung out with whores and tax collectors. He turned water into wine ... indeed, if he were here right now he might turn water to drugs or something equivalent.

ER: Some reviewers and viewers of the film did not like it because they seemed scared by the themes you present.

ZL: The only thing a person has to remember is that a film is a wide-reaching medium. Not every film will make it fun for the viewer. A conscious attempt was made to make it as difficult as possible for the viewer to escape. The use of real time is an example.

ER: Being an independent film, was there a conscious attempt to stray away from the easy selling realm of exploitation?

ZL: The only thing I can say is that the film was what it was to be and that's all. I had a great deal of control and unlike my billing, wrote every word.

ER: What about your character, Zoe, who in the film is the Lieutenant's mistress?

ZL: There was a lot of rewriting done on the set. Two other characters were cut, and my character modulated and took on more and more. A lot of things had to be changed and improvised. The vampire speech, which is crucial to the Lieutenant was written two minutes before it was shot. I memorised it and did it in one take. The speech is important because she is acute in knowing the journey the Lieutenant makes. She shoots him up, sends him off, knowing of his passion, she lets him go.

ER: The film is truly an emotional ride. Are you concerned about it possibly pushing audiences away?

ZL: I think the idea of carnal love versus hieratic love are issues we all deal with and are very strong throughout the film. In the beginning, the Lieutenant is pursuing carnal love, and at the end, finally experiences the greater of the two, the hieratic. In terms of viewers, if you leave halfway through, fine, you shouldn't be there anyway. At the Rotterdam Film Festival I had to tell audiences not to leave until the end, because it's like reading the gospel up to Gethsemene and then you shut the book. If you buy the ticket for the ride, you might as well see it through to the end.

ER: Without giving away too much of the end, there is a sign in camera view that states IT ALL HAPPENS HERE. I thought it only proper to end the film with that sign in view.

ZL: That wonderful sign also echoes the gospel IT ALL HAPPENS HERE and it truly does. The city gave us the sign for the shoot which, by the way, was shot with a hidden camera. The reaction of that scene is of everyday New Yorkers. You must never bore the audience, I am adamant about that rule. You must make things entertaining and have a joy about your work. Audiences want a character they can travel with, make love to. They want to join the character's odyssey and have that odyssey become part of them once they leave the theatre. *Bad Lieutenant* works because we deal with the most powerful questions ever asked by mankind while still being down and dirty, raunchy and funny, and a little crazy thrown in.

Snake Eyes a.k.a *Dangerous Game* 1993

"It's *Who's Afraid Of Virginia Woolf* on acid or *The Player* meets *Contempt* meets Cassavetes" – Abel Ferrara to *Neon* magazine.

"I thought I could take that role and do a great performance. It was going to be this great thing for me. And even though it's a shit movie and I hate it, I am good in it" – Madonna.

"For as far back as I can remember, the line between fantasy and reality has been hopelessly blurred" – Roman Polanski.

A film-within-a-film. Jean-Luc Godard's *Contempt*, a film-within-a-film about the marital breakdown between a film's screenwriter doctor and his idealistic wife. Godard's *Passion*, a film-within-a-film that pits the way in which circumstantial barriers block a director's creative vision from fully materialising against the issue of purpose that preoccupies cast, crew and local inhabitants. François Truffaut's *Day For Night*: a light, playful film-within-a-film about the politics, intrigue and romantic dalliances that surround a shoot. John Cassavetes' *Opening Night*: a troubling play-within-a-film about an actress suffering a nervous breakdown as her handle on the line between 'performance' and reality becomes increasingly confused. Abel Ferrara's *Snake Eyes* or as it has since been re-titled, *Dangerous Game*, is a sprawling addition to this unnervingly wonderful quartet of stylistic predecessors. It concerns a New York film director called Eddie Israel who is making a film in Los Angeles called 'Mother Of Mirrors' about the breakdown of a suburban New York couple's marriage. Ferrara films *Snake Eyes* as a documentary of the filming of 'Mother Of Mirrors', focusing on an increasingly blurred line between actors and acting, director and directing, plot and real life, the shoot and the real world.

The film opens with a family dinner scene, the kind of scene regularly featured within the framework of French and Italian cinema. 'Blue Moon' plays in the background. Israel (Harvey Keitel) sits at the head of the table, facing the camera. His little son, Tommy (played by Reilly Murphy who also played the son in *Body Snatchers*), sits to his right and our left. His wife, Madlyn (played by Ferrara's own wife, Nancy) sits to his left and our right. They are huddled at one end of the table. The camera, placed at the opposite end of the table from Israel forms a cross out of Israel, his family to his left and right and the long stretch of dining room table. It's as if the camera is positioned at the base of a cross and is staring up at a cross. Only in this instance, the three humans and the table replace any kind of man-made material. The family is the holy trinity, the sign of the cross. This symbolic framing implies that Israel is a 'Christ'-like figure, being crucified by family life. He oozes power, control and confidence. His wife appears insecure, eager to please and fusses neurotically about whether Israel will like the pasta she has just cooked. She is the mother of Israel's son; the women that Israel later confesses to having cheated on her with are whores. The classic Catholic male polarisation of women as either mother or whore emerges once more in Ferrara's work. To reinforce the point, St. John calls the film-within-the-film 'Mother Of Mirrors'. Reduce 'Mother Of Mirrors' to an acronym and you get 'M.O.M'. This is why Israel's marriage breaks down: he sees Madlyn as a 'Mom' and actress Sarah Jennings (played by Madonna) as a 'whore' or as he memorably puts it, "a commercial piece of shit". To reinforce the 'mother' symbol that Madlyn comes to represent to Israel, he often calls her 'Maddy', an abbreviation of Madlyn but also of the Madonna, the Virgin Mary.

We later see the men in *The Funeral* remain distant and cold with their wives and then alive and sexual with whores. In a similar way, here we see Israel as distant and cold with Madlyn and alive and charismatic as he's lulling Jennings into his bed by way of over-

148

played compliments and a poolside bout of serenading and dancing. After they've slept together, we see Israel sitting in bed,
smoking a cigarette, a picture of post-coital masculinity. Minutes
later, Jennings has left without saying anything more than a
throwaway line about seeing him on the set the next morning. It's as
Israel likes it: empty sex with no strings and no personal demands.
No sooner has she left than his hotel door bell rings. Israel opens it
to find that Madlyn and Tommy have come to see him on a
spontaneous visit. He fakes being glad to see them and makes an
excuse about having to go and hang up the phone while the porter
brings their bags in.

He then frantically sweeps the bedsheets, hides an ashtray, hides
glasses and runs back in. The change in his behaviour and mood as
we see him shift from a meaningless sex scene to being a father and
husband is dramatic. He reads to his son. A bedroom scene follows
in which the cracks in Israel's marriage are clearly showing. Ferrara
again has the camera capture his wife's exposed nipple, the second
time in the film that he plays this trademark shot on his own wife. In
the opening scenes, after dinner, we saw Israel and Madlyn making
love. There, Ferrara also had the camera capture a shot of one of her
nipples. That scene also makes for uncomfortable viewing, as we
watch Harvey Keitel lying between Abel Ferrara's wife's thighs and
acting out a love-making scene. Her right leg raises, she wraps her
arms around Keitel's back. This encourages us from the start to see
the film from Ferrara's perspective.

Several times during the film, the boundary between the filming
of 'Mother Of Mirrors' and the filming of *Snake Eyes* collapses. In
one scene, we see Eddie Israel sitting and discussing the character
'Clare' with the actress, Sarah Jennings, who plays her. Or so we
think. He says that the relationship between Clare and Frank is
an "argument between heaven and hell". Clare has undergone a
religious conversion. She has sworn off a past of drink, drugs,
multiple sex partners and all manner of pleasure-seeking indul-
gence in favour of her faith in God. Her husband Russo/Russell
(his name is never given definitively) played by actor Frank Burns
(James Russo) still sees drink, drugs and wild sex as "the truth." He
is hell, she is heaven. She can't find redemption with him in her
life, he can't get off anymore without her co-operation. She is 'the

mother of mirrors', showing him how corrupt and debauched his life is. He is also her mirror, reflecting her past back at her.

After making this statement about how he sees their relationship, Israel looks at someone off camera and says, "Right, Nick?" The unseen 'Nick' laughs. This is obviously the writer of the screenplay, Nicholas St. John. Ferrara is messing with the line between reality and film here. When the title PRINCIPAL PHOTOGRAPHY flashes up on a blank screen, Israel calls out to another unseen person: "Ken, she's over there, is that OK?" 'Ken' calls back, "That's fine." This is obviously Ken Kelsch, Director of Photography on *Snake Eyes*. It's a surreal moment because Israel's Director Of Photography is played by Victor Argo. Ken Kelsch is Ferrara's D.P.

Another scene begins with Sarah crying on set. She asks what she is meant to do. A take is about to start. The clap-board comes into the shot. It has two names on it: A. FERRARA and K. KELSCH. In every other scene in the film where the clap-board is shown, the credit is E. ISRAEL and V. NOTO. It's a moment of madness that happens so fast that lazy viewers won't even catch it. In another amusing scene, the clap-board appears upside down.

Each time Ferrara has Israel call his wife 'Maddy', he is also calling to mind Madonna's nickname 'Maddy'. The very fact that Ferrara's own wife plays the director's wife makes it clear that Israel is a self-portrait. When he baits and shouts at his cast in order to get a better performance out of them, we are witnessing the infamous Ferrara method of direction. When Israel tells Frank Burns that he wants him to "dig down into fucking hell" for the film, it's the essence of Ferrara's militant Polanski-inspired directorial technique.

In another scene, Israel plays back video rushes of himself talking about joining the Marines as a young man. This is a biographical detail taken from Harvey Keitel's real-life experiences: he *did* join the Marines as a young man. This separates Keitel and Israel. There is a similarly unnerving scene where Sarah and Israel are talking. She is confessor, he the 'priest'. She recounts a tale of being sexually terrorised by an unidentified man. Is this a fictitious tale that St. John feeds the character Sarah Jennings? Or a candid moment where Madonna is talking about an abusive ex-lover? Again, Ferrara edits the scene to leave room for teasing ambiguity. In a centrepiece scene, Sarah repeatedly fluffs her lines. Israel reads

Burns' lines and baits her. He starts to become abusive. The look on Sarah/Madonna's face is part-bemusement, part-shock. It's as if Madonna is totally thrown by what's happening. Israel repeatedly calls her a "commercial piece of shit". Is this Keitel as Israel attacking Madonna's status as a pop icon or Israel attacking Sarah Jennings, a commercial B-grade telemovie actress? In the disturbing scene where Burns forcibly rapes his wife (and also his co-star), Sarah tries to stop him from tearing at her clothes before he wrestles her to the floor. In an odd moment (and it's odd because Frank Burns' character in 'Mother Of Mirrors' doesn't ever get called by a clear name) Sarah/Madonna starts crying and says, "Stop Russo!" Is Burns playing a character called Russo? Or is this Madonna asking James Russo to stop? Or is Burns playing an abusive husband called Russell? Ferrara never deigns to clarify any of these ambiguities. The same thing happens in another scene too, where she again addresses him as Russo/Russell. Is it sloppy film-making? Inspired brilliance? Lazy editing? Or a deliberate attack on the simplicity of modern film?

The film-within-a-film framework is typical St. John material. It's rather like an Arthur Miller play. The husband has just lost his $200,000-a-year corporate job. He also feels that his wife is (in Israel's words) "abandoning him". Her religious conversion spoils his taste for dark excess as much as his taste for dark excess taints her bid for redemption. It is never made clear why she doesn't just leave him. Instead, she stays around to suffer his physical, sexual and psychological abuse. He hits her, chops her hair off with scissors, takes a piss on their lounge carpet, violently rapes her, drinks constantly, takes drugs and even goes so far as to force her to watch old camcorder movies of their group sex sessions.

In one of these grainy shots, Sarah is lying down and kissing another woman's legs – one more instance of this Ferrara trademark where two women become sexually intimate. In another shot, we see her bending over a sofa and getting spanked; in another she is sodomised by an anonymous man. All of this seems to allude to Madonna's *Sex* book. In another scene in the film, where Sarah leaves Burns' hotel room after sleeping with him, Burns lets his dealer-girlfriend come in, after keeping her waiting for an hour. She is riled about the fact that he's been next door sleeping with his co-star (who even complains that she thinks Burns was sleeping with "the girl in the script"). The dealer-girlfriend ribs him, asking him if Sarah gave him 'head'. She then mimics how she imagines Jennings would have given head to him using one of his fingers. There is an allusion here both to the *Bad Lieutenant* masturbation scene and also to Madonna's *Truth or Dare* film in which the singer simulates fellatio on a coke bottle. The scene ends when Burns hits his dealer-girlfriend, desperate to get his coke. This is one of many off-set and on-set moments when Burns appears to be identical to the character he is playing. The more he drinks and takes drugs (and during one pre-take shot, we see a crew member slip a wrap of coke into Burns' hand), the more he becomes his character.

When Israel lectures Burns on delivering the right degree of "despair", he advises him to either cut down on the coke and booze or increase his intake. Similarly, when Burns sleeps with Sarah, he is also blurring reality and performance. After Sarah sleeps with Israel (and ensures that Burns sees her leave the party with the director) Burns is almost jealous. This veiled jealousy surfaces as rage when it comes to the rape scene which is so graphically violent that a quick shot of the crew shows them all to be astonished and very uncomfortable. When the couple cannot resolve their relationship in light of her religious conversion, Burns shoots Sarah. According to the lines that Sarah/Madonna repeatedly fluffs in the reality/film breakdown scene with Israel/Keitel, Burns is planning to shoot her, then burn the house down and then commit suicide. We assume at the end that Burns is going to commit suicide.

Ferrara layers the film in so many ways that it eventually topples; St. John's screenplay is rather like a house of cards waiting to fall. When Burns plays Clare one of their home porn movies, we are watching Ferrara's *Snake Eyes*, in which Israel's 'Mother Of Mirrors' is showing a suburban couple's camcorder home sex video. We see grainy footage of rehearsals, of the crew preparing for a scene, of Sarah and Burns getting stoned in a hellish glow of red light, of Israel trying to beat performances out of his cast. This video/film interplay would become Ferrara's new toy and would be used to dazzling effect on *The Blackout*. We see Israel watching dailies on two TV screens in his hotel room, drinking wine or beer and picking at some food. We see him sitting on a plane, watching rushes on a tiny monitor, drinking a glass of wine. He works constantly; film surrounds him.

Tellingly, when Israel flies back to New York for his wife's father's funeral and confesses to having slept with Sarah as well as with dozens of other women from other films (actresses, models, wardrobe, make-up), this confession and emotional break-up is played out in front of a blank, turned off TV screen. Madlyn has no involvement with his work. Ferrara has several shots, where the dead screen is exactly positioned between the rowing couple. His wife and family represent stagnancy to him. Just as the Fellini *8½* poster in *The Blackout* represents stagnancy with Susan, so the dead TV here tells us that Israel is in an environment that is stifling him as a person. Understandably, Madlyn throws him out for having the insensitivity to break all these infidelities to her on the morning of her father's funeral. To underline how cold their relationship has become, Ferrara frames Israel's early morning return home by taxi, within a beautiful shot of a snow-lined New York street.

Madlyn's surprise trip to Los Angeles is a disaster. She asks Israel why he's distant, he testily shrugs her question off. They aggressively make love in the back of a car up in the Hollywood Hills and Israel isn't able to reach orgasm. (Earlier, he had sung a song to Sarah in the poolside seduction scene which had lines about sex in the back of a car.) St. John's screenplay suggests that making love in the back of a car is something that has significance for Israel and Madlyn. That he is violating that marital code by using the essence of it to seduce an actress tells us how spiritually bankrupt he has become.

When Madlyn and he lie in bed on the night of her surprise visit, she asks him if Sarah is "beautiful". Israel is lying on the side of the bed that Sarah got out from. His place is taken by Madlyn. To have her ask if Sarah is beautiful while lying in the bed in which Sarah and her husband have just made love is Ferrara-esquely perverse; the 'mother' and the 'whore' have shared his bed in one night. He's as happy as the Lieutenant is when he spies on the naked nun in *Bad Lieutenant*. It's a twisted get-off; Israel shares his bed first with Sarah (Madonna) and then his wife (the Madonna). It's another reality/film moment. When they go driving in Los Angeles, before the love-making scene in the car, they pass a billboard that reads

DOOMSDAY HAS ARRIVED! in a sly echo of the IT ALL HAPPENS HERE billboard in *Bad Lieutenant*.

Their relationship is so doomed that when the phone rings in the middle of the night, she is asleep in the bedroom and he is sitting up drinking and watching yet more rushes. They both pick up, and Madlyn says she's got the call; the fact that they're in the same hotel suite and yet talking via two separate telephones shows us that their own marriage is as damaged as that being played out in Israel's film. She comes into the room, but Israel says he doesn't want to discuss anything with her, as he's too busy working. Then Madlyn tells him that she has just found out her father has died from a heart attack. Israel gives her an insincere hug and she decides to return to New York.

The conclusion to Israel's mental breakdown runs parallel to the approaching climax of 'Mother Of Mirrors'. Shots of Israel's hotel suite nearly always contain a mirror. The film he is making is all about mirrors; he directs one scene in which faces are lit in a manner straight out of a horror movie; in another scene he provides an arrangement of mirrors that allows us to see two of each of the couples, suggesting a body/soul divide.

During his date with Sarah, he tells her a story about having a nosebleed during sex (we guess with Madlyn). Sarah replies that she didn't know that he was "romantic". There is a pause and then Ferrara cuts to some footage of a boxing match. He is telling us that he sees romantic relationships and sexual relationships as a fight, a series of battles and blows, a pugilistic and emotional warzone. The boxing match turns out to be playing on a TV screen at a party – a party at which Israel's date is Sarah Jennings. Ferrara keeps three active layers of film running throughout: (1) *Snake Eyes* (2) 'Mother Of Mirrors' (3) Random video footage: this includes shots of Clare being sodomised, Werner Herzog talking about the film-making process and its insanity, a boxing match, the rehearsals and the rushes. This layer of three provides one of the many trios in the film. As we fathom from the opening scene, Israel, his wife and son form a trio. On set, Sarah, Burns and Israel also form a trio. Video, TV and film form yet another trio in Israel's life.

By the time Israel experiences his own form of conversion, all three layers of the structure have blurred into one layer. He has

become the abusive husband, chasing new sexual kicks, constantly drinking and taking drugs. Madlyn has become Clare, a clean, wholesome wife. During one take of 'Mother Of Mirrors' (always shot in a different film stock), Sarah's husband yells at her "your tits bore me, your mouth bores me, your face bores me", but his words could also be spoken by Israel to Clare. Ditto when Russo tells Sarah that he just wants things back the way they once were.

The redemption scene in *Snake Eyes* takes place in the hotel suite. After a long pan shot of a smog drenched Los Angeles (representing the cloud of impurity destroying the Israels' marriage), Israel stands before the shuttered windows, blinded by the light, his arms outstretched in a slight recreation of the similar crucifixion pose in *Bad Lieutenant*. He is bathed in white light: the white pure light of God. Again, Ferrara frames the scene to make Israel's outstretched arms combine with the positioning of the window shutters in the camera angle, to create an illusion of the sign of the cross. It's a faint underlining of the crucifixion which is taking place inside of Israel. In a hallucination, Israel sees Madlyn sitting in the room with him; she is the Madonna, the mother, the symbol of purity and virtue. She becomes like Jean in *The Funeral*, a pure wife trapped in a marriage to an impure husband. Some of her lines are acutely revealing: "If you think drugs and alcohol are so wonderful then I want you to go out and buy some for our son. If you think infidelity is such a virtue in a person then I want you to bring one of your girlfriends over here and fuck her in front of our son." We assume this to be a *Bad Lieutenant*-esque moment of enlightenment which will lead to redemption.

However, in the next scene, we find it wasn't. Israel is watching TV with another girl he's picked up. The next scene returns to the director and cast discussions about the film. Israel sums up 'Mother Of Mirrors' as a film about someone destroying a love that they have, as a kind of death. Ferrara then shows us Israel's unconscious body sprawled out on the bathroom floor, his binges on booze and pills having taken their toll. The final scene shows Russo pressing a gun to Sarah's forehead, its point between her eyes. Ferrara has Kelsch focus on Russo as the shot rings out, leaving us to assume that he has blown her brains out. The film plays out as it began, with the song 'Blue Moon' playing, this time sung by Bob Dylan. The ending is ambiguous. Has Israel experienced Clare's religious conversion? Has he abased himself to a degree that he is ready to be redeemed by God? Is Russo/Russell's shot also a shot which kills him? Or his marriage? All we can know is that Israel confesses his sins to his wife (the Madonna), experiences some kind of religious experience in his hotel room bathed in white light and is then saved. The death of the non-believer inside Israel and of the evil inside Israel is symbolised when Russo/Russell shoots Clare in the head. She, like the Lieutenant, dies for Israel's (the rapists) sins and consequently saves his soul.

6

BIG BUDGET, LOW ART

Body Snatchers: The Invasion Continues 1993

"The story concerns alien beings taking over the bodies of humans. The aliens assume the exact likeness of real people while gestating in pods. But these pods possess no soul, emotion or culture. They exist like cows munching grass, without a care plaguing them. They are incapable of love, passion is unknown. They simply live – breathing, eating, sleeping" – Don Siegel talking about his original 1956 version of *Invasion Of The Body Snatchers*.

"My films are expressive of a culture that has had the possibility of attaining material fulfilment while at the same time finding itself unable to accomplish the simple business of conducting human lives. We have been sold a bill of goods as a substitute for life. In this country people die at the age of 21. They die emotionally at 21, maybe younger" – John Cassavetes.

Ferrara's *Body Snatchers* is the second re-make of Don Siegel's uncopyable and brilliant film, *Invasion Of The Body Snatchers* (1956). Since Ferrara has only ever spoken of the Siegel original and never mentioned Philip Kaufman's 1978 re-make which starred Donald Sutherland and Brooke Adams, I'm only going to compare the first and third versions. Siegel's black and white masterpiece was a chilling metaphor about the bland homogeny of fifties American society. By setting the film in a small American town where everyone knows everyone and everything runs like clockwork, the

157

message of the film is rendered more intense. Siegel's direction had the milieu bristle with sinister normalcy: the 'pod' people mow lawns, read metres, pump gas and tend bar. Ferrara's re-make, which is based around a storyline knocked up by pulp-meister Larry Cohen and Raymond Cistheri, is set on a US military base.

In the Siegel original, Doctor Miles Bennell (pronounced throughout the film as 'banale') and his old British flame Becky Driscoll were the only remaining citizens of Santa Mira not to become pod people in the original. When Becky also became a 'pod' person, the Doctor managed to escape the town and tell others. The film opens with him at a police station trying to convince a psychiatrist of what he has just experienced in Santa Mira. It is his voice-over that relays what has happened to the inhabitants of Santa Mira and thus tells the story in flashback.

In Ferrara's version, the voice-over belongs to a rebellious teenage girl, Marti Malone (played by Gabrielle Anwar), who is first seen in the film reading Ian McEwan's *The Cement Garden* and listening to her Walkman. Instead of having two lovers fight the onset of the pod people, Ferrara's screenplay (written by three writers including barely recognisable input from Nicholas St. John) has a very poorly developed romantic sub-plot in which Marti and her uninfected chopper pilot boyfriend fight the pod people and at the end, fly away from the base, bomb a convoy of pods and land safely in Atlanta.

The success of Siegel's original was anchored in the way he took a regular small town and everyday life scenarios and injected both with a subtle macabre tension. The citizens are all fairly regular Americans so as they become pod people, their transition is harder to notice. Siegel plays on the 'are they/aren't they?' factor to create masterful suspense. Ferrara's version is absurdly set on a military base where everyone is meant to act exactly the same anyway! No matter how hard Ferrara tries, he can't get the film off the ground. The irony is devastating: with his biggest budget to date ($20,000,000) Ferrara screws up in majestic style.

Marti Malone and her half-brother Andy (played by Reilly Murphy) and stepmother Carol (played by Meg Tilly) are dragged to the military base by Doctor Steve Malone (played by Terry Kinney), an environmental scientist. He is posted to the base so he can check that the chemical warfare laboratory there is environmentally safe. From the start, Carol is an impostor to Marti (and Steve) because she has replaced her mother who died when she was seven. This regular family are impostors on the military base too, because they are non-military, non-pod people and to the General in charge they are snoops. Ferrara fluffs the creeping tension that crackles throughout the original by having Dr Collins (played with increasing psychosis by Forest Whitaker) ambush Marti in a gas station rest room, half strangle her, hold a knife to her throat and warn her that "they get you when you sleep." Already, we are bored.

A barrage of horror genre special effects (heads deflating, worm-like talons growing out of pods and crawling into noses and mouths, pod people pointing at non pod-people and roaring like B-movie devils, several scenes where the replicas share a scene with the victims) doesn't do much to brighten the dullness of the movie. We don't know anything about the family and so we don't care about them. In the original, having a town doctor narrate the increasingly odd goings-on involved us, because a doctor is someone we instinctively want to have faith in. An environmental scientist is not. Kinney also fails to capture one dot of Kevin McCarthy's intense performance in the original version. Tilly has little to do. When she gets taken over and her head crushes on a pillow before her son's eyes, a cropped shot of what is meant to be her naked body walks into the room. This was a body double, which in light of what the film is about, seems faintly comic. By not wanting to do a naked scene, Tilly's double lends the performance an unintended and humorous double meaning.

Marti's relations with the General's punky daughter Jen (Christine Elise) and her romance with chopper pilot Tim are both paper thin. When Tim finds her in the hospital with pod worms crawling over and into her face, a naked, seductive replica appears on the next bed. Ferrara can't resist a topless shot of Anwar, again framing to bring attention to her breasts and nipples. When Tim untangles the worms from her face, the seductive replica dies and Marti is saved; it's a B-movie moment at best. Likewise, when punky Jen's alcoholic mother turns into a pod woman, she airs her suspicions to Marti that she knows something is wrong, because her mother leaves a glass with water in it on a ledge (instead of the usual booze) and takes up playing bridge with a bunch of military wives. It's all absurd stuff, more camp than satirical.

The military base is bathed in a perpetual orange-red-purple heat glow and the army housing is suitably bland. Recreations of some aspects of the original (people running out of their houses and into the street, the fact that the General lets Marti and Tim escape in the chopper) offer occasional reminders of just how brilliant Siegel's work was. The finale – complete with exploding trucks, jeeps, shooting, criss-crossings of search lights, hundreds of people running aimlessly about, fireballs and a slow-motion shot of an exploding building that is an explicit reference to the famous multi-camera exploding building scene in Antonioni's *Zabriskie Point*, is big budget crap.

The ending, which has the chopper landing in Atlanta and a teary-eyed Marti offering her voice-over conclusion, wraps up with a shot of the military air traffic controller, waving them in with precision procedure, a reminder of the regulated society they still live in. Siegel's version took a pop at McCarthyism (even cheekily having the lead role played by an actor with the same name) and a society which tries to repress individuality, Ferrara's wanders aimlessly in search of meaning. Is the film an AIDS allegory at heart? Is it a satire on the military and those who join it? Does it attempt to be a comment on government repression, or an attack on the secret military manufacture of chemical weapons and the civilian lives these experiments may be endangering? Could it even be a comment on the threat of nuclear war?

Siegel chillingly drove his point home in moments such as Becky's poetic speech about human emotions and by having the Doctor look straight into the camera – addressing the viewer directly – and shouting: "You're next!" Ferrara leaves us with the sight of a uniformed soldier conducting a military chopper pilot to a safe landing. Like the entire film, it's poorly thought out, empty and mind-numbingly dull.

7

THE GOSPEL ACCORDING TO ST. JOHN

The Addiction 1995

"Born-again vampires is really what the film's about. It's a very Catholic message. Nicholas St John wrote it and Nicky doesn't see the vampire as a romantic image. It's the embodiment of pure evil and for him, it's spirituality that's going to be the saviour. How else do you overcome pure evil? Intellectuality – how far can it get you, over your primal being? Without the spiritual side, there's really not much hope. There's only the word of God. That's your only salvation" – Abel Ferrara, talking to *Film Ireland*.

"You are what you're addicted to. All we are are addictions. Addictions to evil, the desire not to be evil, to whatever" – Abel Ferrara, talking to *Film Ireland*.

"Man being condemned to be free carries the weight of the whole world on his shoulders; he is responsible for the world and for himself as a way of being" – Jean-Paul Sartre, *Freedom And Responsibility*.

"Vampires are lucky. They can feed on others. We gotta eat away at ourselves" – Zoe to the Lieutenant after shooting up both him and herself in *Bad Lieutenant*.

The Addiction uses vampirism as a metaphor with which to address addiction. Lead character Kathleen Conklin (played quite brilliantly by Lili Taylor) is a philosophy post-graduate student at New York

University. Once again, this creates an allusion to Godard's work. The lead character in his seminal 1967 film, *La Chinoise*, was a philosophy student. She is hungry for knowledge. When we first see her, she's in a dark lecture theatre watching a documentary about the My Lai Massacre. The massacre, along with repeated stills and footage of the Holocaust, comes to represent a symbol of the world's evil for Kathleen as she struggles to understand how mankind can commit such atrocities and also how responsibility for these atrocities is addressed. The film as Cédric Anger suggested in his review of the film in *Cahiers du Cinéma* concerns itself with polarities: "good and evil, day and night, black and white."

Early scenes follow this train of polarity. We see Kathleen watching the My Lai footage, shadows casting an impression of the cross on her face. She sees herself as the polar opposite of what she's watching: the soldiers killing these women and children are pure evil, she is pure good, studying their actions and trying to learn from them. After the lecture, she and her college student friend Jean (played by Edie Falco) discuss the ramifications of what they've just seen. Kathleen says that she doesn't understand how one or several of the soldiers that were responsible could have been brought home and tried for these 'war' crimes. She wants to know why a handful of soldiers were held responsible for such an atrocity. What about the men they took orders from? What about the top rank of the army? What about the government? Kathleen tells Jean that she sees everybody as equally to blame.

The next scene also milks suspense from the juxtaposition of polar opposites: Kathleen, a privileged post-graduate student, walks along a street where men from another walk of life leer and stare at her. Ferrara uses a hip hop track by Cypress Hill (about smoking dope, naturally) to soundtrack this edgy street scene. Kathleen's discomfort is reminiscent of Thana's unease in a similar street scene at the start of *Ms. 45*, and provides the first of several parallels between *Ms. 45* and *The Addiction*. The jittery, rough cinematography underlines how intimidated Kathleen is. Then the screen goes black. The camera comes out from behind a wall, suggesting that she is being secretly observed. She crosses a street and pauses on the sidewalk; she's hesitating, immobilised. Why does she stop? What is she thinking? If she was finding the streets intimidating, then why stand still, inviting trouble? The implication is that she is 'asking' for what happens to her; she makes the choice to have her life altered.

A mysterious woman appears behind Kathleen, wearing a long black dress. She has short hair and looks nothing like any other character that we've seen so far. The woman approaches Kathleen. There is a sexual, predatory sway to her walk. She mutters something in a foreign language and makes some small talk ("nice night"). After all the threatening males that Kathleen has walked past, she isn't bothered by a female stranger talking to her. Why is she still standing there? The stranger suddenly pulls Kathleen off the street and into a dark alleyway. This is a shot we've seen time and time again in Ferrara's films: a dark alley, a menacing street, the city as a dangerous place. The most obvious comparison out of all of Ferrara's alleyway/street snatch shots (many of which were in *Fear City*) is the first rape scene in *Ms. 45* where the rapist grabs Thana from the street and drags her down a dark alleyway. The same thing happens here except that the alleyway is dark and the black and white photography immediately lends the scene a sinister *Nosferatu/Vampyr* air.

Shadows from the criss-cross patterns of the wire fence throw patterns across the faces of both Kathleen and her attacker, rhyming the scene with the earlier shot of the shadow cross on Kathleen's face as she watched the My Lai footage. This use of shadow and reflection also sets the film up for what is to come: a study of the prison of addiction and dependency. The attacker, her face also beautifully toned with shadows from the fence, says, "Look at me and tell me to go away. Don't ask, tell me." This hypnotic, rhetorical statement becomes a motif of addiction throughout the film. When a vampire says these words, they become symbolic of any addiction: the words could be coming from a bottle of wine, a bottle of pills, a lover's mouth, a cup of coffee, a syringe filled with heroin. The idea of addiction itself telling the addict to reject it is an ingenious play on the addict/addiction equation.

Kathleen says, "Please" as if she wants her attacker to go but the tone of her voice is expectant, pregnant with longing. The expression on her face – undeniably one of fear – is torn between longing and terror. She wants to go free but she also wants what is threatening to happen. The delivery of the word is key to the free will theme that litters St. John's screenplay like a trail. Kathleen 'wants' whatever her attacker is offering just as she 'wanted' to be attacked and dragged into the alley. Casanova the attacker (played with sultry, erotic menace by Annabella Sciorra) slaps Kathleen across the face. Kathleen, her face now entirely imprisoned by the shadows of the fence, looks terrified but still hungry. She says, "Please" again to Casanova. We assume that she means, 'Please Go', but the implication is that she is also saying, 'Please do what you're going to do'. In effect, she wants to be attacked. She is excited. She looks in need. Casanova whispers something.

The vampirism then begins as Casanova bites Kathleen's neck. The camera stays with Kathleen's face as Casanova is biting her neck. Kathleen looks 'high', elevated, delirious, blank and in a kind of rapture. There is a trace in this scene of the sexually charged eroticism between Catherine Deneuve and Susan Sarandon in *The Hunger*. Casanova pulls back and smiles, her earlier impatience replaced with a sickly grin. Blood drips down her chin. She wipes the blood on her lips in a sexual manner and licks her fingers, all the while smiling woozily. Her hunger is appeased. The way she licks and wipes her lips recalls the scene in *King Of New York* where Wesley Snipes wipes a cop's spit from his face and licks his fingers. Both characters exhibit the same obscene relish in their actions. There is a pause and then Casanova stares at Kathleen and whispers the word "collaborator". She walks slowly away and starts climbing up the steps, waving her finger at Kathleen like a mother scolding her child. She calls out, "Wanna know what's gonna happen to you? Wait and see." It's ominous. This scene's closing shots are of the empty steps which, due to the lighting, look even more claustrophobic and menacing than before (a deliberate attempt to quote from the suffocating shadowy menace of Carl Dreyer's *Vampyr*) and of Kathleen holding her neck, her face a mixture of shock and disturbing calm.

Ferrara cuts to a hospital corridor where a large, old woman is hobbling along on a walking stick. In the background we see a cop talking to Kathleen who is holding a huge bandage to her neck. The cop says there's nothing they can do but look out for her attacker. As usual in Ferrara's films, the police are of no use to the troubled victim. Kathleen complains to the cop when he says there's nothing they can do. She sits down alongside a man holding a bandage to his head. What happened to him? Was he attacked? Is he a victim or an attacker?

The next scene, again recalling Carl Dreyer's *Vampyr*, begins with a shot of a door slowly opening from the inside. Kathleen enters the room, a look on her face that is equal parts terror and shock. She locks the door behind her (as Julian West does at the Inn in *Vampyr*). She seems dazed, in shock. She shuffles around her apartment, almost lost. She stands before the bathroom mirror and peels the bandages off. The wound has been bleeding badly; she cries at the sight and tries to clean the wound with a wet tissue. Her transformation is already evident. Ferrara also used a mirror scene in *Ms. 45* to show us the effect that the double rape has had on Thana. From the self-confrontation of the mirror scene, Ferrara cuts to an exquisitely composed shot of Kathleen lying on her bed. She is still crying. She writhes about, gripped by sickness. An overhead shot looks down on her as she writhes and contorts feverishly. She has a flashback to the attack, just as Thana hallucinates the rapist's hand reaching out of the mirror and grabbing her breast.

Everything is designed at this point to illustrate the profound transformation that Kathleen is undergoing. She is, as Cédric Anger suggested, becoming increasingly possessed by evil. She has been 'bitten' by something she indirectly called upon herself. St. John's thematic implication that Kathleen's attack is a result of free will and determinism is already under way. A person chooses to take heroin, to snort cocaine, to drink vodka, to smoke a cigarette. Nobody forces someone else to become an addict: regardless of genetic and behavioural theories, at a certain point the addict chooses to continue being an addict. It is this hunger for self-destruction that St. John is addressing. Kathleen wanted to be bitten by the vampire (wanted to take drugs); the vampire's fangs are St. John's metaphorical interpretation of a drug user's needle. The vampire and the needle both prey on the human bloodstream, both 'take over' the victim and both 'prick' or 'bite' a human's veins.

Kathleen is next seen in a classroom, where her professor (Paul Calderon) is talking about determinism and argues that, "the unsaved don't recognise the sin in their lives", that such people don't suffer "pangs of conscience" because they aren't even aware that evil exists. For the Professor, the unsaved are predestined to hell, and can thus never be brought to conversion. The acceptance of guilt necessitates pain, but can result in forgiveness and freedom – redemption. Then, in a key point of the film, the Professor observes that, "guilt is a sign that God is working out your destiny." This marks a return to the ideas of *Bad Lieutenant*: pain and suffering must be experienced before redemption can become a possible option. When the Professor says that only a 'foolish person' would ignore this, Kathleen has to run out of the classroom; she goes to the bathroom and vomits. Blood trickles out of her mouth. She retches and throws more blood up onto the bathroom floor.

Ferrara cuts from this shot to a shot of Kathleen in hospital where a doctor tells her that the tests they've run show nothing. He also says that it's too early for the AIDS virus to show up. Many critics pounced on this scene and decided that St. John was using vampirism as a metaphor for AIDS: someone 'bites' you with the virus and you become a vampire (dead from the neck down due to the virus). The doctor tells her that she's probably anaemic and leaves. The background music is an ominous drone. Kathleen gets out of her hospital bed, dresses and flees.

The darkly lit scene in her apartment that follows underlines that she has undergone a transformation. She is sitting in a catatonic, trance-like state in the shadows. We next see her having lunch with Jean. She eyes everyone's food with disgust. She looks unwell and tells Jean that she's been in the infirmary. The Kathleen that we saw calmly discussing My Lai in the opening scenes has been replaced with a bitter and hostile Kathleen. She and Jean talk about a paper that they've got to do. Kathleen attacks the free will concept by arguing that she would like to see free will advocates 'get cancer' and then re-appraise the concept. Kathleen is starting to question free will. She resents her choices. She makes an angry aside to Jean about the futility of knowledge. Kathleen then asks Jean if she wants to see an exhibition.

Ferrara cuts to the exhibition which features stills of the Holocaust. Black and white photographs of mass graves and mass murders hang from the walls. Kathleen, narrating via a voice-over, quotes philosopher George Santayana, saying, "those who don't learn from history are doomed to repeat it." Almost as soon as she has said this, she corrects herself: "It is a lie. There is no history. Everything we are is eternally with us." This voice-over accompanies agonising close-ups of skeletons and mountains of bodies, some of the faces of the massacred victims frozen in horrific expressions as they lie piled up on other corpses. St. John is asking us to consider the true nature of evil and Ferrara is putting images to that question. How can we understand such atrocities? How can we understand the Holocaust? How can we understand My Lai? How can we understand such true evil? Kathleen rejects all history and thereby refuses to accept the exhibition as valid. She doesn't believe that she is witnessing documentation of the world's atrocities; she believes that the atrocities live on. As a human being, she sees herself as part of the continuing guilt. Mankind committed these atrocities collectively and mankind lives with the atrocities. The Nazis didn't massacre the Jews, the American soldiers didn't execute women and children at My Lai: we all did. Mankind committed these crimes and the guilt is eternal. Evil, like vampires, can never die. It is condemned to eternal life. The Holocaust, like My Lai, will always be with us. This is something that Cédric Anger also tackled in his *Cahiers du Cinéma* review, writing of Kathleen: "She engenders a civilisation that eliminates all distinction between good and evil. A system where ethical disorder is king and favoured by the forces of destruction. America's moral confusion is the real subject of *The Addiction*."

The way in which Ferrara chooses to present Kathleen's first actions as a vampire hark back to the footage of street bums which floated like a spectre over *The Driller Killer* and *Ms. 45*. Kathleen chooses a down-and-out man as her first victim. In a deliberately contemporary action, she sticks a syringe into his arm and draws blood. When she's finished, blood trickles out of his vein suggestively; we recall the scenes of the Lieutenant and Zoe shooting up heroin in *Bad Lieutenant*.

Kathleen returns to her apartment, places the needle on the sink, sits on the toilet, rolls her sleeve up, seeks out a vein and with shaking hands, injects herself with the blood. Her bony, skinny arm trembles as she forces the needle into a stubborn vein; it is an act of self-rape, self-violation. The trembling shows us how excited, how hungry, how desperate she is to get high. Once she's injected the down-and-out's blood, Kathleen sits back on the toilet, eyes closed, smiling, her eyes all whacked out, a blissful expression on her face. Ferrara and St. John got the idea for this from Dreyer's *Vampyr*. In one scene from Dreyer's film, a doctor drains some of Julian West's blood so that he can inject it into a sickly vampire. As if to reinforce the negative connotations of Kathleen's spiralling habit, Ferrara frames this shot with a dying plant lingering behind Kathleen on the toilet, some of its dead, fallen leaves gathered on the toilet lid. The pulsating music underlines her high. The percussion sounds like a heartbeat. She stares at the painting of a woman hung on the bathroom wall. A montage of drug-induced images cascade through her mind (an early version of similar colour montages that plague Matty when he's high in *The Blackout*): Super 8 footage of a young girl (presumably memories of her childhood) running happily in a garden, until Casanova suddenly attacks her. She gets up and looks in the mirror: there is no reflection (one of Ferrara's vague concessions to the formula of the vampire flick genre). Kathleen has become a vampire.

Her astonished look dissolves into another classroom scene where the Professor is giving his class a reading list: Jean-Paul Sartre's *Being And Nothingness*; Heidegger's *Being And Time*; Kierkegaard's *Sickness Unto Death* and Nietzsche's *Will To Power*. He asks them to read the first 120 pages of *Being and Nothingness* for the next class and then dismisses them. This quite brilliantly adds the suggestion that a person can become addicted to knowledge in a quest for answers. Learning becomes another form of addiction. Kathleen is wearing dark sunglasses even though she's in a dingy classroom (another concession to the vampire genre). The Professor says that he's heard that she's been sick. He checks that she's still on for a date that they've arranged for that night. Kathleen answers his questions in a numb monotone. Before the date, we see her in her apartment, where she has covered every mirror. Kathleen has taken on a blank, expressionless tone and personality – like the infected in *Body Snatchers*, she has become 'one of them'. In a wonderful piece of acting, Lili Taylor stands with her fists raised, like a boxer and announces, "It makes no difference what I do. Whether I draw blood or not." Then she cocks her head, in mock regal, theatrical fashion. It's a bizarre moment, implying that she likes what she's become. She is happy with her choice, indeed, she enjoys it. Her concluding sentence, "It's the violence of my will against theirs", drives home St. John's point. It's free will again – Kathleen has chosen what she has become. Her vampirism is a reassuring certainty in an uncertain world. It's as empowering as any substance or addiction. Her addiction defines who she is. She walks backwards, admiring herself in the non-existent mirrors, her head slightly tilted at an angle. She sees what she wants to see. She stands back and theatrically throws her arms in the air like a dancer.

As she throws her arms in the air and closes her eyes in a blissful moment of joy, a cello breaks into play. Ferrara cuts to a classical painting, then another one, in a moment which recalls a similar sequence from Jean-Luc Godard's *Passion*. A scene in which Kathleen and the Professor sit having coffee is intercut with shots of an old man playing the cello. Kathleen is hostile towards the Professor, jostling with him intellectually and declaring, "I'm coming to terms with my own existence, applying what I've learned to my own being." She says the music is 'sad' and is making her 'depressed', so they leave. On the street outside her apartment, the Professor says he thinks he should go home because he's had a lousy evening, but Kathleen seduces him into coming back to her apartment. Her manner is flirtatious, coy, persuasive. He accepts her invitation; again, he chooses to go inside, even though he doesn't really want to. We're thrown back to Casanova's earlier statement: "Look at me and tell me to go away. Don't ask, tell me." Like Kathleen, the Professor chooses his fate. When we see him going into her apartment, she leads him down steps into a basement, just as Casanova led her down steps and attacked her earlier in the film.

Once inside Kathleen's apartment, Ferrara composes a beautiful shot: the two of them stand in silence, facing each other. A lattice pattern is reflected as a shadow onto the wall behind the two of them, near where a vase of flowers stands on a dresser. The criss-cross shadow again recalls prison bars and refers back to the same shadowplay which fell on the faces of Casanova and Kathleen during the earlier attack. They stand about a foot apart, Kathleen staring seductively at the Professor, hands on hips. She is willing him to be seduced. She offers him a drink, he accepts. He reaches out to touch her chin, she pulls his hand away and grabs him, kissing him passionately. (A glaring editing error follows: the Professor loosens and takes his tie off, throwing it on a dresser; while Kathleen fixes the drinks, the Professor notices the covered mirrors; he is then seen with his tie back on, and he loosens it.) He looks puzzled by the covered mirrors. Kathleen reappears, carrying a tray with a silver candlestick on it, in one of the more obvious references to the vampire genre. Seductively sprawled across her bed, Kathleen drawls, "Dependency is a wonderful thing. It does more for the soul than any formulation of doctorate material." Again, St. John is presenting addiction as a stabilizer, a constant, something which has answers, unlike the My Lai massacre, the Holocaust or academia. The simplicity of chemical addiction replaces the uncertainty and fallability of academic pursuit. Kathleen asks the Professor for his arm. He volunteers it, rolling his sleeve up, choosing to let her inject him with a drug. The next we see of him, he's laid out on the bed. His arm bears two wounds: one is marked 'IN' and the other marked 'OUT'. Kathleen sits on the bed, more vamp than vampire – dark nail polish, hair long and elegant – flicking through his wallet and taking dollar bills out.

Ferrara then cuts to shots of Kathleen walking along a street, rap music blasting out in the background. She gets harassed by a couple of black youths. She talks to one, who starts coming on to her. This time, falsely strengthened by her addiction, Kathleen is confident and as brash as those trying to intimidate her. This threatening scene is followed by a cut to a silent, dimly lit library. As Kathleen walks around the library, she delivers a deadpan voice-over: "This is a graveyard. Rows of crumbling tombstones . . . we're all drawn here like flies." The timbre of her voice recalls Martin Sheen's voice-over in Coppola's *Apocalypse Now*. She sits down next to a fresh-faced anthropology student (played by Kathryn Erbe). They talk for a while and the student invites Kathleen back to her dorm for an all-night studying session. (Again, she chooses to invite Kathleen back – it's an issue of free will.) At this point, Ferrara abruptly interjects more atrocity footage. We see dead bodies lying everywhere in a hospital. It turns out to be a report on TV. Kathleen is watching it with blood on her lips. The anthropology student is in the bathroom, holding a cloth to the wound. She is in shock and as distressed as Kathleen was after being attacked by Casanova.

Ferrara sets up a perfect shot. Kathleen comes into the bathroom. The student has the door to her bathroom medicine chest open. The camera focuses on Kathleen's face while the student's face is seen only as a reflection in the mirror. This is, of course, playing on the fact that Kathleen, as a fully fledged vampire, has lost her reflection. This girl still has hers, but not for long. Kathleen barracks the weeping student, snapping: "What the hell were you thinking? Why didn't you just tell me to go?" She's attacking the student for being shocked at the outcome of her choice, taking on Casanova's role. The student becomes hysterical, says she didn't tell Kathleen to go because she thought that if she did, then Kathleen would hurt her. She then asks Kathleen if she's going to get sick. This was clue number two for critics favouring the film as a drawn-out AIDS metaphor. Kathleen tells her that she won't be any sicker than she already is. The student gets angrier, asking Kathleen how she can be so glib after inflicting such a wound. Kathleen responds by telling her that it was her own decision. Kathleen then says that it isn't her 'indifference' that should be considered, it's her 'astonishment'. What she is attacking is the girl's shock at what happened. As far as she's concerned, the girl asked for it to happen. She 'wanted' it, so why is she now so surprised and guilty?

In the following scene, Kathleen and Jean run into each other in a corridor. Kathleen wants a fix of blood, but she runs off to escape having to attack Jean. She goes back and finds the black kid who came on to her on the street. She tells him she wants him. She takes him out into the street and attacks him. Is St. John attacking the male's promiscuity or Kathleen's revenge on someone who sexually intimidated her? Her predatory nature bears a hint of Thana's reactive murder spree in *Ms. 45*. As she overpowers him, she again asks him to tell her to leave, but he is no different to the Professor: he wants her, and by implication wants what she will do to him. After this scene, a get-well plant from Jean is delivered. Kathleen tips the soil all over the floor and plays with it, while Cypress Hill thunder away in the background, singing: "I want to get high." Ferrara throws subtlety to one side and goes for the jugular of St. John's screenplay by cutting to a shot of two guys getting high. Kathleen sits to one side of them shooting herself up.

Jean and Kathleen talk again. Jean asks Kathleen when she started smoking; she doesn't respond. Kathleen says that she's dating a Vietnam Veteran who works in a slaughterhouse and that he kills cows for a living. (This takes us back to the atrocity footage. She says that he was turned into a slaughterer after his service in Vietnam.) Jean is on a different wavelength, asking Kathleen why she isn't working on her dissertation. This prompts Kathleen to launch into an attack on philosophy: "guilt doesn't pass with time – it's eternal." This follows on from the story about the Vietnam Vet as well as the atrocity footage – it is a further denial that mankind can learn from history, and is therefore capable of redemption. A Vietnam soldier is taught to kill: once the war is over, he's stuck with the hunger to kill. It doesn't go away. Kathleen then tells Jean about the mirrors and how she can't stand to see herself. This is as much a reference to vampirism as to an addict who is losing control and consumed with self-contempt. We assume that she has dabbled in heroin before but has now got out of control with it. In an interview, Ferrara commented of her character: "She dabbles in heroin. She's one of those white intellectuals who has a chippy habit" (i.e. that she plays around with it and then loses control).

Kathleen takes Jean into the bathroom on campus and dramatically pulls out a tooth, explaining that she's 'rotten' inside. Jean begs her friend to get some help. This time, as Kathleen grabs Jean, she amends the usual 'tell me to go' line to: "Look sin in the face and tell it to go." Kathleen believes that she has become a living embodiment of evil. As before, Jean's pleading (and she pleads more than the Professor or the library student) is mostly led by the ambiguous use of the word 'please'. Kathleen eventually bites her, but this time we don't see her smiling afterwards. Sombre piano notes are picked out as she sits alone in her apartment. The hunger has become habit. She now needs the fix of blood more than she needs the high. It's become an issue of maintenance over hunger. There is no pleasure to be derived from the act anymore: nothing is enough. She is simply sustaining her habit. This development recalls Zoe's monologue to the Lieutenant about vampirism: "We gotta' eat away at ourselves 'til there's nothing left but appetite."

Ferrara introduces Christopher Walken's incendiary cameo as a vampire (Peina) with a high-angle shot that quotes straight from the scene in Howard Hawks' *Scarface* where Tony Carmonte's sister throws change down to an organ grinder. Peina is wandering along a windy street, talking to himself, a book in hand. Kathleen approaches to attack him but he simply turns to face her and mocks her, using the recurring vampire motif. He says that he's been 'fasting' for forty years, lectures her on her addiction and then invites her back to his apartment. They journey up in an elevator; Kathleen doesn't speak. Peina talks of learning to live on a little, of controlling dependency with a disciplined self-will. Until he takes his coat off, Peina has been standing lecturing her with his book still in his hand. This was Kathleen's world: books, knowledge, education and learning. Now she has a vampire professor, who lectures her as her professor-boyfriend did. Peina talks of Nietzsche's ideas: how mankind has always struggled to go beyond good and evil; to view the world in terms other than 'good' and 'evil'. He is an experienced vampire: he is able to eat, to work, to go out in the daylight, to 'defecate'. He drops in various obvious literary references that relate to the twin themes of vampirism and addiction: Beckett, Sartre, the drug addicted prose of William Burroughs' *The Naked Lunch*, the syphilitic despair of a line of poetry by Baudelaire. When Kathleen asks Peina who he is and what he wants from her, he corrects her, asking her what she wants from him. This takes us back to the issue of free will: she 'chose' him. She sought Peina out, first as a victim, but allowed herself to be brought back to his apartment because she felt that he could teach her something. By asking him what he wants from her, Kathleen is really admitting that she no longer believes in free will. She now believes in 'good' and 'evil'. Peina has arrived to explain what happens when you take ideology beyond good and evil.

The next scene shows Peina in a bathrobe, hair messed up, washing his face. Kathleen is slumped down, bleeding. He is trying to detox her, to teach her how to control her habit. Peina is enforcing a 'cold turkey' scenario onto her. His actions (biting her, draining her of her blood) contradict his lecture about discipline. In draining Kathleen, supposedly in the name of help, he has revealed his own inability to resist a fix. The paradox that lies at the heart of his actions and words is yet another of the film's complex polarities. Peina lectures Kathleen on what comes beyond dividing the world into good and evil: discipline. As Kathleen lies writhing in agony on the bathroom floor, Peina explains to her that he controls his 'habit' with his 'will'. He has replaced insatiable appetite with discipline. Again, this is a choice, an exercising of free will. In one very disturbing scene which follows, Kathleen tries to cut her wrists and suck her own blood. Peina mocks her, pointing out that she can't kill 'what's already dead' and that she'll live eternally now that she's a vampire. Peina then leaves the apartment. Kathleen is left inside, seemingly a captive of his attempts to forcibly teach her what he has learned. It's like academia at gunpoint.

The assumption that Peina has locked her in his apartment is immediately overturned when Kathleen, soon unable to survive without a fix, flees Peina's apartment. Again, she is exercising her right to free will. If she wanted to learn to control her addiction, then she had the option to stay with Peina. Instead, she chooses to further her addiction. She is next seen staggering along a deserted street, banging on store grills and writhing on the sidewalk. A passer-by stops to help her, thinking she must be having a fit and she attacks him. The emotive droning music emphasises Kathleen's aching hunger for her high. Ferrara fades to more atrocity footage and there is another Kathleen voice-over as she studies the photographs at the exhibition once more. While looking at a photograph of a mass grave, she comments, "I finally understand what all this is. Now I see, Good Lord, how we must look from out there. Our addiction is evil. The propensity in our evil lies in our weakness before it." She then quotes Kierkegaard saying that she believes he was right when he said that, "There is an awful precipice before us", but offering the qualification, "He was wrong about the leap. There's a difference between jumping and being pushed." These lines are delivered in an ingeniously framed shot: the camera aligns Kathleen with a long dug-out trench of a mass grave. The lighting and camera angle combine with the placing of Kathleen within the shot to create the illusion that she too is a body in the mass grave.

Ferrara then dissolves to a scene where Kathleen is sitting at a desk and typing her dissertation into a lap-top computer. Her previous comments are now revealed to be far from random musings – they are part of her work. The voice-over completes her train of thought on Kierkegaard's theories: "You reach a point where you are forced to face your own needs and the fact you can't terminate the situation settles on you with full force." Addiction has now become her *raison d'être*; she is defined by what she needs. Her dependency no longer gives her pleasure, it is a necessity. Nothing else matters. This is what Ferrara was talking about when he said, "You are what you're addicted to. All we are are addictions. Addictions to evil, the desire not to be evil, to whatever."

Ferrara then cuts to a scene where Kathleen is explaining her paper to the departmental examination board. She concludes that her analysis is all about, "Our impact on other egos." As this sentence trails out, the screen fades to black. The truth has dawned on Kathleen. We see her staring at her doctorate certificate, her hair put up in a tidy bun. She looks icy, different, in control. We start to wonder if she has built on Peina's advice, if she has learned to conquer her addiction. She invites an elderly professor to a gathering that she says she's having later that evening to celebrate her doctorate. Her boyfriend-professor, also now a vampire, interacts with her in a strangely blank manner, rather like the emotionless exchanges of the pod people in *Body Snatchers*.

We next see Kathleen in the back of a taxi cab, putting on earrings. Her voice-over floats above an acoustic guitar. She puts on lipstick (just as Thana applied lipstick before the Halloween party in *Ms. 45*). She is getting dressed up for her graduation party. We have never seen her seem so composed, so in control, so feminine (another parallel with *Ms. 45*). The voice-over suggests that Kathleen has come to terms with her addiction by intellectualising it: "There is a dual nature to *The Addiction*. It satisfies the hunger which evil engenders but it also dulls our perceptions so we are helped to forget how ill we really are. We drink to escape the fact we're alcoholics. Existence is the search for relief from our habit. And our habit is the only relief we can find." St. John is no longer hiding his ideas or intentions behind the veils of free will, determinism, existentialism and phenomenology but instead expressing his ideas simply and obviously. A vampire and an addict are one and the same thing. Both need an external substance to stay alive; both drain the people who surround them. Kathleen has reached the catch-22 of addiction. In order to seek relief from alcoholism, an alcoholic must turn to more alcohol. The disease feeds *The Addiction* and vice versa. This is the entrapment that Kathleen was talking about in her dissertation. She became an addict and now has to suffer the consequences of her choice. When she was pondering Kierkegaard's idea about the existential precipice, she was debating the question of whether someone becomes addicted to something because they choose to or because they are 'pushed'. Does an addict leap into addiction? Or is an addict pushed into addiction?

After this scene in the taxi cab, St. John raises the possibility of Kathleen's redemption, her passage from 'unsaved' to 'saved'. She gets out of the cab and approaches a missionary (played by Michael Imperioli) who is preaching God's word on the street. He is a believer. Kathleen takes his hand and asks him to 'come inside'. He turns her down, saying he can't and then adds, "God loves you." He is the first of her intended victims who "looks her in the eye and tells her to go away . . . and means it." His will is stronger than hers. He disproves her theory that she has done evil simply because she is inherently evil. Unlike her other victims, the missionary does not choose her or what she might do to him. His faith has led him to be saved. The fact that he can reject her advance makes Kathleen realise how weak she is. She chose to become a vampire, an addict. He has chosen not to. He presses a leaflet into her hand.

Ferrara cuts to a close-up of the leaflet which Kathleen is holding. The front of it portrays a painting of Jesus Christ on the cross. Kathleen is holding this leaflet in her hand. In the background, we hear the missionary saying, "God loves you, brother." The heavily symbolic tranquillity of this moment is interrupted by a dissolve to a chilling scene in a cluttered room. Kathleen is screaming and acting in a deranged fashion. It's a magnificent piece of acting by Lili Taylor. She snarls and howls like one possessed. She tears at her clothes, lashes out at the objects in the room, all the while shouting, "I will not submit!" St. John is suggesting two things here that she doesn't want to 'submit' to: God and her addiction. The realisations that came from encountering the stronger personality of the missionary have shaken her up. She now wants to choose God but her vampirism wants her to choose addiction. Her pain is intense enough for her to want God. The guilt which she recognised during the writing of her dissertation ("Our impact on other egos") has now come full circle from the first classroom scene where the professor said, "guilt is a sign that God is working out your destiny."

Kathleen is trying to go cold turkey in a back room at the party, where Jean finds her. Kathleen is bouncing off the walls. She orders Jean to go and find a female victim whose clothes Kathleen will fit because she's torn her own while thrashing about violently. Jean finds a woman who goes straight to the room without questioning why. Kathleen attacks her, bites her and then walks out into the party wearing the woman's dress. She also has her hair fully down now, making her look seductive and 'ripe'. Once high, she is confident and in control. When she's craving her fix, she's withdrawn and sickly. The party is mostly full of Kathleen's victims. She gives a short speech thanking the faculty and saying how glad she is to have attained her doctorate and then grabs the elderly professor who she specifically invited and bites him.

This triggers a vampiric orgy as the vampires (including Casanova and the earlier victims) prey on fresh victims, and blood gushes freely. Asked about this blood-overload, Ferrara chuckled, "I like that black blood. We used Hershey's syrup." The carefully orchestrated chaos of the vampiric frenzy is very similar to the Halloween party at the climax to *Ms. 45*. Again, as in the earlier film, the party head-count is made up of Ferrara's family, friends and friends of friends. At one point, the mass writhing of the vampires almost replicates some of the disturbing atrocity material, where bodies were stacked up on one another. To reinforce the full ideological circle that St. John is trying to create using this parallel, Kathleen overdoses on the victims' blood. After the party, we see Kathleen, her face and clothes soaked in blood, wandering about in the street. She falls to the sidewalk. Passers-by call an ambulance. A very disturbing slow-motion shot of Kathleen being wheeled through a hospital corridor on an emergency trolley lends further parallels between the atrocity footage and the atrocities that we inflict on ourselves. Kathleen begins the film wondering how people commit such atrocities. How did American soldiers do what they did in My Lai? How did the Nazis do what they did in the Holocaust? Now, laid out on the trolley, she is as disturbing an image as some of the sights in the footage. St. John's message seems to be that we are all capable of atrocity and evil, but only if we choose to be.

The final scenes show Kathleen in a hospital bed. A nurse tends to her. Kathleen mutters, "Let me die." The camera pulls back to reveal a crucifix on the wall above her bed, a classic Ferrara trademark shot. From somewhere out in the corridor, a child is singing the nursery rhyme 'London Bridge Is Falling Down'. Kathleen asks the nurse to open the blinds: either to die as vampires cannot tolerate light or as Peina suggested, to learn to live with the light; to learn discipline and control. She lies in bed, gasping for breath once the blinds are open: she's seen the 'light'. Just as we think she might die or become 'saved', the camera first shoots back to the crucifix above her bed and then suddenly to the blinds being roughly snapped shut by Casanova who stands in shades, with a cigarette in her mouth. She picks up Peina's literary thread by paraphrasing Dante's *Inferno*. After sarcastically addressing Kathleen as 'doctor' (as in her doctorate), Casanova snarls a quotation at her: "we're not sinners because we sin but we sin because we are sinners . . . we're not evil because of the evil we do, but we do evil because we are evil." Annabella Sciorra delivers this monologue in the same charismatic, rhetorical terms that Peina used. She also delivers her lines in a kind of purring sexual fashion: she's a seductive vampire, her posture and words pregnant with pure evil, and she confuses Kathleen. She offers the opposite path: telling Kathleen to forget 'divine rest' and just accept that she is evil. Casanova advocates acceptance over a quest for redemption. Kathleen can't accept this however, because of her encounter with the missionary and also because of the extent to which *The Addiction* grips her. She has lost all control of herself. She cannot attain Peina's degree of discipline but then again, if Peina had abstained for forty years as he said, then why did he attack her? He claimed it was to help her but in the light of Casanova's speech, we now wonder if it was just another deceit of evil, another 'junkie' line.

Once Casanova has gone, Ferrara shows us a priest in the hospital corridors. He comes in to see Kathleen; sinister, ominous music marks his arrival, underscoring a meeting between good and evil, priest and vampire, each an implement of God or the Devil. The priest asks her how she feels, if she wants something. He has a rosary and a bible with him. She whispers that she wants to make a confession. He asks her if she is a Catholic. She simply replies that she was 'baptised'. He asks her what she wants to confess and she says, "God. Forgive me." His response – and this is black humour indeed on the part of Ferrara and St. John – includes the line, "and by the power of the holy spirit, keep you in eternal life." This is of course a darkly ironic blessing for a priest to give to a vampire who is doomed to eternal life anyway. The priest puts the chafer in Kathleen's mouth and says, "the body of Christ". Kathleen then says, "Amen", accepting God and, apparently, dies.

However, we should regard the ending as metaphorical. We see Kathleen in a cemetery, placing a flower before her own grave, on which is written: "Kathleen Conklin. October 31st 1967–November 1st 1994." Taken literally, this means that she died just as she turned twenty-seven years old. The other inscription on the tomb reads: "I am the Resurrection. John XI: 25." It's tempting to wonder if the dates on the gravestone relate to a period of addiction in the life of someone that St. John knew or knows. Kathleen walks away from her own grave. Her voice-over closes the film with the lines: "To face what we are in the end, we stand before the light. And our true nature is revealed. Self-revelation is annihilation of self."

There are twin meanings at work here. For a vampire to 'stand before the light' the act itself would be one of self-annihilation. For an addict to 'stand before the light', the act would be one of simultaneous self-revelation and self-annihilation. To relinquish an addiction is to undergo a death of self. It is the death of an element of the addict's identity. Taken literally, the voice-over originates from Kathleen after she has accepted God, quit heroin and started an entirely new 'born again' life as one who was saved. It seems likely that St. John intended us to read the closing scenes as a movement towards redemption as Kathleen accepts God and is reborn, moments before death.

Alternatively, in having Kathleen visit the grave of the 'self' she discovered and lost through addiction – the self she subsequently annihilated in order to start a new life after the revelation granted to her by her encounter with the missionary, St. John could be suggesting that the death is entirely metaphorical. He could be saying that Kathleen's life up to the point where she accepted God and conquered her addiction was negated by her twin choices: God and the abandonment of addiction. Her 'will' was stronger than addiction and evil. The will to convert/to be born again was stronger than the will to 'use'. Consequently she was freed from the prison of her addiction and began a new life. In visiting her grave, she is visiting who she was and mourning the death of a reliable self, an identity created to keep despair at arm's length.

The Funeral 1996

"Johnny was out there, he was asking to die. Screwing the wife of a mobster, breaking with traditions, how long did he expect to live? It's a just end for him" –Abel Ferrara, talking to *Time Out*.

"It isn't the style of gangster films that interested me for *The Funeral*, only their foundations. Stories about families and vengeance" – Abel Ferrara, talking to *Cahiers du Cinéma*.

The Funeral is centred around three gangster brothers: Ray (played by Christopher Walken), Chez (played by Chris Penn) and Johnny (played by Vincent Gallo) and is set during the Great Depression in the 1930s. Great attention is paid to recreating period detail. Shots of Johnny in his coffin bookend the film. Early scenes that roll with the credits show the coffin being delivered to Ray's house; the closing shot is of someone shutting the coffin's lid. In between lies a three-day period of open casket mourning, during which Ray quenches his thirst for revenge, his wife Jean (played by Annabella Sciorra) tries to talk him out of it, the women mourn Johnny's death, the men look sombre in public and crack up in private and Chez loses his mind and kills Ray, himself and their bodyguards.

   Johnny, who we learn was only 22 years old, is killed by a young gangster, who in turn is killed by Ray. It's hard not to see the death of Johnny as a reference to the death of St. John's own son. The scene in which Ray sits alone by Johnny's casket and delivers a monologue of devastating intensity feels as though it must have been written from personal experience. Indeed, Ray, assuming the paternal role that he has always adopted with Johnny, talks to his dead brother like a son. It's chilling. There is nothing remotely 'created' about it, it flows freely, as if St. John was re-living his own son's death.

Every aspect of the *mise en scène* reflects the funereal mood. Ray's house is filled with flowers of all colours which contrast with the browns, greys, blacks and whites of everything and everyone in the house. Scenes around the coffin are beautifully lit in a soft golden yellow and earth brown light. The soundtrack score's mournful tone has the mood of an elegy to it. There is a great focus on the family in *The Funeral*. The characters are believable; the details of their everyday lives are flawlessly integrated into the narrative, something which cannot be said of much of Ferrara's previous work – he seemed to experience some difficulty in creating warm family settings. Much of this new-found warmness can be attributed to the wonderful acting of Annabella Sciorra and Isabella Rossellini (Clara, Chez's wife).

Jean is tough, assertive, intelligent, at odds with her husband's past (as a gangster and, as a flashback tells us, an unwilling inheritor of a Mafia lifestyle) and his lust to avenge Johnny's death. He wants revenge, she wants peace. At one point, after he argues on the porch that everything wrong in the world is God's fault and that if he commits a sin then it's God fault for not stopping him, she tells him that she will take the children and leave him after the funeral. Ray doesn't answer, he simply sits staring into the night; like Frank White, Ray is introspective and closed off. He knows that, in his own words, he will "roast in hell" when he dies, so as far as he's concerned, it's already too late. The flashback to Italy or Sicily where a man (presumably his father) orders the young Ray to shoot an equally young enemy tells us that he never had any choice in the matter. As he tells Johnny's killer before shooting him, "once you pull the trigger, there's no going back." As much as he believes that he is damned and accepts it, Jean prays and hopes for his repentance and redemption.

The Funeral is a grandiose tragedy. It is a gangster film that is being eaten away from the inside, consumed by its characters. This Nicholas St. John screenplay sets spiritual torment in the midst of the gangster genre. Ferrara has said that he received the screenplay from St. John and barely had to touch it because, "it was so sweet, so beautiful that I didn't really find it necessary." St. John plays off the kinds of scenes and scenarios that the audience expects from a gangster film against his own personal trademark battle between good and evil. The women in the film suffer because of their husbands and the men suffer because of their fathers. St. John strips these men of the superficial seductiveness of the gangster lifestyle – Jean tells Helen at one point that there's nothing 'glamorous' about being a gangster – and makes them vulnerable. The kid brother Johnny is a Communist and aspiring intellectual, middle brother Chez is mentally ill (like their father, who eventually killed himself) and Ray is the closed off, steely figure who has taken on the paternal role. These are not muscular, brutal gangsters: Johnny says books, the radio and the movies are all he lives for; Chez repeatedly breaks down; Ray is tormented by his absent faith and imminent damnation.

When a priest visits the open casket gathering, Ray goes outside and sits alone in his car. Jean comes out and asks him to come in. He says he won't go inside until, "the asshole leaves". Jean pleads with him to go in, but he snaps, "I'm not about to start with all that stuff at this point." For Ray, it's too late; for Jean, it's never too late. She is a devout Catholic, he is damned to hell.

Shortly after, when they talk on the porch late one night, Ray responds to her pleas to let Johnny's killers go free, by offering a theological critique of Catholic teachings. Ray is well versed in the subject, but can't accept the teachings. He avoids the priest, Jean is on first name terms with him. As Ray sees it, if he does something wrong or commits a sin, it's God's fault for not giving him the 'grace' to do the right thing. He blames God for his predicament, in a denial of free will which recalls both Kathleen's dilemma in *The Addiction* and the bad Lieutenant's crisis of faith. When Jean, like his brother's killer, suggests that by not killing someone to avenge Johnny's death he would be making the world a better place, Ray retorts simply that he didn't create the world. Ray is at war with God, Johnny was at war with his legacy (and also society) and Chez is at war with his father's legacy and ultimately himself. Jean and her values and beliefs are at war with Ray's values and beliefs.

Clara is a victim, frequently terrorised by her husband Chez. The scene towards the end of the film where he subjects her to what is essentially marital rape makes for horrific viewing. Just watching Clara's clasped hands is enough to turn the stomach (and brings to mind Thana's clenched fists during the first rape in *Ms. 45*). She appears to love Chez blindly, and even kisses and comforts him after her ordeal. Clara, like Jean, is repeatedly seen with a small cross hung around her neck. Both women are devout Catholics, witness the scenes of them praying and mourning beside the coffin and with the Catholic priest. Even when Clara tries to persuade Chez to go to an overseas treatment hospital for the mentally ill, she has to finish her monologue by begging him not to get angry. The suggestion is that her abuse is long term.

Clara is the victim; Jean is the worldly-wise woman. Early on when her sons make too much noise on the stairs playing with toy guns, she is the one to take the guns away from them and scold Ray for even buying such toys for them in the first place. She also blames Ray for turning Johnny into a gangster. We can tell from Johnny's death scene and his interest in workers' rights, Communism and the cinema, that he isn't a typical gangster. He's playing at being an intellectual but ultimately he is trapped within a male legacy that can only end in despair. Chez's final shooting spree is an attempt to put an end to the legacy. The only problem is that we have already seen Ray's kids playing gangsters with their guns. A flashback shows us that Chez has been traumatised ever since he eavesdropped on a conversation (which took place beside another open casket) from which he learned that his father committed suicide by shooting himself in his car. He was subsequently denied a Catholic burial. By killing himself and Ray at the end of the film, he provides Ray's sons with the potential to lead the same emotionally damaged lives.

The Funeral opens with a scene of Humphrey Bogart in *The Petrified Forest*. Bogart delivers a classic macho line: "The first time any of you makes a wrong move, I'm gonna kill the whole lotta you." Another character calls out that he wants to get his life insurance papers first; Bogart's character snaps back, "What do you want with your insurance papers? Are you expecting to die?" The voice pipes back, "You guessed it, Mr. Maple." We get a sneak shot of Johnny sitting in a cinema watching the film. It's a dark touch: the dialogue from the film anticipates its viewer's fate. Johnny will end up being gunned down as he comes out of the performance. The opening scenes of the film show Johnny's coffin being taken into Ray's home and are accompanied by a second prophetic clue: Billie

Holiday singing 'Gloomy Sunday', an infamous torch song about suicide. In using this piece of music, Ferrara makes two subtle suggestions to his audience. Firstly, he implies that Johnny committed suicide, in the sense that he brought his own death upon himself. Secondly, he mischievously alludes to Chez's suicide at the film's climax. These early scenes of Johnny's coffin being carried into the house and opened link specifically with the film's closing shot, which is of the lid to Johnny's coffin being closed. It's as if St. John wanted the coffin to be open and then closed, like the covers of a book being opened at the beginning of the story and closed at the end. This also compares with the way in which Johnny has been living his life, like an open book: blatantly having an affair with Gaspare's wife, championing Communism in spite of his brother's disapproval, firebombing Enrico's trucks.

When we first see Ray, his face wears a deep frown and his tie is undone, suggesting that his character is that of an inwardly troubled man. He sees off *The Funeral* parlour workers and then stands alone with Jean who is sitting before a brightly coloured spread of food on the kitchen table. The composition of this shot brings out the reds of the tomatoes which clash with Ray and Jean's black clothes and the white walls. The almost painterly composition inevitably recalls Jean-Luc Godard's wonderful use of colour.

These early scenes set Jean up as a beautiful, contemplative, thoughtful woman and Ray as a dark, complex individual. Two ensuing scenes show us what is going on behind Ray's wrought iron exterior. Firstly, flowers are delivered for the funeral and secondly, his young sons run around playing with toy guns and making a noise. In both scenes, the steely, introspective wall that surrounds him is replaced by a volcanic rage. He explodes, for reasons that we can only guess at. All we can sense is that he is coming out from behind his frozen reserve, emotion overwhelming him. We realise that although Chez demonstrates his father's legacy and temper most explicitly, Ray also has the rage in his blood. Later, after it seems as though he has let rival gangster Gaspare go free, he coldly orders one of his henchmen to kill Gaspare, adding that he wants him killed on his 'front lawn'. You can feel his rage gaining momentum as he then corrects himself, saying he wants Gaspare killed in front of his wife. All three brothers have inherited their father's madness, literal and otherwise. Johnny is the odd one out and he gets killed because of it; he wants to break the cycle but he doesn't know how. We see him go from attending a Communist meeting to helping to raid and firebomb a delivery truck – all in support of the 'workers'.

The two homes (Ray's and Chez's) are overrun with religious iconography: crucifixes, statuettes of saints and religious paintings. In one telling scene, Jean lectures Johnny's girlfriend, Helen, over whiskeys about the wrongs of the gangster lifestyle. Jean tells her that they should almost be celebrating the fact that she won't be marrying into the family. Jean has a crucifix necklace hanging around her neck, Helen doesn't. St. John revels in these contradictions: he conspires to make Jean, the most religiously devout character in the film, the wife of a criminal. The tension in their marriage, a struggle between purity and impurity, is explicit.

When Jean comes out of their home to talk to Ray in his car, after the priest arrives at the funeral, the scene is shot to mimic a confession. An exchange of technically brilliant reverse shots alternately places either Jean or Ray in close-up while the other is out of focus. She sticks her head in through the passenger door window, Ray sits at the wheel staring straight ahead. She is like the priest at the confession booth window, he is the sinner who doesn't want to confess. When Jean asks the priest to pray for her family, he is firm with her, saying, "The only way anything is going to change is if this family has a total reversal of heart." He calls her family 'atheists'. Questions are demanded of the viewer here: why is a devout Catholic living with an atheistic, murderous gangster? And vice versa. It's the same tension that weaves throughout *Snake Eyes*: the virtuous or reformed woman and the impure, troubled man.

Clara is less openly religious compared to Jean and in the scene in which she talks with the priest, her conversation is mundane and revolves around a type of food that the guests are eating. The priest appears irritated by her and by what she is saying. His speech about the family being doomed follows only minutes later. Jean is the only one who wants to escape. Her whiskey-fuelled confession to Helen about how she'd gone to college for two years before meeting Ray is both sad and regretful. She says that she has nothing left but memories and ideas. She is trapped in her relationship with Ray.

When she stands on the porch and tells him that maybe she might take the kids and leave after *The Funeral*, he says nothing. She goes inside, smashes a glass and then unburdens herself to Helen over the whiskey. Jean is lonely and isolated, she seeks redemption for her family. Her wish is made all the more desperate as she knows that Ray is doomed as clearly as he does.

The confessional conversation between Jean and Ray through his car window coincides with a flashback to Ray's childhood. This is the most explicit homage to *The Godfather* trilogy in the film. We see the young Ray in Italy. An older man, we presume his father, hands him a gun. A young beaten and bloodied man sits tied to a chair, and the older man tells Ray to either shoot and kill him or let him live. This scene provides the seeds for Ray's problems in adult life. Ferrara doesn't make the outcome of the scene clear. After a gunshot, the father figure hands Ray the bullet from the gun, telling him to keep it because it will cost him dearly. We assume that Ray has killed the bloodied captive. However, later we see a member of Ray's intimate circle (played by Victor Argo) who bears a striking resemblance to the victim. Did Ray spare him? If so, then Ray's downfall is that he can't just kill without contemplating his actions first. He lacks a cold-blooded killer's instinct; a part of him must still believe in hell and in damnation. He can't share Jean's blind faith but neither can he admit to himself that he's an atheist. He's neither a true gangster nor a true Catholic. He's suspended in a moral no-man's-land.

When Ray's henchmen tell him that they've picked up a mechanic who they believe killed Johnny, he is eager to go and see the suspect. Again, Ray is confronted with a beaten and bloodied young man, in a scene that relates directly to the flashback. As the henchmen beat the kid, Ray asks him if it's true that he killed Johnny. The kid replies that he killed Johnny only because Johnny beat his girlfriend up and raped her. The camera closely follows Ray's face as he tries to digest this information. We can see his thoughts reeling. He is thrown by this new story and being a man of honour, he finds his thirst for revenge stalled. He asks the kid who his girlfriend is, when the incident took place, how he knew it was Johnny who did it. After receiving answers to all his questions, we see Ray turn to his henchmen for support. His resolve is weakening in the face of what sounds like a plausible story. It's his human spirit coming through. Ray has a conscience – it's clearly damaged, but it stalls his 'success' as a gangster.

Ray decides to take the kid off on his own. His tone of voice changes: we feel that he's prepared to let the kid go if the story is true. He asks the kid what he'll do if he lets him go. He asks him if he'll marry the girl, and the kid plays Ray (and us as viewers) along. The turning point comes when Ray stops the car at a deserted space. They get out of the car and in a telling moment, Ray asks the kid to tell the truth as, "God sees it." This is not Ray's language, it's the language of his wife. He is struggling with the situation. He tells the kid that he wants to believe him, that his wife who doesn't even know him has pleaded for his freedom. Ferrara stretches audience belief: we begin to feel that Ray's theological debate may lead to forgiveness. We feel that Ray will forgive the kid and in turn be forgiven for his own sins by Jean. Shades of the bad Lieutenant's dilemma spring to mind. Jean's plea for forgiveness loosely mirrors the nun's act of forgiveness. Then St. John introduces a killer twist, by having the kid admit that it was a bullshit story, that he made it up, that he was sore at Johnny for beating him up. Our sympathies instantly shift. When the kid, like Jean, tries to talk Ray into letting him go on the basis that he will be doing a good turn, Ray says that he already knows that he's going to "roast in hell" and shoots him.

When we first see Chez, he arrives at Ray's house with his wife, Clara, and their children. Of all the men present, Chez gives the most emotional reaction when he sees Johnny's corpse laid out before him. First he gets tears in his eyes and then he explodes into such a rage that Ray has to calm him down. A later scene, beginning with Chez sitting alone in his car, explains the depth of feeling demonstrated here – a flashback shows Chez learning of his father's suicide. Thus his psychotic reaction when he sees Johnny in his coffin: it triggers memories of his father's death. This also suggests why we so often see Ray and Chez brooding alone in their cars. They are both reliving their father's suicide. In Chez's case, he is preparing to follow in his father's footsteps.

St. John uses the female characters as ciphers for his more explicitly religious material. Ferrara delivers a marvellously composed shot of the women praying in Italian and weeping over Johnny's coffin. Jean looks striking in her black veil and dress. Another scene has Helen with Jean in her bedroom and comes after a scene of Chez alone in his car. That scene fades to darkness; then we become aware that another scene has begun in the dark. Suddenly light appears as Jean strikes a match and lights a candle before a statuette of a saint. This is perhaps the most breathtakingly beautiful scene in the entire film, a moment of staggering visual richness. The statuette's red dress is wonderfully framed by the golden and brown tones of the lighting. Helen asks Jean who the statuette represents. Jean replies that it's Saint Agnes, who slit her throat rather than accept the unwelcome advances of an older man. Chillingly, when Helen asks Jean if she prays to the saint, Jean says that she doesn't and that she only has the statuette to remind her what happens, "when you say no". This captures the degree to which Jean feels trapped by her marriage. Choral music plays in the background, complementing her sad and regretful mood.

The scene closes with Helen and Jean getting into Jean's bed together and trying to get some sleep. The next scene shows Ray sitting downstairs alone beside his brother's coffin. It's a direct reference to the scene in Bertolucci's *Last Tango In Paris* in which Marlon Brando sits beside his dead wife and talks to her. Again, the same earthy hues frame the scene and a blue candle adds an eerie atmosphere. When asked by *Cahiers du Cinéma*, "If there was a single moment – no matter how fleeting – that encapsulates cinema for you, what would that be?", Ferrara responded, "Robert De Niro and Harvey Keitel in the back room in *Mean Streets*; the incredible long take inside the small room from a low angle in *Touch Of Evil*; Christopher Walken sitting at his brother's casket in my new movie *The Funeral*; the scene where I kill a sleeping bum with a power drill in my old movie *The Driller Killer*."

The third scene which Ferrara alludes to is undoubtedly one of the great moments of cinema. Christopher Walken conjures up a performance which is hair-raising. Various elements contribute to this dramatic effect: gestures that he makes with his hands; facial expressions – particularly the way Walken uses his eyes; the act of covering the bullet-holes in Johnny's corpse with his hands; the way he whispers; the climax to the monologue where he sounds simultaneously angry at Johnny for getting himself killed and jealous of Johnny for being at peace. It's undoubtedly Walken's finest piece of acting and testimony to Ferrara's reputation for getting the best out of an actor or actress. It's also worth noting that Walken's performance, which seems like the result of much thought and preparation was in fact pulled together in a very short space of time. His character unleashes a torrent of feeling in this scene but, tellingly, he is entirely alone when he does so.

As so often with the work of the Ferrara/St. John partnership, we know that Ray would never let his family see these emotions. He's as lonely and isolated as Thana, Reno, Frank White or the Lieutenant. When he breaks down and reveals what's inside, it's before his dead brother. It is in this scene and also in the scene where he prepares to kill his brother's killer that he appears most human. The fact that he doesn't react when Jean says that she may leave with their children tells us that either he knows that she would never do that, or that he's unable to feel. Like Chez, he only seems to know how to deal with women on sexual terms. When Jean comes out to see him in the car early in the film, he concludes their conversation by making her get in the car. Then he kisses her. Ferrara takes this scene of them tentatively kissing each other and transports it back into the house where a guilty looking Jean sees the priest off; she goes from sexual feelings, aroused by Ray's kiss, to spiritual ones, inspired by the priest. After seeing the priest out, Jean then stands outside with him, asking him to pray for her and her family. The priest tells her to pray for herself. Ray's monologue peaks when he asks Johnny, "What's it like", meaning "What's it like to be dead?" He's thinking of his father too now, as well as his brother; Ray can't move on. It becomes clear that for him to abandon the gangster lifestyle, which is what Jean wants of him, he would also have to abandon his father and what he stood for. He is his father's son and that legacy survives as long as he continues the criminal tradition.

Of the three sons, Chez is most like their father. Johnny is the youngest and farthest removed from the pain of having a father who committed suicide. He has the least memories and is therefore best equipped to try to break the cycle. Ironically, his death occurs because of a business deal his brothers make with mobster Gaspare (played by Benicio Del Toro who seems deliberately dressed and made up to resemble Tony Carmonte in *Scarface*) and a factory owner, Enrico (played by Robert Miano) that he is involved with. Not only was Johnny having an affair with Gaspare's wife but he was also involved in firebombing the trucks of a company who were laying off a great number of workers. Johnny is a Communist and his impulse would be to *support* the workers. His beliefs clash with his family's business engagements.

When he turns up at Chez's house in the early hours of the morning with Gaspare's wife, Chez is incredulous. Johnny seems to be symbolically inviting death by such a rash gesture. His buddy Gouli was knifed to death by Gaspare and his henchman and Johnny knows that he's treading on toes that he shouldn't tread on. Ray's coffin-side monologue dissolves into a flashback of Johnny's death. We see him come out of the cinema. A billboard above him reads *The Petrified Forest*; he stands outside the theatre, beside a poster for *Kiss Kiss Bang Bang* which suggests symbolically that he is shot dead for having illicit sexual relations. A car pulls up. The driver calls out to Johnny and he walks up to the door.

Ferrara brilliantly cuts from this scene to one of Chez driving alone. From this scene we go to one at a bar where a lock-in crowd are watching a projected grainy black and white reel of vintage erotica. The men in the bar are all messing around with prostitutes; we see Ray, Johnny and Chez with different women. Chez takes a clearly underage prostitute into a corridor at the back of the club. There are three unpleasant sex scenes in the film. One, as we've already seen, is when Chez more or less rapes his wife Clara. This is the second such scene – again, it involves Chez, but this time it's with a young prostitute. They start making out but he stops, saying that she's a "baby" and a "child". She hustles him to carry on and pay her the money. He says he'll give her $5 if she goes home; she says he can fuck her for $10. At this Chez goes berserk and says he'll pay her $20. His face turns an ugly red and he tells the girl that she has "sold her soul". He presses her face-first against a wall, abusing her; as she cries out, he screams, "Don't fuck with the devil!" It's a disturbing scene, Chris Penn almost histrionic.

After brutalising the young prostitute, we see Chez sheepishly arriving home. Clara is in their bed, a large crucifix on the wall above her. It is then that she tries to persuade him to seek help for the madness that he has inherited from his father. She says she wants him at peace. Chez points at a black-and-white photograph of his parents and says that his father is at peace. He then ominously takes a razor into the bathroom, hinting at the suicidal impulse that is about to explode within him.

In the third sex scene, Johnny and Gouli are with a prostitute. Gouli is screwing her on the bed, her legs pointed up in the air, shoes still on, nails a harlot rouge. Ferrara fetishistically aims the camera primarily to focus on the girl's nipples and breasts. Johnny sits next to the couple, talking to Gouli. It's perverse and typical of Ferrara that the Catholic teaching of intercourse as a sacred means to procreation is subverted and turned into a banal get-off. Johnny talks about all manner of things while Gouli screws the prostitute. When he's finished, she wipes herself off with her hand (another sleazy touch) and gets ready for Johnny. When he kisses her (and his friend Gouli has only just stopped kissing her, so he's almost kissing Gouli) her lipstick smears across his mouth. All three of these scenes seem particularly degrading to women.

The film's ending is explosive. After nearly taking an axe to Gaspare in a bid to find out if he had Johnny killed, Ray kills the mechanic whom at one point he had considered sparing. The next morning, the day of the funeral itself, is bright and sunny. The dark mood has lifted. We see Ray shaving. We see him tell Chez that he has avenged Johnny's death. We then see Chez at the site where Ray killed Johnny's murderer, digging the dead boy's grave. Then Chez comes home. The kitchen is brightly lit, almost white. Out of the blue, Chez pulls out his gun and shoots the bodyguards. He then shoots Ray, before going to the open casket and pumping Johnny's corpse full of bullets. Finally he kills himself by sticking the gun in his mouth, repeating his father's suicide. The shot of blood spurting out of his nose and mouth is especially gory. Jean and Clara, clad in black, go to their injured men. Clara is more hysterical than Jean; it's as if Jean knew this was coming. When the coffin lid finally closes on Johnny, it's closing on the legacy, although only for the time being, bearing in mind that Ray's children were earlier seen playing with guns in a manner that suggested that they were already conditioned to continue their family's violent legacy. Jean has won her war, been handed the salvation she was praying for. She can save herself and her sons from the family legacy. The adult men in the family are dead, damned and gone to "roast in hell".

8

INTO THE BLACKOUT

Mylène Farmer/Promo Video For 'California'

In February 1996 Ferrara shot his first music promo video for French Canadian artist, Mylène Farmer, in Los Angeles. The shoot took place in a motel room as well as on external location on Sunset Boulevard and Hollywood Boulevard. A fascinating accompanying documentary was shot by French company Toutankhamon/S.A. Films about the making of the video. This 26-minute film (made with French sub-titles) shows Ferrara at work. He stands stony faced by a monitor screen throughout the early part of the documentary, scowling or waiting for cinematographer Ken Kelsch to capture the right shot. In his baseball cap, tatty black blazer, denim shirt and haven't-been-to-bed-for-days grimace, his fascination with Rolling Stone Keith Richards is evident. He has Richards' laidback posturings and when we see Ferrara slumped in a chair, half asleep, Richards' perpetually bored attitude too. When he speaks he sounds exactly like his other rock'n'roll hero, Bob Dylan.

Only when the camera is rolling, does Ferrara come alive. As soon as a scene is 'cut', Ferrara rushes to the actors and tells them what he wants. He takes a similarly authoritative role with Kelsch, although the mutual respect that lies at the heart of their long-term friendship is easy to pick up on. He comes across as intimidatingly stern when things aren't working to plan. When someone from outside the set is taking flash photographs, Ferrara goes berserk and tells somebody to get outside and stop whoever it is. Likewise, when a mirror gets broken on the set, Ferrara also becomes edgy and tense, asking first what had broken and then immediately checking that Farmer is not injured.

Everything about his working method suggests an unsettling mix of complete control and laidback ennui. On occasions he sits in an armchair, looking restless and bored, chomping on a piece of gum. On others, he seems animated and totally engrossed with what he's seeing on the monitor. When they shoot the outside scenes on the second and third days of the shoot, he becomes an animated director, cooing at the actresses lined up to play prostitutes one moment and then advising Kelsch to switch to 24mm the next. Early on, we see him and Kelsch clowning around on the balcony outside the hotel room and, again, the history between them is evident.

Ferrara also jokes around, sticking his baseball cap on the third actor's head and laughing when lead actor Giancarlo Esposito's yard long hair falls out from under his hat. Ferrara also seems concerned throughout with Farmer's feelings and mood, even giving her a friendly, encouraging kiss on the cheek at one point. His method seems intense and restless. Once you've seen this documentary, it becomes very clear why Ferrara is able to shoot films like *Bad Lieutenant* and *The Addiction* in three weeks flat: he gets too irritated to spend too long on any one scene. To combat possible frustration, he pushes his cast to the limits, to force the perfect performance out of them before he grows restless and starts falling asleep in his armchair. He seems like a grumpy old bear, slouching around the set, bad tempered and demanding yet acutely focused and extremely talented.

The video opens with a montage of slow motion nocturnal street shots of Los Angeles. As the neon signs pass by, we are reminded of Ferrara's work on Miami Vice but also of the beginning neon drenched shots in *Fear City*. As the song begins, we see Mylène Farmer (playing the 'Rich Woman') and actor Giancarlo Esposito (playing her rich lover) in a hotel room composed of red, orange, black, brown and white. He is dressed in a smart businessman's outfit. She has long orange-red hair and is trying on various outfits for their night out. She sits down at a dresser before a mirror. Again, Ferrara returns to his obsession with mirrors, even in a five-minute promo video. She stares at herself in the mirror. Her lover criticises what she's wearing, they argue. Ferrara captures the lover standing behind her, pulling her hair from her neck. We see her face in the dresser mirror. As he starts kissing her, she closes her eyes and a fantasy sequence begins in which she's a prostitute and he's a pimp.

We see her standing at a doorway, wearing thigh high red PVC boots, her hair now messy and shorter and dyed electric red, wearing only a black slip. She's with a pimp (dressed in suitably sleazy attire). They fight over what she's wearing. He tries to get her to wear a leopard skin jacket, she doesn't want to. Ferrara intercuts scenes where she's being kissed by the pimp in the fantasy sequence and then wearing a black dress with her lover. In those shots, they are in a hallway bathed in an orangey glow. The lover undresses her in the hallway and they start to make out. In the fantasy sequence, the pimp roughly feels up her ass, pulls her leopard skin jacket off and lifts her off the ground, supporting her by her thighs.

Next we see the bright red doors (another Godard reference) of a motel. In the fantasy sequence, the pimp and his prostitute leave. In the next shot, the rich woman and her rich lover, both immaculately dressed, leave an expensive looking house and get into a Jaguar car. Ferrara has then filmed in the moving Jaguar, first as a blur of lights on a Los Angeles boulevard (recalling the way he filmed Crockett in *The Home Invaders*, driving around Miami at night) and then with a shot of her staring out of the passenger door window, her face faraway in thought. Ferrara then weaves in shots of advertisement billboards for generic brands like McDonalds and Marlboro. In this rapid succession of shots of advertisements and billboards, Ferrara is again quoting from Godard, whose obsession with advertising has surfaced frequently as a motif throughout his career.

After juxtaposing the last of this run of shots with Farmer's melancholic gaze, Ferrara shows a gaggle of prostitutes on a boulevard. As the documentary illustrated, Ferrara had this scene shot in 24mm, giving the prostitutes a grainy quality. The women pout and tout for business as the pimp hovers behind them. Farmer is seen, in the leopard skin jacket, swinging her handbag. The way Ferrara has this scene filmed, recalls the early scene in *King Of New York* where White's (just out of jail and being driven around) limo swings past a bunch of prostitutes on a street corner, one of whom lifts her skirt up and shows her ass. It also recalls the scene in *The*

Home Invaders where Trudy and Gina were working undercover as prostitutes.

As the rich woman and her rich lover drive slowly past the prostitutes on the boulevard, the fantasy sequence and reality sequence become blurred. Ferrara has the prostitutes touting for business in slow motion. The camera crawls along each of the girls, cutting back and forth from the rich woman in the car looking at them and then a reverse shot of each girl leering back. Finally reality and fantasy collide and the rich woman stares at the prostitute. As each looks at the other (again, the split between the two versions of Mylène Farmer explain Ferrara's use of mirrors as a symbol), the two versions of the same man (rich man/pimp) get angry. The pimp pulls a switchblade on the prostitute while the rich woman throws her door open, tries to get out but her lover restrains her.

After this, she and her lover argue in the car and then arrive at their big party. Photographers are hanging around the entrance. It's a big black tie affair. Her lover enjoys the attention, she is bored. She stares at herself in a mirror and then goes to the ladies room. She goes into a cubicle as the well dressed rich woman and comes out looking more like the fantasy prostitute version of herself. Ferrara intercuts some quick flashbacks to the prostitutes and to how the rich woman looked as a prostitute in her fantasies.

Finally, the rich woman (now looking like a cross between her rich self and her prostitute self) checks herself out again in a mirror and then we see her standing in a fantasy sequence within the fantasy sequence. In this, the other prostitutes stand around looking bored, in a 'V' shape. Furthest from the camera, stands the hybrid of the two personas in prostitute's clothing. Ferrara then cuts to a shot of a sheet being pulled over her corpse: she is dead. Ferrara has Kelsch film her corpse being taken away with an overhead shot. After a montage of already seen images, Ferrara takes the narrative into *Snake Eyes* territory by showing the rich woman (well-dressed, although in prostitute's clothes) kissing the pimp from the parallel fantasy sequence. She takes a hairclip from her hair and stabs the pimp to death after another montage of clips including a flashback to the pimp threatening the prostitute with a switchblade. The video ends on a shot of the prostitute persona from the initial fantasy sequence, wearing the leopard skin jacket.

The video is interesting for several reasons. Firstly, Ferrara infuses every shot with the stylish boudoir sensuality that has become part of his trademark style. Secondly, the footage of Farmer dressed as a prostitute and also the actual scene featuring the prostitutes again takes Ferrara's vision of sleazy erotica very close to the realm of exploitation. Thirdly, even in a five-minute promo video, Ferrara still manages to create complex results, mostly by again blurring the line between fantasy and reality. It is clear that the narrative concerns a passive woman and her dominant male lover. The fantasy sequence explores the psychology of the relation- ship (her as prostitute, him as pimp). When they arrive at the black tie dinner, she feels like a prostitute. Earlier, when we saw the lover criticising her choice of outfit for the dinner, it was no different to a pimp wanting his prostitute to dress up in a certain way. The intercut sex scenes show us that in the fantasy sequence she is aroused by the pimp's roughness but in the reality sequence, she is bored by her rich lover's domineering and selfish attitude to sex. This promo video feels as though it might have been an early draft of the Annie 1 and Annie 2 concept in *The Blackout*: two women blurring into one woman. Lastly, it feels like Ferrara's miscroscopic take on Bunuel's 1967 film *Belle De Jour* in which Catherine Denueve plays a bored rich French housewife who moonlights by day as a prostitute in order to explore/release her sexuality.

Subway Stories: *Love On The A Train*

This five-minute short stars Rosie Perez (as The Girl), Gretchen Mol (back again as The Wife after playing Helen in *The Funeral*) and Mike McGione (playing John T.). Their names ('The Girl', 'The Wife') recall the married couple in Robert Bresson's *A Gentle Woman* who were simply credited as 'She' and 'He'. *Love On The A Train* is one of ten short films made by ten directors (the others were Bob Babalan, Patricia Benoit, Julie Dash, Jonathan Demme, Ted Demme, Alison Maclean, Craig McKay, Lucas Platt and Seth Zvi Rosenfeld) for HBO's Subway Stories feature.

The project began with an advertisement inviting New Yorkers to send in any stories they had about an experience on the New York subway. Of the 1,000 stories they received, the best ten were picked and then contracted out to interested directors. Ferrara's story was knocked into a five-minute screenplay by his girlfriend at the time, Marla Hanson. Ken Kelsch filmed it and Ferrara co-wrote two bluesy instrumentals with Joe Delia for the brief soundtrack. It's a radical departure in style for Ferrara. Indeed, after the deeply dark St. John films, it's light relief.

The subway A train pulls in. A couple walk through the station, hand in hand. She, The Wife, has short blonde hair and is wearing a bland blue cardigan. He, John T. (Mike McGione), is in a suit and tie, has slicked-back hair, looks clean cut and is carrying a briefcase. He asks for *The Daily News* and two coffees at a kiosk, while she straightens her necklace. Each of the coffee cups has 'I Love New York' emblazoned on the side.

A voice-over kicks in; it's John T. talking. We discover that the couple are newlyweds and that they live in Brooklyn. Every morning they walk up to the station together and catch the A train. She goes South to her job as a kindergarten teacher, he goes north to his job as a Trader Of Municipal Bonds. As we see John T. climb onto the subway and grip the handrail, his voice-over explains that the story is being recounted in flashback style and that the story begins on what was their three months' anniversary.

A rush of passengers get on the train. Various hands grip the rail. We see a surprised look on his face. Ferrara cuts the camera so we can see why: a woman's crotch is pressed up against his hand. She's wearing a creamy beige dress and a pin stripe blazer. The camera returns to a close-up on John T.'s face. He takes another look: this time the camera frames her breasts. She's not wearing a bra and we see a nipple poking up against the fabric – one of Ferrara's favourite shots.

We see John T.'s face again – he's uncomfortable – and then the camera goes back down to his hand. Now, the woman is rubbing her crotch against his knuckles, getting off on the sensation. Up to this point, we've yet to see her face. Each framed shot of either her crotch or breast recalls Robert Bresson's trademark cropping of shots of the human body. The camera returns to John T. who is now looking to his left and right and pulling an 'is this really happening?' expression. Finally we see the woman's face: it's Rosie Perez, The Girl. She flicks her hair and goes back to reading her newspaper. We get another close-up of John T's face. Then the camera returns to her crotch. Now we see her rubbing her crotch on his knuckles but also her hand pressing on his.

This shot of their hands dissolves to a shot of John T.'s wife straightening her necklace. It's the following morning and the same routine is playing out. He orders the coffees and the newspapers. She is telling him a story about a kid in her class. He nervously checks the clock. She is again in pale blues and looks bland and homey. John T. kisses his wife goodbye and gets on his train, his voice-over telling us that he was sure that the encounter with The Girl was just a "coincidence".

We see another very Bressonian shot of the handrail, then of his hand, a wedding ring on his finger. He is reading his newspaper, gripping the handrail when the next station comes along. The Girl gets on, her hand appears above his. She pushes his hand slowly down the rail, in a sexually suggestive manner. His voice-over asks, "coincidence or fate?" and then tells us that these "chance encounters" carried on every day for nine months. They never speak, they only encounter each other in these oddly restrictive physical ways. The anonymity of their meetings recalls the relationship between Marlon Brando and Maria Schneider in Bertolucci's *Last Tango In Paris*. To accompany this information, Ferrara pulls together a montage of rendezvous shots as well as shots of the subway speeding through a tunnel to symbolise the passing of several months.

After this montage, we get a third early morning husband and wife scene. This time, while he buys coffees and a newspaper, her hand twitches around her neckline as if fiddling with the necklace as she did in the same earlier scenes, only this time she isn't wearing the necklace. This is a sign that something has changed. Her nervous habit of fiddling with her necklace while he bought the coffees and a newspaper, continues even though she is not wearing the necklace. Why isn't she wearing it? Was it a gift from her husband? As if to answer these questions, they are tense with one another. He doesn't kiss her goodbye nor do they speak. She is not wearing blue now, but a washed-out green. He is in a dark grey suit. His voice-over explains that he wants to finally speak to his mystery subway woman, to see if anything lies behind their ritualistic touching. He breaks the spell by pulling his hand away when she puts hers on his; he wants to "spoil the mystery" and have a conversation. However, The Girl moves away from him, takes a seat and gets off at the next station – all in silence. After that, the spell is broken and they return to their covert sexual interplay on the subway.

John T. reaches a crossroads: two shots juxtapose The Girl and The Wife. His voice-over tells us, "I guess I thought I'd found something with her that I could not find in my own marriage but I was wrong." He stops taking the A train and starts taking the F train. We then see him walking along with his wife, who is dressed in grey and heavily pregnant. As they pass through the ticket turnstiles, he sees the girl, who opens her mouth to say something. He freezes too. It's clear that they both miss the ritual. His wife jealously pulls on his arm at this, asking, "Did you know her? Honey, who was that?" His response ("I don't know who that was") ends the film.

The short is mostly notable for the Bresson-inspired framing, a crystal clear, almost clinical grey and white composition, some typical Ferrara breast/nipple focus, a kinky storyline and the theme of romantic deception which would be more fully played out in Ferrara's next work, *The Blackout*.

The Blackout 1997

"It's another one of our genre of cry-baby men who lose their bitches and don't stop fuckin' crying about it" – Abel Ferrara, talking to *Neon* magazine.

A man is swimming further and further out to sea in total darkness. He doesn't know where he's going, we don't know where he's going. Everything goes black. He reappears on the shore, standing with a naked woman, who asks him, "Did ya miss me?" This is the final scene in *The Blackout*, a film co-written by Marla Hanson, Christ Zois and Ferrara. The scene almost perfectly describes the film itself, the darkness of the waves and the lone thrashing of a directionless, suicidal "coked-up drunk" paralleling Ferrara's continued voyage into increasingly fractured narrative, fiercely non-commercial subject matter and a 'screw the audience' dependence on film/video interplay that recalls a complex Jean-Luc Godard film like *Numéro Deux*.

Ferrara used the AVID digital editing program to layer the film with the dream-like quality that he was after and was subsequently able to build layer upon layer of film, stockpiling shots into a series of recurring haunting montages. *The Blackout* began as Ferrara's homage to *Vertigo*, but explicitly borrows from two other films: Jean-Luc Godard's *Contempt* and Larry Cohen's *Special Effects*.

Cohen's *Special Effects* boasts two films-within-a-film. It stars Zoë Tamerlis as a struggling actress called Andrea who flees her smalltown husband and child for New York to pursue her dreams of becoming a movie star. She soon becomes involved with big-shot director Christopher Neville, who offers to give her a trial run on his casting couch. When she discovers that he's filming them in bed with a secret camera, they fight and he strangles her. To throw the police off his scent, Neville decides to make a film based on Andrea's life and death. He casts Andrea's grieving husband (the police's chief suspect) as himself and then casts a lookalike, Elaine, (also played by Zoë Tamerlis) as Andrea. Cohen took the idea of having Tamerlis playing both women from *Vertigo*, in which Kim Novak famously played twin roles.

After Neville dies by falling from his apartment balcony, the chief detective on the case (Phillip Delroy) completes Neville's film and Cohen ends the film with the title 'A Film By Phillip Delroy', therefore introducing the second film within a film. Cohen's film shares the same tension between reality and film as *The Blackout*. Both films pay homage to Hitchcock's *Vertigo*, both feature the strangulation of a woman by the lead character and in both the strangulation is filmed. The similarities don't stop there. Neville is played by Eric Bogosian who had a small part in *Crime Story*. Cohen wrote the storyline for Ferrara's *Body Snatchers* remake and Zoë Tamerlis is part of Ferrara's inner circle.

The allusions to Godard's *Contempt* are also fundamental to *The Blackout*. In *Contempt*, a writer (Paul, played by Michel Piccoli) is seduced by a smarmy film producer's (Prokosch) lucrative financial offer into working as a screenplay doctor on a treatment of The Odyssey being filmed by Fritz Lang. His wife Camille (Brigitte Bardot) neither approves of Paul prostituting himself for money (which Paul needs so that the couple can buy their apartment outright) nor of Paul's flirtations with Prokosch's assistant Francesca, nor of Paul's use of her as a 'bargaining chip' with Prokosch who finds her attractive.

As mentioned earlier, *Contempt* also has a film-within-a-film structure. Ferrara borrows the following elements from Godard's film: Camille is first seen with long blonde hair (Bardot's trademark). Early on, she surprises Paul by putting on a wig of short black hair, which Godard had her wear because it made her look like his wife at the time, Anna Karina. In *The Blackout*, Claudia Schiffer's character, Susan, has exactly the same long blonde hair as Bardot's Camille, while Béatrice Dalle's Annie 1 has exactly the same short black hair as Bardot's Camille when she wears the black wig. Godard had the split within the same actress/character; Ferrara divides the two 'looks' into two completely different women who are loved and in love with Matty (played by Matthew Modine), a Hollywood movie star.

In *Contempt*, Paul and Camille travel to Capri to work on Prokosch's production, the blue seas and sunny climate providing a breathtaking backdrop to their romantic drama and increasingly fragmented relationship. Ferrara makes Miami his 'Capri', using the same beautiful blues to create a luminous backdrop. The third lift from *Contempt* is the fight scene between Annie 1 and Matty in their hotel room (a setting which loosely borrows from Paul and Camille's Rome apartment). The specifics of this allusion will be examined later in the chapter.

The Blackout is built around Matty who arrives back in Miami to meet up with his French actress/model girlfriend, Annie (played by Béatrice Dalle with her trademark mix of pouty sensuality and melancholic detachment). We understand that before they parted the two were very much in love, and that Annie is pregnant. We see them reunited by a hotel swimming pool, where Matty ignores his perpetually gossiping groupies (a dig at Madonna here) and mawls Annie.

Later, in their hotel room, we see Annie lying up on the bed, dressed in all black, half asleep or too drunk to keep her eyes open. Matty hands her a glass of champagne (despite her pleas to him to let her sleep) and asks her to say that it's a toast to their future together. She, bleary-eyed and sad, replies using incorrect grammar, toasting him and saying, "Here's to your future together" which he angrily corrects. In one of the film's seediest scenes, Matty then scrambles around on the floor, and pulls an engagement ring out of a wrap of coke. He rubs some coke on his gums, snorts a tiny bit and then proposes to her.

Annie starts crying and says, "Why do you ask me now?" Matty presumes that she's saying this because they've been apart for a while (presumably he has been off on a shoot or a promotional trip). Earlier by the pool, Annie has casually mentioned that she knows Matty's been screwing other women. To explain why, we're given a close-up of the real-life Modine out on the town with Bruce Willis and Demi Moore, another shot that plays with our notions of film and reality. The photo tells us that 'Matty' is a major movie star (as Modine is). Annie appears to accept his proposal, albeit sadly, although we have no idea why she's crying. He climbs on top of her, mounting her clumsily and without feeling: she wants romance, he simply wants sex. Throughout the whole scene, Dalle is the picture of dark romantic despair, her gigantic bird trapped-within-barbed-wire tattoo screaming from her shoulder. It's as if Ferrara wanted the tattoo in as many shots as possible to emphasise Annie 1's predicament.

The couple go to see a sleazy porn film-maker called Mickey Wayne (played with veins-standing-out-on-forehead psychosis by Dennis Hopper) who is shooting a video porn re-make of the old French film *Nana* (made in 1934, directed by Dorothy Arzner and kicked into action by Sam Goldwyn's backing), which itself was based on a story by Emile Zola. The film concerned a woman who rises from poverty to become a notorious Paris whore. She is torn apart by her love for two brothers (mirroring the two Annies as well as the conflict between Matty's feelings for Annie 1 and Susan). Dan Wolman re-made the film in 1982 with the same title. As the *Time Out Film Guide* notes, the setting was changed and Nana was now the: "porno-protégé of a certain bleu-film-maker." Mickey is effectively bastardising the original but by out-pornoing Wolman's re-make.

Mickey's studio, like Ferrara's set, is in constant chaos. There are five cameras running and as many, if not more, monitors and play-back screens on the walls. A band are playing, a huge cast and crew are following his orders, which are a barked mess of banal encouragement and director-speak. Through Mickey's cameras and their monitor screens, we observe women making out together, threesomes making out, straight couples making out, girls dancing, two crew members talking (one of whom is Nancy Ferrara) and in a blink-and-you'll-miss-it shot on one screen, what looks like Ferrara's face in black and white talking to a crew member. This is another teasing reference to the collapsing boundaries between film and reality.

To flesh the point out, Ferrara even has Matty later deliver a few lines to Annie 2 in the back of his chauffeur-driven limo about how the difference between acting and real life has become blurred for him. In this respect, Ferrara is still back in *Snake Eyes* mode. Mickey, shouting at his cast to deliver better performances and spouting ideas about video film-making, must be loosely based on Ferrara himself. Kim Newman, in his review of the film for *Sight and Sound* saw this as a key moment in the film: "Hopper brings along 40 years of movie baggage as he embarks on what could be seen either as a caricature of the Ferrara method or a self-aware critique of the dangers of stepping half into a sea of madness in order to capture on film the thrashing of the poor souls who can't make it back to the shore."

In one scene, Mickey takes Matty to see two of his regular porn actresses in one of their apartments and has them act out a scene where they have sex. Before the knock at the door, the girls are dressed and snorting coke off a table. One is wearing blue, the other wearing black. Both colours have 'blackout' associations; together they make the colour of a bruise. After a series of rapid cuts and even faster dissolves, time passes, a lot of coke is snorted and then Mickey gets his video camera out. He points it at the girls who start performing. They kiss, one licks the other's stomach, one rubs the other's genitals, one fondles the other's breasts, one spanks the other's ass while it's stuck out at the camera. One of the girls performs a personal erotic show up on a counter. As Matty snorts coke and bemusedly tries to follow Mickey's salivating enthusiasm for degrading the women, Mickey 'directs' them with frenzied instructions – "keep rubbing, baby", "now make her nipples hard", "that's sweet", "spank her, man", "make it pink! Give it to her! Slap her!", "Say 'Fuck me, baby!' "

When Mickey orders one of the girls to perform a personal show for him to film, he disturbingly tweaks and pulls on both of her nipples, as if she's a toy to be played with. It's hard to tell what's worse: his drooling lecherous behaviour or her disinterest. He is, however, a porn director, so we have to imagine that Ferrara and his co-writers were trying to give him an authentic persona. Via Mickey, it's as if Ferrara's fondness for female nudity and especially breast/nipple shots and sex scenes between two women is being exorcised through Mickey's video monitor.

Modine later told *Neon*'s Jim Shelley that the scene wasn't even in the screenplay. He and Hopper began the scene by being told to enter a hotel room. Once inside they were met by the two women, as Modine recalled, "These girls started taking their clothes off and spanking each other. Dennis is improvising, going 'Yeah baby go on!' This girl starts to pull down my pants and go down on me. I say, 'Hey, slow down!', 'cos no one told me that was going to happen. This girl looks over at the focus-puller and says, 'Oh right! A guy telling a girl to slow down – what the fuck is that?' which is a good line and is in the movie. So when we finally ran out of film, I asked her, 'Who told you to do that?' She said, 'Nobody, it's a porno flick, right?' She couldn't believe it when we told her it was a real movie."

This is typical Ferrara, dragging brilliant performances out of his cast by duping them. Ken Kelsch told *Neon* that this was Ferrara's knack: "The actors go to the limit. Some of them don't even know their limits until they get on the set and Abel works it out of them." The very idea of two porno actresses thinking they were making a porno with clean-cut Matthew Modine is hilarious. The confusion on all sides makes for a bristling tension as Hopper wings it, the girls do their thing with stoned nonchalance and Modine sits uncomfortably throughout, clearly unnerved by a scene playing out that wasn't scripted.

The violent break-up scene with Annie 1 in the hotel room features similar improvisation. The scene is like many of the sparring couple scenes in Godard's *Contempt* dragged through hell and back, and Modine looks like he was flying by the seat of his pants throughout. After a lengthy crowded outdoors fashion show by a swimming pool, in which Annie, looking beautiful in a blue dress and shades, is one of the star models, Ferrara shows the couple in their hotel room at the end of the night. Earlier on, Matty and Annie (wearing a white dress that makes much of her shoulder tattoo) had hung out with Mickey who had tried to talk Matty into being in the film and declared Annie the 'star' of his re-make, shooting her through some of the multiple video cameras. The hotel room is bathed in golds, whites and soft brown light. A painting sits unhung on the floor, a quotation from Schrader's *American Gigolo.* Matty's shirt is hanging out, his appearance dishevelled. He is telling Annie (from the bathroom) about a friend of his (tellingly called 'Nicky') who had a run-in with a prostitute. She interrupts in broken English, her husky, deep French accent purring the grammatically incorrect question, "You want to marry me because I was still pregnant?" She asks this with her hands on her hips; she's in a white dress, against a background of white walls, with white curtains behind her blowing in the breeze, the colour-coding of the scene heavily symbolising purity. Matty is in the bathroom, before a mirror, a flash of red wall (symbolising hell) visible. He snorts some coke, drinks his beer and continues with the story. She repeats her question. Suddenly realising that she has had an abortion, Matty goes berserk and they fight. Annie says she terminated her pregnancy because she didn't want their baby to have a father who is a "junkie". Their fight is violent, Annie striking back as hard as he attacks her. At one point, she even smashes a champagne bottle on Matty's head. He goes to hit her, she cowers, raises her arms to protect herself. She breaks into French, tears at his hair, he wrestles her, she slaps him across the face repeatedly. Annie's outbursts in French have the feel of a spring unwinding, as though Dalle, restrained by English language improvisation and an ever-changing script, suddenly erupted, all her frustration as a French actress in an English language film pouring out in one of the most inspired pieces of acting in the entire film.

This scene is a violent extension of the brief fight scene in Godard's *Contempt,* mentioned earlier. In that film, Paul and Camille argue in their Rome apartment. Paul, having previously announced that he is declining Prokosch's offer to work on the Odyssey production because he knows Camille will cease loving him if he does, decides to take the job. Camille immediately retracts the tenderness that she has been displaying. Paul and Camille argue. She says she doesn't love him anymore. He asks why. She says there is no reason. He asks if it is because she saw him slap Francesca's ass; she says that can be the reason if he wants it to be, and announces that their relationship is over. They both stand up; Camille suddenly explodes and thrashes her fists at Paul. The violence of this outburst and the way in which Godard has Coutard film it, is a starting point for the way in which Ferrara directed Matty and Annie 1's fight. Dalle flails her arms at Modine as Bardot does with Piccoli. Annie 1 also 'stops' loving Matty (out of necessity rather than because she no longer feels anything for him) because she has contempt for him. She doesn't want the father of her baby to be strung out on drugs.

When the fighting stops, Annie 1 crosses her arms and stands by the window. Matty retreats to the bathroom. He goes to the mirror and then immediately turns to come out of the room. Considering Modine's considerable acting experience, the next shot is fascinating. He flashes a look at the camera, that says, 'What the fuck was that?', as if he's pleading for the scene to be cut. Other directors might have cut this out but Ferrara opts for the Cassavetes approach and leaves it in; again, it plays with the tension between film and real life. Modine later explained to *Uncut* that this scene was improvised by Dalle with an intensity he wasn't banking on: "I bet she's been in some big fights with some big guys. In one scene she walloped me, smacked me. That was never scripted. It didn't say, 'Then Annie hits Matty', or anything. Across the face, again and again. I went home in pain. I was thinking, Jeez, why does my neck hurt? I got a splitting headache. Oh yeah, right. I got the shit beat outta me by Béatrice. It was like fighting Mike Tyson. And she's got a mouth like a horse. Another day she bites my chin, it swells up like a balloon. We had to stop until it stopped bleeding. Then they put plastic skin on my jaw and painted over it."

The scene ends with Annie taking out a mini-tape recorder and playing back a recording of Matty's violent and abusive insistence that she abort their child. As he hears himself saying lines such as, "If you were any kind of woman you'd take a knife and cut that baby out of your stomach" and "Better yet, give me a knife and I'll cut it out for you", Matty shouts back at the recording, unable to accept that he has said any of this. The man shouting (during what turns out to be one of his blackout periods, of which he subsequently has no memory) is a Matty he doesn't understand or know.

Annie leaves. Matty slumps down on the floor, pathetically whining excuses and answers to the horrific things ("it ain't my baby", "fuck you, fuck the baby, fuck everything") he's saying on the tape to an Annie who had already gone. A synth plays ominously in the background as he walks over broken glass, pausing to pick up the engagement ring Annie's thrown down. After this, he goes back to Mickey's studio and paranoically asks him if he's slept with Annie. Mickey, after playing the answer back at him ("Which will make you feel worse? If I say yes or no?") says that it's not a question of whether he slept with Annie but a question of whether he remembers sleeping with Annie. He then turns Matty's paranoia back onto him by asking him, "More importantly, do you fuckin' remember?" This is a reference to Matty's blackouts, another one of which is imminent.

Mickey and Matty go for a drive in a convertible with the roof down. It's a moody Miami day. Matty tells Mickey that Annie is the one for him. He refers to her as "the other half of me". Mickey, seeing a great confession from a wasted Matty, deviously pulls his video camera out and films Matty via a wing mirror, his grainy, bestubbled face pinned against a brooding, cloudy skyline. After the scene with the porno actresses, Matty gets even higher back at Mickey's studio where the *Nana Miami* shoot is about to wrap up. He smokes crack in a back room (in slow motion against a backdrop of hellish red walls). As he slumps stoned to the floor, his head presses against a mirror (another Ferrara trick) and we see Matty's double. This is the Jekyll And Hyde shot: a shot where there are two Mattys, one who gets so fucked up that he has blackout periods during which he is capable of telling the woman he loves to get an abortion, and the other his everyday movie star persona. Ferrara throws in some Lynch-esque shots of dark oceans and a lone swimmer. It's creepy premonition stuff, acid flashback meets *Lost Highway*. Mickey comes in with his video camera and focuses on Matty. Presumably seen through Mickey's lens, Ferrara throws in a pacey fade-out by having the screen shrink until Matty has vanished.

Vincent Gallo, who acted in *The Funeral*, would use a similar effect in his superb directorial debut *Buffalo 66*.

The fade-out delivers a sweaty, wasted Matty to a diner where he falls for his 17-year-old waitress (played by Sarah Lassez) – her name badge tells us that she's called Annie as well. This Annie is a fresh-faced home-girl. She and Annie 1 share no similarities. She looks sweet – the kind of girl who'd be fun but would take care of him. The brightly lit diner, her pink uniform and soft face all clash with Matty's wasted visage; it's like a horror story sitcom moment. Meanwhile, Mickey, alone at his studio is watching (à la Godard in *Numéro Deux*) two playback screens. On one, the original *Nana* film plays – significantly, it is caught at a moment in which a man is strangling a woman. On the other screen is footage of Annie 1 and Matty. As the strangling becomes more intense, Mickey grins ("this is real") and on the playback screen the message 'shot missing' (an in-joke alluding to the 'scene is missing' sub-title that appears in Dennis Hopper's epic *The Last Movie*) appears. We can tell from this that Mickey is planning to shoot a scene in which a man strangles his lover.

Matty picks Annie the waitress up (she is clearly star-struck by him) and takes her to Mickey's studio. Mickey dupes the messed-up Matty by christening her Annie 2 and by making her replace her brown hair with a short black Annie 1 wig (again alluding to Godard's *Contempt*). The associations between the two Annies had already started at the diner, where Matty is so high that he starts hallucinating in a series of shots that, again, recall David Lynch's most sinister work. At one point, while he's sitting in the diner, Annie 1's face keeps appearing in place of the waitress's face. In another surreal moment, when the waitress speaks Annie 1's voice comes out of her mouth. At Mickey's studio, Annie 2 can't understand it when Matty paws at the screen when Mickey's rushes of the footage he shot of Annie 1 are playing back. Matty talks to her image, tries to kiss her and touches her face. He talks to Annie 2, dressed as Annie 1, as if she was Annie 1, and asks her why she left him.

In a moment of director-speak (and, no doubt, of insight into the Ferrara method) Mickey comments on how many directors won't let their actors and actresses see rushes. He says he doesn't care about that because it gives an actor a gauge of their performance:

"Know when your acting is shit, know when you're faking it." Mickey asks Annie 2 if she wants to be an actress because, in his eyes, "everyone wants to be in pictures." He starts videoing her; he asks her if she's ever had candle wax dripped on her and offers her a joint. Matty holds Annie 2, dressed in the wig which makes her look like Annie 1, certain that his first love has come back to him. A dreamy, stoned scene of Matty and Annie 2 in the back of a car, superimposed on a nocturnal backdrop of Miami has her talk of meeting him as a romantic moment of fate. This strongly contrasts with an earlier limo scene in which Matty fondled Annie 1's breast and nipple.

Matty passes out and a series of nightmares flash through his mind: Mickey tells a distressed Matty (who has been asking him where Annie 1 is) that Annie 1 (really Annie 2) is right with them in the studio. Matty, confused by Mickey, asks Annie 2 if she had an abortion. Ferrara gives us a peach-toned close-up of Annie 2 and then fades to black.

We now fast-forward 18 months. Matty is at an Alcoholics Anonymous meeting, collecting a coin which celebrates his one year sober. He introduces himself in the language of the group: "Hi, my name's Matty and I'm an alcoholic and a drug addict." Matty is telling the meeting his 'story', explaining that he got into drink and drugs on the sets of films. Then he makes an interesting comment: he says that as an actor, the great thing is that he's fed lines of dialogue, told what to say. Just before he falls off the wagon in Miami, we see him meet up with Mickey on the beach. He is inarticulate and talking nonsense, and one of his lines is, "My guts are coming out of my stomach." Some reviews highlighted this as a terrible line of dialogue in *The Blackout*. It is meant to be terrible, to make us cringe. Matty needs to be fed lines of dialogue like a baby, just as he needs to be fed lines of coke and bottles of alcohol. Without this prompting in all aspects of his life, he's dead. The symbolism of Matty at an 'A.A.' meeting is also darkly humorous. The 'A.A.' stands for Alcoholics Anonymous, but also for Annie 1 and Annie 2.

After the security of the A.A. meeting, we see Matty with Susan (his art dealer girlfriend, played by Claudia Schiffer) at their New York home. It could be a scene from a TV show like *Thirtysomething*.

He cuddles up to her, talking about how A.A. have rewarded his first year sober with a coin. In a moment of bittersweet irony, Matty reads the quotation on the coin, "To thine own self be true." Within the context of the cute-wife-and-husband domestic scene, a first viewing of the film makes the quotation seem to be further testimony to how much Matty has changed. He's off the drugs, off the drink and off Annie 1. He's given up all of the bad things. He's also in therapy.

However, in reality Matty feels stagnant and bored. The crazy, full-ahead lifestyle that he had been enjoying is now replaced with its polar opposite. He is somewhat contemptuous of what he's turned into. He talks with his therapist about Annie 1 and when asked if he would like to "bury" her, Matty says he wants to, "cut the umbilical cord" between them. This choice of words is deliberately perverse in light of why they broke up; the therapist's choice of verb "bury" is equally dark and also prophetic. Ferrara is playing with the notions of narrative, pumping us with morsels of information and then closing off. After a nightmare in which he strangles Annie 1, Matty wakes up in a cold sweat. Susan comforts him. A gentle acoustic guitar plays on the soundtrack, again mimicking or parodying the mood of *Thirtysomething*. Ferrara is laying on the sugar-coated topping with gusto.

The rest of the film concerns the drink- and drug-induced blackout that Matty had at Mickey's studio 18 months earlier. He is haunted by nightmares and flashbacks that suggest to him that he killed Annie 1. He has nightmares in which he is strangling Annie 1. The baby they might have had together had he not abusively driven her to abort it, also haunts him. In a nightmare sequence, a baby appears to him in a montage that includes juxtaposed shots of Annie 1 and Susan.

The only person he shares these nightmares with is his therapist. To get to the therapist's office, Matty has to pass through some security gates. Amusingly, a sign on the gate which reads NO PARKING has been graffitti'd so that it reads NO FUCKING. The therapist chairs the sessions in what Matty calls a "bunker". A giant poster of Fellini's 8½ leans up against the wall; this was Fellini's epic 'writer's block' film, all about creative juices drying up. In a connecting scene, we see Matty rudely turning down a $75,000-a-week TV

211

acting role, despite Susan's enthusiasm. She tells him he has to go back to work at some point, and we realise that since quitting drink and drugs, he hasn't worked. Maybe he's unable to work. Hence, the Fellini poster.

As if to drive the point home, after passing on the TV offer, Matty attacks the 'art' hanging on the walls (and thus attacks Susan through her profession: she deals in art whereas he believes he creates it) and then stands in the lounge doorway, swigging on a bottle of mineral water in the same manner that we have seen him, in the earlier Miami scenes, repeatedly swig on a beer bottle. Ferrara is rhyming shots. We can feel the cracks starting to appear again in Matty's character. When Susan goes away for three days, we see first a tender parting by the cab. Matty stands on the steps of their home having waved her off and fidgets with his nose (a coke addict's mannerism) as he did earlier in the film. Subconsciously, he's already drinking and taking coke again. In these few scenes, Ferrara has Modine recreate the physical language of addiction to anticipate where the narrative is heading.

Matty uses the fact that Susan is away to take a trip back to Miami and to the person he was and misses. This trip is inspired by his therapist who also video records his sessions with Matty, although we don't find out why. It's presumably nothing more than a nar-ratorial device which allows Ferrara to capture Matty squirming through the grainy lens of the video camera. (These video sessions recall the earlier scene in Mickey's car, in which the porn director videos a 'confession' from Matty about his feelings for Annie 1.) The grainy, rough video film is used to give us access to, and symboli-cally reflect, just how raw Matty's feelings are; he's an open wound. He tells the therapist about the nightmares and the therapist sug-gests that he goes to Miami to see if Annie is dead or alive and to lay old ghosts to rest.

After a scene in which Matty is reunited with Mickey on a crisply shot sunny beach, he falls off the wagon in his hotel room, just after Mickey has just warned him to take it easy. In typically per-verse Ferrara style, Hopper, himself a recovering alcoholic and drug addict, delivers the line, "You A.A. people!" to Matty after hearing about how Matty has to make "amends" with Annie 1. Ferrara is mocking the infamous A.A. twelve-step programme which includes one step in which the recovering alcoholic has to make 'amends' to all those he or she wronged while drinking. That he offers his own comment on this type of programme through a character played by an actor who must surely be familiar with twelve-step programmes is trademark Ferrara stuff. Who better to 'find' the correct delivery of such a line than someone who knows exactly what the line refers to?

Again, right at the end of the film, when Matty has been played the video footage of himself actually strangling Annie 2, Mickey delivers a demented monologue, telling Matty to live with what he's done. The performance is so intense, so hair-raising, that even after repeated viewings, it seems that Hopper is being himself on-screen, rather than playing the part of Mickey. When he's shouting at 'Matty' (perhaps a part of himself) to, "learn to live with it!", you feel that he's stepped outside of the scene and is drawing on his own experiences as a recovering addict.

Mickey's speech seems to follow directly on from his parting quip at the beach reunion when he calls after Matty, "You look real good straight, man." That line is immediately followed with a shot of Matty standing at the window in his hotel room. He turns and eyes the mini-bar. Then he hesitates and opens the door. He pulls out a miniature bottle of alcohol, pauses and then tips it down his throat. We feel as though we're sitting in the room with Matty, watching him from the sidelines, on the edge of our seats, willing him not to take the drink but also perversely to *take* the drink. It's the way that he downs the miniature that makes the scene so haunting. There is no evidence of pleasure in his actions. He drinks it as though it's oxygen. Then he gasps, breaks into a mischievous smile and opens the next one. This mini-bar scene brings to mind a passage from Tom Charity's interview with Ferrara that ran in *Time Out* to accompany the simultaneous British release of *The Addiction* and *The Funeral*. Here is his description of arriving in Ferrara's hotel room: "the PR hastily clears away the circumstantials: overflowing ashtrays, beer bottles and the remnants of a well stocked mini-bar." The scene seems grounded in personal experience.

Hours later, Matty is slipping into hell: guzzling from two bottles at once; masturbating to the memory of having violent sex with Annie 1, his hands wrapped tight around her throat; answering the door to his coke dealer (who tells him he liked a scene in his last film where he shot coke addicts, again blurring the line between film and real life); hanging out of the window and rocking back and forth as U2's 'Miami' blasts on the soundtrack; calling dozens of people who might know where Annie 1 is; shouting on his mobile at somebody on the beach as a new day begins and he hasn't yet been to bed.

The drugs and drink go hand in hand with Annie 1. Matty's love for Annie 1 is also a love for all things bad. She represents all profanity; Susan represents the sacred. When Susan calls him on his mobile in the middle of this degeneracy and realises that he's drunk, Modine's jumpy twitches and face-pulling tell us everything we need to know about his relationship with her. She is a maternal figure to him, although earlier Matty agrees when his therapist suggests that Matty's mother's refusal to return his calls or answer his letters, mirrors the way Annie 1 has vanished from his life. Is this Ferrara's real-life relationship to his mother or just a scene in a movie? The phone call with Susan degenerates into hallucination as Matty starts to believe that she is telling him she's pregnant. He tells her, falsely, that he has booked a flight back to New York and asks her not to come to Miami.

As in *Love On The A Train* there is a 'wife' figure and a 'girl'. Susan, who Matty describes to his therapist in sarcastic tones as a "whole food store", is the responsible homey, wife. Matty tells the therapist that she doesn't drink, smoke or "get high". Annie 1 is tattooed, carnal, sensuous and dark; she drinks, smokes and is into rough sex. She oozes sensuality, Susan oozes comfort and homely values. We see Matty fondling Annie 1's breast and having violent sex with her; we only see asexual domestic scenes between Matty and Susan. As so often in Ferrara's work, the two women symbolise a tug-of-war in Matty between the impulses towards good and evil. Susan is good for him, Annie 1 isn't. Susan is New York, Alcoholics Anonymous meetings, being clean and sober, therapy and a pleasant, though often darkly lit, home. Annie 1 is Miami, alcohol, drugs, sex, and a sparkling white hotel room. Scenes with Susan are steeped in darker colours, scenes with Annie 1 in light colours, this coding reinforcing how Matty sees Annie 1 as exciting and Susan as dull.

The film is, as Ferrara has said, a tale about "obsessive love". Matty cannot forget Annie 1. When he returns to Miami to find her, we first see him meeting up with Mickey in a beautifully shot beach scene. After the dreary street scene in New York, the blue sky that lies behind Matty reminds us that Miami is Matty's former playground. He says he has to see Annie 1; Mickey says she's in Mexico City with her new man and tells Matty to forget her. However, in a surreal twist, the next morning, he shows up in Matty's hotel room with Annie 1. She's wearing all black, as beautiful as ever. Mickey says he tracked her down in Acapulco; that she was willing to travel to see Matty (mostly, she admits, because Mickey told her that Matty quit drinking) tells us that she too, in spite of how he treated her, could not forget him either. He, lying in broken glass and hungover, is relieved that she is still alive; however, she sneers with disgust that he is so weak that he's already fallen off the wagon, and leaves. Matty's dream came true, only to fall apart again abruptly.

After a brown-tinted flashback to a beach scene where Matty and Annie 2 play around on their 'romantic' date, presumably before going to Mickey's, we see Matty at Mickey's studio. He's showing Matty video footage of what happened when he blacked out. Modine pulls off a jittery performance laden with self-disgust, as he watches himself strangle Annie 2, mirroring the earlier footage of *Nana* that we saw Mickey watching. Matty finished Mickey's film for him, turning it into a porno snuff film. This footage is his secret just as Chris Neville's genuine footage of him strangling Andrea in bed in *Special Effects* is kept as his secret footage. Why don't Mickey and Neville erase their incriminating films?

In the playback footage, as Matty strangles Annie 2, he keeps asking her why she had an abortion, at which Annie 2, terrified, screams and says she doesn't know what he means. In one great line, she asks, "Is this acting?" as Matty starts to maul her. Matty breaks down and Ferrara rhymes the original shot of him touching Annie 1 on screen at the time of the murder with a shot of him now touching the dead Annie 2 on the screen. Mickey becomes a combination of conscience, God and the Devil as he delivers a ferocious monologue which concludes that Matty is a "piece of fucking filth!"

The film ends at night on a beach, as it began. Susan has arrived. Matty, wasted again, tells her he doesn't love her and that he's a murderer; in a brief tussle, he grabs her by the hair (recreating the strangling of Annie 2 and the pseudo-strangling which formed a part of his sex games with Annie 1) and then runs into the sea, swimming to suicide. The tacky reunion with a naked Annie 2 in the afterlife somewhat mars the ending because it seems so artificial. Ferrara has commented ironically of Matty's connection with Annie 2, "He knows Annie 2 is somebody he actually might have an opportunity of having a decent relationship with. So he kills her."

The film is also Ferrara's attempt to separate his twin leanings. On the one hand there's video porn maker Mickey who spouts Godard quotations, is obsessed with film, revels in video technology and delivers various pro-video lines. On the other hand there's the flash of the 'star system' represented by the opening scenes in which we see Matty arrive at the airport in Miami, transported in a VIP cart, snort coke in the back of a chauffeur-driven limo and shoving handfuls of complimentary sweets into his pocket (even though he's presumably rich enough to buy the company that makes them). The uneasy alliance between Matty and Mickey (their names representing Ferrara's original intention to have Matt Dillon and Mickey Rourke play the Modine and Hopper roles) which is best captured in the tense 'did you fuck Annie?' speech (playfully recalling the infamous 'did you fuck my wife?' scene between De Niro and Pesci in *Raging Bull*) is symbolic of the conflict between Ferrara's dual fascination with mainstream work (*Body Snatchers*, Miami Vice) and the kind of low-budget films that have earned him his tag as a 'maverick' and 'outlaw' director.

ABEL FERRARA FILMOGRAPHY

The Driller Killer (1979)
Production Companies: Rochelle Films Inc/Navaron Films Ltd
Screenplay: Nicholas St. John
Cinematography (colour): Ken Kelsch
Editor: Christopher Andrews
Music: Joe Delia
Running Time: 94′
Cast: Abel Ferrara a.k.a Jimmy Laine a.k.a Ferrara (Reno Miller); Carolyn Marz (Carol); Baybi Day (Pamela); Harry Schultz II (Dalton Briggs); Alan Wynroth (Landlord); Maria Helhoski (Nun); James O'Hara (Man In Church); Richard Howorth (Carol's husband).

Ms. 45 a.k.a *Angel Of Vengeance* (1981)
Production Companies: Rochelle Films Inc/Navaron Films Ltd
Screenplay: Nicholas St. John
Cinematography (colour): James Momel
Editor: Christopher Andrews
Music: Joe Delia
Running Time: 84′/78′/76′ (depending on cut)
Cast: Zoë Tamerlis (Thana); Albert Sinkys (Albert); Darlene Stuto (Laurie); Helen McGara (Helen); Bogey (Phil); Nike Zachmanoglou (Pamela); Jimmy Laine a.k.a Abel Ferrara (Rapist #1); Peter Yellen (Burglar/Rapist); Editta Sherman (Mrs Nasone); Vincent Gruppi (heckler on the corner); Nicholas St John (detective); Karen O'Shea (model); Jack Thibeau (man in bar); Mariana Tripaldi (buyer's assistant).

Fear City (1983)
Production Companies: Zupnik-Curtis Enterprises
Screenplay: Nicholas St. John
Cinematography (colour): James Lemmo
Editor: Anthony Redman
Music: Richard Halligan
Running Time: 93'
Cast: Tom Berenger (Matt Rossi); Billy Dee Williams (Wheeler); Jack
    Scalia (Nicky); Melanie Griffith (Loretta); Rossano Brazzi (Car-
    mine); Rae Dawn Chong (Leila); Joe Santos (Frank); Michael V.
    Gazzo (Mike); Jan Murray (Goldstein); Janet Julian (Ruby); Daniel
    Faraldo (Sanchez); Ola Ray (Honey); Mar Conchita (Silver); John
    Foster (Pazza).

Miami Vice (1985)
Episode Title: 'The Home Invaders'
Production Companies: Universal/Michael Mann
NBC Air Date: 15 March, 1985
Episode #19 of Season One
Executive Producer: Michael Mann
Produced: John Nicolella
Co-Producer: Richard Brams
Screenplay: Chuck Adamson
Music: Jan Hammer
Cinematography: James A. Contner
Editor: Joel Goodman
Cast: Don Johnson (Crockett); Philip Michael Thomas (Tubbs);
    Edward James Olmos (Castillo); Olivia Brown (Trudy Joplin);
    Gina Calabrese (Sandra Santiago).

Miami Vice (1985)
Episode Title: 'The Dutch Oven'
Production Companies: Universal/Michael Mann
NBC Air Date: 25th October 1985
Episode #26 of Season Two
Screenplay : Maurice Hurley
Music: Jan Hammer
Cinematography: James A. Contner

Editor: Robert Daniels
Cast: Don Johnson (Crockett); Philip Michael Thomas (Tubbs); Edward James Olmos (Castillo); Olivia Brown (Trudy Joplin); Gina Calabrese (Sandra Santiago).

The Gladiator (1986)
Production Companies: Walker Brothers/New World Company
Screenplay: William Bleich
Cinematography (colour): James Lemmo
Editor: Herbert Down
Music: David Frank
Running Time: 94'
Cast: Ken Wahl (Rick Benton); Nancy Allen (Susan Neville); Robert Culp (Frank Mason); Stan Shaw (Joe Barker); Rosemary Forsyth (Loretta Simpson); Bart Braverman (Dan); Brian Robbins (Jeff Benton)

Crime Story (1986)
Production Companies: Michael Mann Company In Association With New World Company
Screenplay: Chuck Adamson, David J.Burke, Gustave Reineger
Cinematography (colour): James A. Contner
Music: Todd Rundgren
Running Time: 96'
Cast: Dennis Farina (Lieutenant Mike Torello); Anthony Denison; William Smitrovich; Steve Ryan; Bill Campbell; Paul Butler; Stephen Lang; David Abrams; Joseph Wiseman; Darlanne Fluegel; Jon Polito; Johann Carlo; William Russ; Eric Bognosian; Martin Ferrero; David Caruso.

China Girl (1987)
Production Companies: Vestron Pictures, Street Lite, Great American Films Limited Partnership
Screenplay: Nicholas St. John
Cinematography (colour): Bojan Bazelli
Editor: Anthony Redman
Music: Joe Delia
Running Time: 90'

Cast: James Russo (Alby); Richard Panebianco (Tony); Sari Chang (Tye); David Caruso (Mercury); Russell Wong (Yung Gan); Joey Chin (Tsu Shin).

Cat Chaser (1988)
Production Companies: Vestron Pictures
Screenplay: James Borelli based on the novel by Elmore Leonard
Cinematography (colour, black and white): Anthony B. Richmond
Editor: Anthony Redman
Music: Chick Corea
Running Time: 90'
Cast: Peter Weller (George Moran); Kelly McGillis (Mary DeBoya); Tomas Milian (Andres DeBoya); Charles Durning (Jiggs Scully), Frederick Forrest (Tyner).

King Of New York (1990)
Production Companies: Reteitalia SPA, Scena International
Screenplay: Nicholas St. John
Cinematography (colour): Bojan Bazelli
Editor: Anthony Redman
Music: Joe Delia
Running Time: 100'
Cast: Christopher Walken (Frank White); David Caruso (Dennis Gilley); Laurence Fishburne (Jimmy Jump); Victor Argo (Bishop); Wesley Snipes (Thomas Flanigan); Janet Julian (Jennifer); Joey Chin (Larry Wong); Giancarlo Esposito (Lance); Paul Calderon (Joey Dalesio); Steve Buscemi (Test Tube); Theresa Randle (Raye); Leonard Lee Thomas (Blood); Roger Smith (Tanner); Carrie Nygren (Melanie).

Bad Lieutenant (1992)
Production Companies: Edward R. Pressman
Screenplay: Abel Ferrara, Zoë Lund
Cinematography (colour): Ken Kelsch
Editor: Anthony Redman
Music: Joe Delia
Running Time: 96'
Cast: Harvey Keitel (Lt.); Brian McElroy (Lt.'s Son 1); Frankie

Acciario (Lt.'s Son 2); Peggy Gormley (Lt.'s Wife); Stella Keitel (Lt.'s Daughter); Victor Argo (Bet Cop); Leonard Thomas (Cop 2); Vincent Laresca (JC); Robin Burrows (Ariane); Victoria Bastell (Bowtay); Frankie Thorn (Nun); Paul Hipp (Jesus); Zoë Lund (Zoe); Detective Bo (Bo Dietl); Heather Bracken (Nurse); Eddie Daniels (Jersey Girl Passenger); Bianca Bakiia (Jersey Girl Driver).

Body Snatchers: The Invasion Continues (1993)
Production Companies: Warner Bros US
Screenplay: Jack Finney (novel), Raymond Cistheri/Larry Cohen (Story), Nicholas St. John, Stuart Gordon, Dennis Paoli
Cinematography (colour): Bojan Bazelli
Editor: Anthony Redman
Music: Joe Delia
Running Time: 83'
Cast: Terry Kinney (Dr Steve Malone); Meg Tilly (Carol Malone); Gabrielle Anwar (Marti Malone); Reilly Murphy (Andy Malone); Billy Mirth (Tim Young); Christine Elise (Jen Platt); Forest Whittaker (Dr Collins).

Snake Eyes a.k.a *Dangerous Game* (1993)
Production Companies: Maverick Picture Company
Screenplay: Nicholas St. John
Cinematography (colour): Ken Kelsch
Editor: Anthony Redman
Music: Joe Delia
Running Time: 108'
Cast: Harvey Keitel (Eddie Israel); Madonna (Sarah Jennings); James Russo (Francis Burns); Nancy Ferrara (Madlyn Israel); Reilly Murphy (Tommy); Victor Argo (Dir Of Photography); Leonard Thomas (Prop Guy); Kristina Fulton (Blade); Heather Bracken (Stewardess); Glenn Plummer (Burns' buddy); Nikki Munroe (Girl In Trailer); Anthony Redman (Swinger); Randy Sawasuwa (Producer).

The Addiction (1995)
Production Companies: Distribution, Fast Films, Guild, October Films
Screenplay: Nicholas St. John

Cinematography (black and white): Ken Kelsch
Editor: Mayin Lo
Music: Joe Delia
Running Time: 79'
Cast: Lili Taylor (Kathleen Conklin); Christopher Walken (Peina);
  Annabella Sciorra (Casanova); Edie Falco (Jean); Paul Calderon
  (Professor); Fredro Starr (Black); Kathryn Erbe (College Student);
  Michael Imperioli (Missionary); Father Robert Castle (Priest).

The Funeral (1996)
Production Companies: C & P Productions, WDP Worldwide,
  October Films
Screenplay: Nicholas St. John
Cinematography (colour): Ken Kelsch
Editor: Mayin Lo, Bill Pankow
Music: Joe Delia
Running Time: 95'
Cast: Christopher Walken (Ray); Annabella Sciorra (Jean); Isabella
  Rossellini (Clara); Vincent Gallo (Johnny); Chris Penn (Chez);
  Gretchen Mol (Helen); Benicio Del Toro (Gaspare); Father Robert
  Castle (Priest).

Mylène Farmer, 'California' (1996)
Production Company: Toutankhamon
Promo Music Video
Running Time: 5' 18"
Cast: Mylène Farmer (Rich Woman), Giancarlo Esposito.

Subway Stories: *Love On The A Train* (1997)
Production Companies: HBO
Screenplay: Marla Hanson
Cinematography (colour): Ken Kelsch
Editor: Elizabeth Kling
Music: 'Baby Me Baby' (Abel Ferrara, Joe Delia) & 'Waiting Here
  Forever For U' (Abel Ferrara, Joe Delia)
Running Time: 5' 25"
Cast: Rosie Perez (The Girl); Mike McGione (John T); Gretchen Mol
  (Wife).

The Blackout (1997)
Production Companies: Edward R. Pressman, MDP Worldwide, CIPA, Les Films Number One
Screenplay: Abel Ferrara, Marla Hanson, Christ Zois
Cinematography (colour): Ken Kelsch
Editor: Anthony Redman
Music: Joe Delia, Schoolly D
Running Time: 94'
Cast: Matthew Modine (Matty); Claudia Schiffer (Susan); Annie 1 (Béatrice Dalle); Annie 2 (Sarah Lassez); Mickey Wayne (Dennis Hopper); Mickey's Studio Actor (Nancy Ferrara).

Closed On Account Of Rabies: Poems And Tales Of Edgar Allan Poe (1997)
2 CD album of interpretations of Edgar Allan Poe's writings. Ferrara offers a spoken word excerpt from 'The Raven'. Other figures involved were Marianne Faithfull, Christopher Walken, Iggy Pop, Diamanda Galas, Ken Nordine, Gavin Friday, Ed Sanders, Jeff Buckley, Dr John, Deborah Harry and Gabriel Byrne.

The Phoids, 'Iowa' (1998)
Produced: NG Records
Promo Music Video
Running Time: 4' 23"

New Rose Hotel (1998)
Production Companies: Quandra Entertainment, Edward R. Pressman
Screenplay: Abel Ferrara, Christ Zois based on the story by William Gibson
Cinematography (colour): Ken Kelsch
Editor: Anthony Redman/James Moll
Music: Schoolly D
Running Time: 92'
Cast: Christopher Walken (Fox); Willem Dafoe (X); Asia Argento (Sandii); Yoshitaka Amano (Hiroshi); Annabella Sciorra (Madame Rosa); Gretchen Mol (Hiroshi's Wife).

'JIMMY LAINE' (a.k.a. ABEL FERRARA) FILMOGRAPHY

The Nine Lives Of A Wet Pussycat (1976)
Production Companies: Navaron Films Ltd
Directed by Jimmy Boy L and Holly Yellen
Screenplay: Nicholas George based on the novel *Les Femmes Blanches*
   by Francois DuLea
Editor: K. James Lovttit
Music: Joseph Delia
Cinematography (colour): Francis X. Wolfe
Running Time: 63'
Cast: Pauline Lamonde (Pauline); Dominique Santos (Gypsy); Joy
   Silver (Nacala); David Pirell (husband); Shaker Lewis (Stable
   Boy); Nicholas George (chauffeur); Tony Richard (attendant);
   Peggy Johnson (Younger Sister); Jimmy Laine (Old Man);
   Everrett East (Attacker I); Ace Ming (Attacker II).

(This film is widely rumoured to be directed by Abel Ferrara,
   written by Nicholas St. John, scored by Joe Delia, shot by Ken
   Kelsch and to feature acting performances by Ferrara. The British
   Obscene Publications Act prevented the author of this book from
   importing a print of this film into Britain and, therefore, made
   verification of whether it is or is not an Abel Ferrara work an
   impossibility.)

The Driller Killer (1979)
Ferrara played Reno Miller under the acting pseudonym Jimmy
   Laine.

Ms. 45 (1981)
Ferrara played the first rapist under the acting pseudonym Jimmy
   Laine.

BIBLIOGRAPHY

The following periodicals and books were used as source material. Any quotations from *Cahiers du Cinéma* were translated by the author. Any quotation that doesn't have a cited source is taken from interviews conducted by the author. The Zoë Lund interview is reprinted with the permission of Dan Taylor, Josh Long and *Exploitation Retrospect*. It originally appeared in *Exploitation Retrospect* Issue #37, March 1993.

Articles

Adams, Mark: 'Abel Ferrara: The King Of New York' (NFT Theatre Programme, May 1993)

Adam: *'Cat Chaser'* (Variety, December 27, 1989)

Anger, Cédric: 'The Addiction D'Abel Ferrara' (*Cahiers du Cinéma*, July 1996)

Anger, Cédric: 'L'Esprit D'Abel' (*Cahiers du Cinéma*, December 1996)

BBFC: The Driller Killer Press Release (April 1999)

Bentley, Michael: 'The Body Snatchers' (*Cineaste*, Vol. XX. No. 3. 1994)

Bilbow, Marjorie: 'Ms. 45, Angel Of Vengeance' (*Screen International*, January 26, 1985)

Cart: 'Fear City' (*Variety*, May 23, 1984)

Charity, Tom: 'Willing And Abel' (*Time Out*, April 16-13, 1997)

Chute, David: 'Fear City' (*Film Comment*, December 1993)

Dawson, Jeff: 'Harvey Keitel' (*Empire*, November 1993)

Duane, Paul: 'Vampire Chronicles' (*Film Ireland*, April/May 1995)

Deevoy, Adrian: 'Béatrice Dalle' (GQ, March 1998)

Francke, Lizzie: 'King Of New York' (*Sight and Sound*, July 1991)

Hemblade, Christopher: 'Matthew Modine, The Darker Side' (*Empire*, March 1998)

Howe, Rupert: 'Mo' Betty Blue' (*Neon*, February 1998)

Jousse, Thierry: 'Abel Ferrara: New York – Miami' (*Cahiers du Cinéma*, May 1997)

Jousse, Thierry: 'Entretien avec Béatrice Dalle' (*Cahiers du Cinéma*, May 1997)

Kaufman, Anthony: 'Ferrara's Blackout' (indieWIRE, February 1998)

Kermode, Mark: 'Bad Lieutenant' (*Sight and Sound*, February 1993)

Kulkarni, Neil: 'Schoolly D' (*Uncut*, March 1998)

Lalane, Jean-Marc: 'Veillee Funebre' (*Cahiers du Cinéma*, December 1996)

Lalane, Jean-Marc: 'L'Ideal du Manque: Blackout' (*Cahiers du Cinéma*, June 1997)

Lehman, Peter: 'The Male Body Within The Excesses Of Exploitation and Art: Abel Ferrara's Ms. 45, Cat Chaser and Bad Lieutenant' (*The Velvet Light Trap*, Fall 1993)

Levy, Emmanuel: '*The Funeral*' (*Variety*, September 9, 1996)

Long, Josh: 'The Zoë Lund Interview' (*Exploitation Retrospect*, March 1993)

Lor: 'Ms. 45' (*Variety*, May 6, 1981)

Lor: '*China Girl*' (*Variety*, May 20, 1987)

McCarthy, Todd: 'The Addiction' (*Variety*, February 6, 1995)

Maslin, Janet: 'Bad Lieutenant' (*The New York Times*, November 20, 1992)

Maslin, Janet: 'Killer Lady' (*The New York Times*, May 15, 1981)

Morgan, David: 'Abel Ferrara, Director' (*Empire*, March 1993)

Nevers, Camille: 'Entretien Avec Abel Ferrara' (*Cahiers du Cinéma*, May 1993)

Newman, Kim: 'The Blackout' (*Sight and Sound*, January 1998)

Newman, Kim: 'Torn Halo' (*City Limits*, January 18, 1985)

Newman, Kim: 'The Driller Killer' (*Monthly Film Bulletin*, May 1984)

Newman, Kim: 'Angel Of Vengeance' (*Monthly Film Bulletin*, November 1984)

Bibliography

Newman, Kim: 'Ms. 45' (*City Limits*, January 18, 1985)

Newman, Kim: 'The Gladiator' (*Monthly Film Bulletin*, April 1988)

Newman, Kim: 'China Girl' (*Monthly Film Bulletin*, January 1988)

Newman, Kim: 'Bad Lieutenant' (*Empire*, March 1993)

Newman, Kim: 'The Street Where I Live – Abel Ferrara' (*Monthly Film Bulletin*, February 1988)

Newman, Kim: 'The Funeral' (*Empire*, May 1997)

Newman, Kim: 'The Addiction' (*Empire*, May 1997)

Newman, Kim: 'You Know The Drill' (The Guardian, April 14th, 1999)

Petley, Julian: 'Abel Ferrara' (*International Dictionary Of Films And Filmmakers*)

Petley, Julian: 'Fear City' (*Monthly Film Bulletin*, August 1986)

Rauger, Jean-Francois: 'Abel Ferrara: la Passe De Trois' (*Cahiers du Cinéma*, 1993)

Robe: 'The Driller Killer' (*Variety*, July 4, 1979)

Roberts, Chris: 'Matthew Modine' (*Uncut*, March 1998)

Shelley, Jim: 'Back In Blackout, Matthew Modine' (*Neon*, February 1998)

Shelley, Jim: 'The Abel Guy' (*Neon*, February 1998)

Schnabel, Julian: 'Harvey Keitel, Zoë Lund and Abel Ferrara' (*Interview*, December 1992)

Smith, Gavin: 'Moon In The Gutter' (*Film Comment*, July/August 1990)

Smith, Gavin: 'Nobody Rides For Free' (*Film Comment*, July/August 1990)

Smith, Gavin: 'The Gambler' (*Sight and Sound*, February 1993)

Smith, Gavin: 'Dealing With The Now' (*Sight and Sound*, April 1997)

Strauss, Frederic: 'Bad Trip' (*Cahiers du Cinéma*, March 1993)

Strauss, Frederic: ''Entretien Avec Abel Ferrara' (*Cahiers du Cinéma*, May 1993)

Terenzi, Lawrence: 'An Interview With Abel Ferrara' (*Film Nation*, 1996)

Thompson, David: 'Staying Power' (*Sight and Sound*, January 1993)

Uncredited: 'Zoë Tamerlis' (*Interview*, June 1984)

Uncredited: 'Enquete Aupres Des Cineastes: Abel Ferrara' (*Cinémaction*, January 1992)

White, Rob: 'The Addiction' (*Sight and Sound*, April 1997)

Books

Bellour, Raymond & Bandy, Mary Lea: *Jean-Luc Godard; Son+Image* (MoMA, 1992)

Boorman, John & Donohue, Walter: *Projections 7* (Faber & Faber, 1997)

Bresson, Robert: *Notes On The Cinematographer* (Quartet 1986)

Cameron, Ian: *The Films Of Jean-Luc Godard* (Studio Vista, 1967)

Carney, Ray: *The Films Of John Cassavetes* (Cambridge, 1994)

Clover, Carol: *Men, Women And Chain Saws: Gender In The Modern Horror Film* (BFI, 1992)

Fine, Marshall: *Harvey Keitel: The Art Of Darkness* (Harper Collins, 1997)

Katz, Robert: *Love Is Colder Than Death: Fassbinder* (Random House, 1987)

Newman, Kim: *A Critical History Of The Horror Movie From 1968* (Bloomsbury, 1984)

Parker, John: *Polanski* (Victor Gollancz, 1993)

Pezzotta, Alberto: *Abel Ferrara* (Il Castoro Cinema, 1998)

Polanski, Roman: *Roman: Polanksi* (William Heinemann Ltd, 1984)

Quandt, James: *Robert Bresson* (Cinematheque Ontario, 1998)

Siciliano, Enzo: *Pasolini, A Biography* (Bloomsbury, 1987)

Siegel, Don: *A Siegel Film* (Faber & Faber 1993)